B & T
11/22/82
17.50

W9-AXF-375

As the
Japanese
See It

As the Japanese See It

PAST AND PRESENT

Compiled and edited by
Michiko Y. Aoki
and
Margaret B. Dardess

THE UNIVERSITY PRESS
OF HAWAII
HONOLULU

Wingate College Library

Copyright © 1981 by The University Press of Hawaii
All rights reserved
Manufactured in the United States of America

The Press acknowledges the assistance of the Andrew W. Mellon Foundation in the publication of this book.

Library of Congress Cataloging in Publication Data
Main entry under title:

As the Japanese see it.

Translated from the Japanese.
1. Japan—Civilization—Addresses, essays
lectures. I. Aoki, Michiko Yamaguchi. II. Dardess,
Margaret B.
DS821.A69   952   81-11526
ISBN 0-8248-0759-6   AACR2
ISBN 0-8248-0760-X (pbk.)

088300

Contents

Preface

This collection of readings is designed to illustrate common human concerns in Japanese society. In teaching Japanese history and civilization, the editors have long felt a need for material that presents a picture of the daily life of ordinary people—those in society who are not likely to appear in history books. There is also a need for materials that illustrate areas of interest to ordinary people because they concern folk heroes or prominent people and events. This book is an attempt to fill that need.

The readings include folk legends, sermons, short stories, and excerpts from novels, interviews, newspaper articles, and autobiographical material. All are primary sources written by Japanese themselves. The book does not pretend to be an analysis of the Japanese social structure. Excellent works are available to serve that purpose. This book is designed to help Western readers appreciate Japanese ways of thinking and acting by offering reading material in English translation in which Japanese people relate their ideals, goals, and experiences. Much of the material is highly personal. By selecting these readings, we hope to provide a means by which Westerners can understand and empathize with Japanese as they respond to problems of common concern to people of all cultures.

The book is divided into four parts: Religion, The Family, The Community, and The State. The readings present many facets of Japanese life including popular beliefs, marriage customs and childrearing practices, interpersonal relations in rural and urban communities, and the response of Japanese who are excluded or feel they are excluded from Japanese society. The section on the state is not intended to explain the Japanese political order but rather to show popular attitudes toward authority above the family and community level. We have not included a separate section on the individual because we believe that the individual can most clearly be seen against a background of family, community, and state. Some of the selections could effectively be extracted to form a separate section on the individual should the reader prefer a different approach to the study of that subject. These would include "Housewife and Woman," "On Becoming an Adoptee," "The Talisman," "One Woman's Outcry," and "A Protest Against My Charge." The reader may find others to add to the list from among these readings.

This sourcebook is interdisciplinary in its conception and its organization. The topical organization we have chosen is one often adopted by sociologists and anthropologists as a framework for studying a culture. Within that framework the selections are arranged chronologically so that the reader may examine change and continuity over time. The earliest selections date from the eleventh century and the most recent from 1976. Each section includes material that was written before the twentieth century. The majority of the selections depict life in the first half of the twentieth century and the years since World War II.

We had the general reader in mind in choosing materials that illustrate important aspects of Japanese life. We hope that the selections are entertaining as well as intellectually stimulating and will guide the reader to a further study and understanding of ordinary people in Japanese society.

We hope, moreover, that the book will be useful for a number of different educational purposes. We believe that when used as supplementary reading in history courses it will be of value to teachers and students who want to deal with a wide range of Japanese experience. Historians who in the past have had primary source materials that illustrate only the elite culture will now have material that deals with the popular culture as well. It is our hope, too, that many social scientists who are now examining traditional as well as modern societies will find these materials stimulating and useful to the study of the social sciences.

Nearly two-thirds of the selections are translated here for the first time and are not available in English elsewhere. We have abridged stories and novels that would have been too long to use in their entirety. To make reading easier, omission has generally not been indicated. A word should be said about the handling of Japanese personal names. We have followed present-day usage—that is, using Western-style order (given name first, followed by family name) for names from the time of the Meiji Restoration in 1868. The customary Japanese order is retained, of course, where it appears in previously published material.

The book was begun in 1975 at the University of Illinois under a National Endowment for Humanities grant for the development of a new undergraduate course on Asia. A great deal of new material was translated for use in the course, and those readings on Japan that proved to be most illuminating and of the greatest interest to students have been included in this book. A group of faculty at the Center for Asian Studies of the University of Illinois have helped in selecting and translating these materials. We would like to thank Professors David Plath, John Pierson, Robert Crawford, and Chieko Mulhern for their suggestions and useful comments. Our special appreciation goes to Professor Patricia Ebrey for her direction of the original project and her encouragement and advice on the compilation of this book. We are also much indebted to Professors Susan Hanley and Kozo Yamamura of the University of Washington, Professor Hiroshi Wagatsuma of the University of California at Los Angeles, and Professor George Akita of the University of Hawaii at Manoa for their valuable advice.

We are grateful to those authors and publishers who have willingly given us permission to use works from their publications. Without their cooperation, publication of this book would not have been materialized.

M. Y. A.
M. B. D.

Part 1
RELIGION

The beliefs and religious practices of the Japanese people combine elements of the indigenous folk religion with aspects of religions that were introduced into Japan from other countries. Between the third and seventh centuries Buddhism and Confucianism were introduced into Japan from China and Korea, and in time, mixing with native beliefs, they produced a rich, multilayered, syncretic religious tradition.

The native religion, called Shinto (the way of the gods or spirits), is at the popular level a simple and unorganized worship of awe-inspiring spirits. Central to Shinto is a feeling of communion between human beings and nature. The spirits often live in nature in mountains, trees, water, and rocks—and control the natural phenomena that affect people's lives. Worship of these spirits is aimed at winning their favor through prayer and offerings. The spirits can take on human or animal form when they choose. Princes and heroes are spirits in human form, and any person might become a spirit by exhibiting supernatural powers.

Friendly spirits function as guardians of rice fields and assure good harvests to the majority of the population—those who, throughout Japanese history, have been involved in agriculture and particularly rice production. Shinto festivals often take place in conjunction with planting and harvesting, when the spirits are asked to assure a good yield. Spirits also watch over fishermen and those in other trades. The spirits of deceased members of a family function as the guardians of the living and are honored when a new family member is born or a new bride enters the family. Malevolent spirits can put a curse on humans or transform them into other creatures. Possession by such spirits, according to folk belief, is a common cause of illness. The *Nihon shoki,* an eighth-century chronicle, described ancient Japan in terms of Shinto beliefs as follows: "In that Land there were numerous spirits which shone with a luster like that of fireflies, and evil deities which buzzed like flies. There were also trees and herbs which could speak."

Shinto has no ethical precepts. Pollution—that is, things believed to be unclean—is the greatest source of evil, ill fortune, and illness. Although humans can never be as free of pollution as some spirits, they can, to a certain extent, cleanse themselves. This cleansing is symbolized in Shinto worship by bathing and by rinsing one's hands and mouth with water. Death is a principal source of defilement, and practices connected with the recently deceased in many parts of Japan often reflect that belief. In one area, for example, two graves are constructed—one for the corpse, a source of defilement, and another for the spirit. Since the spirit is believed to be easily separable from the body, the spirit may then be honored without fear of pollution from close physical association with the corpse.

A number of the stories in this section illustrate aspects of Shinto. The world of the spirits has an important influence on the events described in the "Tales of Tōno" and in "Japanese Folktales." In "Yosoji's Camellia Tree" the spirit of a mountain, in this case Mount Fuji, appears in the form of a beautiful woman to show a young man where to find water with which to purify his mother and the people of his village and thus rid them of disease. A young man who boasts that he is not afraid of fox spirits is tricked by a spirit into having his head shaved and becoming a priest. Retribution in the form of supernatural punishment is also explained in terms of angry spirits as in the "Legend Told by a Fisherman," a tale in which a fire spirit avenges the betrayal of a *daimyō* by local fishermen. In "The Snow Ghost" the spirit of a woman recently deceased returns to admonish her husband for abandoning her father.

Of all the religions imported into Japan, Buddhism has had the most profound impact. To the simple explanation of natural happenings provided by Shinto, Buddhism added a universal teaching of the unity of all beings and the ideal of supreme enlightenment and salvation. The Japanese seem to have had little difficulty accepting the major premises of Buddhism, which maintain that all things are impermanent, suffering is the inevitable result of human desire, and humanity is caught in an endless cycle of death and rebirth from which we can escape only through moral conduct, meditation, and prayer.

Buddhism contributed to the ethics of the Japanese people as well as to their spiritual life. The four cardinal virtues of Buddhism —friendliness, compassion, joy, equanimity—were extolled for the layperson as well as for the monk. Buddhist teachings set forth the ideal of a society in which friendly relations would exist between people and animals and where family love, honesty, and brotherhood would characterize all human relationships. The performance of good deeds in this world and the avoidance of passion, hatred, and false ideas would lead to a happier rebirth and bring both men and women closer to salvation. The *Tales from Uji,* a collection of stories intended to popularize Buddhist teachings, illustrates the tenets. In the story "How a Sparrow Repaid Its Debt of Gratitude," one woman is rewarded for showing kindness to a sparrow and to her neighbors while another woman is punished for jealousy and selfishness. "How the Priestly Nobleman from Mikawa Retired from the World" and "About the Holy Man in the Province of Shinano" demonstrate the Buddhist rejection of desire for status, fame, and wealth.

Until the twelfth century all Buddhist rituals were performed by priests from the great monastic establishments near the court. In the late twelfth and early thirteenth centuries reformers like Hōnen and Shinran broke away from monastic Buddhism because they doubted their ability to achieve salvation through their own efforts at moral conduct and study in the monastery. They turned instead to the worship of the Buddha Amida and emphasized the redeeming power of the recitation of the Buddha's name, the *nembutsu.* Human beings were weak according to the reformers and could not through their own efforts escape from desire and suffering. Only by putting absolute faith in the compassion of Amida could they enter the paradise of the Pure Land over which Amida rules and there, through his help, achieve salvation. Amida worship became the prevalent form of popular Buddhism.

Simple faith in Buddhist figures other than Amida was an important part of the popular Buddhist tradition in Japan. Jizō and Kannon appear frequently in religious tales and were often objects of worship. Kannon was regarded in both China and Japan as a female figure who functioned as a goddess of mercy—Japanese folk legends tell often of her miraculous works. The selection "Nariai Kannon" is typical of these. In Japan Jizō is regarded as the protector of children and pregnant women and especially of poor people. Worship of Jizō increased with the rise of the Amida cult, since Jizō was often considered to personify Amida's compassion. In popular belief Jizō took over the role of the early Shinto spirit of the road and became the patron of travelers. Small statues of Jizō appear along older roads all over Japan. The practice of piling small pebbles in front of the statues and leaving offerings to them is probably a remnant of the pre-Buddhist practice of supplicating the spirit of the road. In the tale "The Jizō with the Bamboo Hats," statues of Jizō come to life and appear before a farmer to reward him for his unselfish offering of hats to keep them warm.

Buddhism took over from Shinto the function of overseeing funerals and ceremonies in honor of the dead. Even today, when Buddhism is viewed by many as an outmoded religion, priests still perform rituals for the recently deceased and for family ancestors. Buddhist altars are set up in many Japanese homes where dead members of a family may be honored, and priests are often invited to perform ceremonies and pray at the altars. This is the case in the selection from *The Buddha Tree*. A communist, who according to Marxist doctrine might be expected to have turned away from religion, nevertheless joins the village priest in celebrating the memory of his father at the home altar. The priest is a member of the Pure Land sect of Buddhism, and together with the man and his wife he invokes the name of Amida in his prayers. In "The Snow Ghost," too, a spirit kneels before the Buddhist altar in a home to assure the household that she means it no harm.

Confucianism was introduced into Japan along with the apparatus of the Chinese imperial state as part of the political and administrative reform of the seventh century. It brought to the ruling classes ideals for formal education, a family code, and a social ethic. Confucianism also offered a set of ethical teachings that were used to support social harmony in the family, in the community, and in the state. Unlike Buddhism, which was primarily other-worldly in its focus, Confucianism was concerned above all with the conduct of human beings here and now. When in the six-teenth century the Japanese gradually emerged from several centu-ries of prolonged warfare, the leaders of the unification eagerly sought political and social stability. In Confucianism as it had evolved in China by that time, Japanese leaders found ethical teachings they hoped would guarantee order. They were attracted to the emphasis Confucianism placed on a hierarchical society that gave the ruler and family head the highest positions. Everyone was to conform to the obligations imposed by the five primary human relationships—that is, the relationships between father and son, ruler and subject, husband and wife, older and younger brother, friend and friend. Of these only the relationship between friends was equal; the others represented the mutual obligations of a supe-rior and an inferior. The highest value was placed on loyalty to one's ruler and filial piety to one's parents. Frugality and diligence were part of one's obligation to superiors.

Especially interesting to the student of popular culture in Japan is the way in which Confucian ethical teachings spread throughout Japanese society after 1600, when Confucianism was adopted as the official ideology of the Tokugawa state (1600–1868). It was the deliberate policy of the government to inculcate Confucian values among the common people and hence ensure their loyalty to the state and their support of family and commu-nity. Signboards throughout Japan carried moral injunctions; vil-lage headmen were encouraged to deliver lectures on proper be-havior; commoner education, too, emphasized Confucian ethics.

The sermons of itinerant preachers were another important vehicle by which Confucian values were translated into popular terms for the peasants, artisans, and merchants of the commoner class. The sermon included here by Hosoi Heishū was delivered in 1783 under the aegis of the lord of the domain of Owari. Hosoi

Heishū was one of the most famous and by all accounts one of the most effective popular preachers in eighteenth-century Japan. Trained as a Confucian scholar, he was able to translate Confucian doctrine into stories that would appeal to the common people. He incorporated concepts from Shinto into his argument for obedience to a political and social structure based on Confucian theory. Central to Hosoi's sermon is the concept of sincerity or *makoto*, a crucial tenet of Shinto as it had developed by the eighteenth century. Sincerity, for the Japanese of Hosoi's day, expressed the idea that there is an innate purity in nature and humankind. People who retain that sincerity are in sympathy with each other and with nature, and this sympathy gives rise to peace and harmony in human society and in the natural world as well. In his lecture Hosoi argues that if we have sincerity we will naturally be able to perform the moral duties taught by the Confucian sages. Having established a basis in the native religious tradition for the values he advocates, Hosoi goes on to discuss those values at length and illustrate their importance in daily life.

Like Hosoi Heishū, Ninomiya Sontoku traveled throughout Japan delivering sermons to the common people and urging them to cultivate the virtues of loyalty, duty, and filial piety. Ninomiya was clearly influenced by Confucian views of society and social ethics. He was less concerned with gaining popular support for the government than was Hosoi, but his ideas nevertheless supported the economic, political, and ethical base of the state. Like the orthodox Confucians of his time, Ninomiya considered agriculture to be the foundation of society and he sought to improve the lot of the Japanese farmer through moral exhortation and practical agricultural reform. Central to Ninomiya's sermons was the idea, also important to Hosoi Heishū, that everyone must repay the blessings bestowed on them by heaven, earth, and their fellow humans. If people repay their blessings with hard work, frugality, and self-improvement, the result will be peace and prosperity in family, community, and state.

In the years of upheaval and reconstruction in the aftermath of World War II, new religions sprang up in Japan and have gained wide support. They appeal particularly to urban Japanese who feel out of touch with their traditional roots and to Japanese for whom the established religions no longer offer answers to modern problems. Especially attractive to contemporary Japanese is the emphasis these new religions place on happiness in this world and on peace of mind and universal brotherhood. The selection presented here is taken from *The Prophet of Tabuse,* the official biography of the founder of one of the new religions, often called the Dancing Religion or *Odoru shūkyō.* Like many of the new religions the Dancing Religion is eclectic, incorporating elements from the popular religious tradition. It emphasizes simple faith, the recitation of religious formulas, belief in awe-inspiring spirits, and ritual cleansing. In *The Prophet of Tabuse* the atomic bomb is explained as a kind of exorcism intended by the spirits to rid Japan of evil.

The Japanese people throughout history, at all levels of society, have shown a great propensity toward religious tolerance and little concern for religious orthodoxy. Individual beliefs and practices often combine aspects of all the religions in Japan. In this respect, Japanese religious attitudes contrast sharply with Western religions, which tend to be exclusive. In Japan a man may be married in a Shinto ceremony and pay his respects to his ancestors in a Buddhist ritual. Even the religious buildings themselves combine elements from more than one religion. Many Shinto shrines include a Buddhist temple on the premises, and Buddhist establishments generally provide water for ritual cleansing before worship. A priest of one religion may officiate at ceremonies of another. The selections offered here reflect the syncretism of Japanese religion. In folk legends and in Japanese literature, as in the minds of the Japanese, beliefs and practices stemming from many sources make up the popular religious tradition.

Japanese Folktales

The following legends were recorded from the Japanese oral tradition by Westerners in Japan during the nineteenth and early twentieth centuries. The first one is from A. B. F. Redesdale's *Tales of Old Japan* (London, 1919) and the next three from R. Gordon Smith's *Ancient Tales and Folk-lore of Japan* (London, 1908). All are representative of folktales that describe supernatural events believed by many people for centuries to have actually happened.

HOW A MAN WAS BEWITCHED AND HAD HIS HEAD SHAVED BY THE FOXES

In the village of Iwahara, in the province of Shinshū, there dwelt a family which had acquired considerable wealth in the wine trade. On some auspicious occasion it happened that a number of guests were gathered together at their house, feasting on wine and fish; and as the winecup went round, the conversation turned upon foxes. Among the guests was a certain carpenter, Tokutarō by name, a man about thirty years of age, of a stubborn and obstinate turn, who said:

"Well, sirs, you've been talking for some time of men being bewitched by foxes; surely you must be under their influence yourselves, to say such things. How on earth can foxes have such power

---

The stories are reprinted here as originally published, with a few minor changes to modernize punctuation and diacritical marks.

over men? At any rate, men must be great fools to be so deluded. Let's have no more of this nonsense."

Upon this a man who was sitting by him answered:

"Tokutarō little knows what goes on in the world, or he would not speak so. How many myriads of men are there who have been bewitched by foxes? Why, there have been at least twenty or thirty men tricked by the brutes on the Maki Moor alone. It's hard to disprove facts that have happened before our eyes."

"You're no better than a pack of born idiots!" said Tokutarō. "I will engage to go out to the Maki Moor this very night and prove it. There is not a fox in all Japan that can make a fool of Tokutarō."

Thus he spoke in his pride; but the others were all angry with him for boasting, and said:

"If you return without anything having happened, we will pay for five measures of wine and a thousand copper cash worth of fish; and if you are bewitched, you shall do as much for us."

Tokutarō took the bet, and at nightfall set forth for the Maki Moor by himself. As he neared the moor, he saw before him a small bamboo grove, into which a fox ran; and it instantly occurred to him that the foxes of the moor would try to bewitch him. As he was yet looking, he suddenly saw the daughter of the headman of the village of Upper Horikane, who was married to the headman of the village of Maki.

"Pray, where are you going to, Master Tokutarō?" said she.

"I am going to the village hard by."

"Then, as you will have to pass my native place, if you will allow me, I will accompany you so far."

Tokutarō thought this very odd, and made up his mind that it was a fox trying to make a fool of him; he accordingly determined to turn the tables on the fox, and answered:

"It is a long time since I have had the pleasure of seeing you; and as it seems that your house is on my road, I shall be glad to escort you so far."

With this he walked behind her, thinking he should certainly see the end of a fox's tail peeping out; but, look as he might, there was nothing to be seen. At last they came to the village of Upper

Horikane; and when they reached the cottage of the girl's father, the family all came out, surprised to see her.

"Oh dear! oh dear! here is our daughter come: I hope there is nothing the matter."

And so they went on, for some time, asking a string of questions.

In the meanwhile, Tokutarō went round to the kitchen door, at the back of the house, and, beckoning out the master of the house, said:

"The girl who has come with me is not really your daughter. As I was going to the Maki Moor, when I arrived at the bamboo grove, a fox jumped up in front of me, and when it had dashed into the grove it immediately took the shape of your daughter, and offered to accompany me to the village; so I pretended to be taken in by the brute, and came with it so far."

On hearing this, the master of the house put his head on one side, and mused a while; then, calling his wife, he repeated the story to her, in a whisper.

But she flew into a great rage with Tokutarō, and said:

"This is a pretty way of insulting people's daughters. The girl is our daughter, and there's no mistake about it. How dare you invent such lies?"

"Well," said Tokutarō, "you are quite right to say so; but still there is no doubt that this is a case of witchcraft."

Seeing how obstinately he held to his opinion, the old folks were sorely perplexed, and said:

"What do you think of doing?"

"Pray leave the matter to me: I'll soon strip the false skin off, and show the beast to you in its true colors. Do you two go into the store-closet, and wait there."

With this he went into the kitchen, and, seizing the girl by the back of the neck, forced her down by the hearth.

"Oh! Master Tokutarō, what means this brutal violence? Mother! father! help!"

So the girl cried and screamed; but Tokutarō only laughed, and said:

"So you thought to bewitch me, did you? From the moment you jumped into the wood, I was on the lookout for you to play me some trick. I'll soon make you show what you really are"; and as he said this, he twisted her two hands behind her back, and trod upon her, and tortured her; but she only wept, and cried:

"Oh! it hurts, it hurts!"

"If this is not enough to make you show your true form, I'll roast you to death"; and he piled firewood on the hearth, and, tucking up her dress, scorched her severely.

"Oh! oh! this is more than I can bear"; and with this she expired.

The two old people then came running in from the rear of the house, and, pushing aside Tokutarō, folded their daughter in their arms, and put their hands to her mouth to feel whether she still breathed; but life was extinct, and not the sign of a fox's tail was to be seen about her. Then they seized Tokutarō by the collar, and cried:

"On pretense that our true daughter was a fox, you have roasted her to death. Murderer! Here, you there, bring ropes and cords, and secure this Tokutarō!"

So the servants obeyed, and several of them seized Tokutarō and bound him to a pillar. Then the master of the house, turning to Tokutarō, said:

"You have murdered our daughter before our very eyes. I shall report the matter to the lord of the manor, and you will assuredly pay for this with your head. Be prepared for the worst."

And as he said this, glaring fiercely at Tokutarō, they carried the corpse of his daughter into the store-closet. As they were sending to make the matter known in the village of Maki, and taking other measures, who should come up but the priest of the temple called Anrakuji, in the village of Iwahara, with an acolyte and a servant, who called out in a loud voice from the front door:

"Is all well with the honorable master of this house? I have been to say prayers today in a neighboring village, and on my way back I could not pass the door without at least inquiring after your welfare. If you are at home, I would fain pay my respects to you."

As he spoke thus in a loud voice, he was heard from the back of the house; and the master got up and went out, and, after the usual compliments on meeting had been exchanged, said:

"I ought to have the honor of inviting you to step inside this evening; but really we are all in the greatest trouble, and I must beg you to excuse my impoliteness."

"Indeed! Pray, what may be the matter?" replied the priest. And when the master of the house had told the whole story, from beginning to end, he was thunderstruck, and said:

"Truly, this must be a terrible distress to you." Then the priest looked on one side, and saw Tokutarō bound, and exclaimed, "Is not that Tokutarō that I see there?"

"Oh, your reverence," replied Tokutarō, piteously, "it was this, that, and the other; and I took it into my head that the young lady was a fox, and so I killed her. But I pray your reverence to intercede for me, and save my life"; and as he spoke, the tears started from his eyes.

"To be sure," said the priest, "you may well bewail yourself; however, if I save your life, will you consent to become my disciple, and enter the priesthood?"

"Only save my life, and I'll become your disciple with all my heart."

When the priest heard this, he called out the parents, and said to them:

"It would seem that, though I am but a foolish old priest, my coming here today has been unusually well timed. I have a request to make of you. Your putting Tokutaro to death won't bring your daughter to life again. I have heard his story, and there certainly was no malice prepense on his part to kill your daughter. What he did, he did thinking to do a service to your family; and it would surely be better to hush the matter up. He wishes, moreover, to give himself over to me, and to become my disciple."

"It is as you say," replied the father and mother, speaking together. "Revenge will not recall our daughter. Please dispel our grief, by shaving his head and making a priest of him on the spot."

"I'll shave him at once, before your eyes," answered the

Wingate College Library

priest, who immediately caused the cords which bound Tokutarō to be untied, and, putting on his priest's scarf, made him join his hands together in a posture of prayer. Then the reverend man stood up behind him, razor in hand, and, intoning a hymn, gave two or three strokes of the razor, which he then handed to his acolyte, who made a clean shave of Tokutarō's hair. When the latter had finished his obeisance to the priest, and the ceremony was over, there was a loud burst of laughter; and at the same moment the day broke, and Tokutarō found himself alone, in the middle of a large moor. At first, in his surprise, he thought that it was all a dream, and was much annoyed at having been tricked by the foxes. He then passed his hand over his head, and found that he was shaved quite bald. There was nothing for it but to get up, wrap a handkerchief round his head, and go back to the place where his friends were assembled.

"Hallo, Tokutarō! So you've come back. Well, how about the foxes?"

"Really, gentlemen," replied he, bowing, "I am quite ashamed to appear before you."

Then he told them the whole story, and, when he had finished, pulled off the kerchief, and showed his bald pate.

"What a capital joke!" shouted his listeners, and amid roars of laughter, claimed the bet of fish and wine. It was duly paid; but Tokutarō never allowed his hair to grow again, and renounced the world, and became a priest under the name of Sainen.

THE SNOW GHOST

Perhaps there are not many, even in Japan, who have heard of the "Yuki Onna" (Snow Ghost). It is little spoken of except in the higher mountains, which are continually snowclad in the winter.

Up in the northern province of Echigo, opposite Sado Island on the Japan Sea, snow falls heavily. Sometimes there is as much as twenty feet of it on the ground, and many are the people who have been buried in the snows and never found until the spring.

Mysterious disappearances naturally give rise to fancies in a fanciful people, and from time immemorial the Snow Ghost has been one with the people of the North; while those of the South say that those of the North take so much *sake* that they see snow-covered trees as women. Be that as it may, I must explain what a farmer called Kyūzaemon saw.

In the village of Hoi, which consisted only of eleven houses, very poor ones at that, lived Kyūzaemon. He was poor, and doubly unfortunate in having lost both his son and his wife. He led a lonely life.

In the afternoon of the 19th of January of the third year of Tempō—that is, 1832—a tremendous snowstorm came on. Kyūzaemon closed the shutters, and made himself as comfortable as he could. Towards eleven o'clock at night he was awakened by a rapping at his door; it was a peculiar rap, and came at regular intervals. Kyūzaemon sat up in bed, looked towards the door, and did not know what to think of this. The rapping came again, and with it the gentle voice of a girl. Thinking that it might be one of his neighbor's children wanting help, Kyūzaemon jumped out of bed; but when he got to the door he feared to open it. Voice and rapping coming again just as he reached it, he sprang back with a cry: "Who are you? What do you want?"

"Open the door! Open the door!" came the voice from outside.

"Open the door! Is that likely until I know who you are and what you are doing out so late and on such a night?"

"But you must let me in. How can I proceed farther in this deep snow? I do not ask for food, but only for shelter."

"I am very sorry; but I have no quilts or bedding. I can't possibly let you stay in my house."

"I don't want quilts or bedding—only shelter," pleaded the voice.

"I can't let you in, anyway," shouted Kyūzaemon. "It is too late and against the rules and the law."

Saying which, Kyūzaemon rebarred his door with a strong piece of wood, never once having ventured to open a crack in the shutters to see who his visitor might be. As he turned towards his bed, with a shudder he beheld the figure of a woman standing beside it, clad in white, with her hair down her back. She had not the appearance of a ghost; her face was pretty, and she seemed to be about twenty-five years of age. Kyūzaemon, taken by surprise and very much alarmed, called out:

"Who and what are you, and how did you get in? Where did you leave your *geta?*"*

"I can come in anywhere when I choose," said the figure, "and I am the woman you would not let in. I require no clogs; for I whirl along over the snow, sometimes even flying through the air. I am on my way to visit the next village; but the wind is against me. That is why I wanted you to let me rest here. If you will do so I shall start as soon as the wind goes down; in any case I shall be gone by the morning."

"I should not so much mind letting you rest if you were an ordinary woman. I should, in fact, be glad; but I fear spirits greatly, as my forefathers have done," said Kyūzaemon.

"Be not afraid. You have a *butsudan?*† said the figure.

"Yes: I have a *butsudan,*" said Kyūzaemon, "but what can you want to do with that?"

"You say you are afraid of the spirits, of the effect that I may have upon you. I wish to pay my respects to your ancestors' tablets and assure their spirits that no ill shall befall you through me. Will you open and light the *butsudan?*"

"Yes," said Kyūzaemon, with fear and trembling: "I will open the *butsudan,* and light the lamp. Please pray for me as well, for I am an unfortunate and unlucky man; but you must tell me in return who and what spirit you are."

"You want to know much; but I will tell you," said the spirit. "I believe you are a good man. My name was Oyasu. I am the daughter of Yazaemon, who lives in the next village. My father, as perhaps you may have heard, is a farmer, and he adopted into his family, and as a husband for his daughter, Isaburo. Isaburo is a

---

*Clogs.

†Family altar, in which the figures of various gods are set, and also the family mortuary tablets.

good man; but on the death of his wife, last year, he forsook his father-in-law and went back to his old home. It is principally for that reason that I am about to seek and remonstrate with him now."

"Am I to understand," said Kyuzaemon, "that the daughter who was married to Isaburo was the one who perished in the snow last year? If so, you must be the spirit of Oyasu or Isaburo's wife?"

"Yes: that is right," said the spirit. "I was Oyasu, the wife of Isaburo, who perished now a year ago in the great snowstorm, of which tomorrow will be the anniversary."

Kyūzaemon, with trembling hands, lit the lamp in the little *butsudan*, mumbling "Namu Amida Butsu; Namu Amida Butsu"* with a fervor which he had never felt before. When this was done he saw the figure of the Yuki Onna (Snow Ghost) advance; but there was no sound of footsteps as she glided to the altar.

Kyūzaemon retired to bed, where he promptly fell asleep; but shortly afterwards he was disturbed by the voice of the woman bidding him farewell. Before he had time to sit up she disappeared, leaving no sign; the fire still burned in the *butsudan*.

Kyūzaemon got up at daybreak, and went to the next village to see Isaburo, whom he found living with his father-in-law, Yazaemon.

"Yes," said Isaburo, "it was wrong of me to leave my late wife's father when she died, and I am not surprised that on cold nights when it snows I have been visited continually by my wife's spirit as a reproof. Early this morning I saw her again, and I resolved to return. I have only been here two hours as it is."

On comparing notes Kyūzaemon and Isaburo found that directly the spirit of Oyasu had left the house of Kyūzaemon she appeared to Isaburo, at about half-an-hour after midnight, and stayed with him until he had promised to return to her father's house and help him to live in his old age.

That is roughly my story of the Yuki Onna. All those who die by the snow and cold become spirits of snow, appearing when

---

*A Buddhist incantation often called a *nembutsu*. It is said in praise of the name of the Amida Buddha. [Ed.]

there is snow; just as the spirits of those who are drowned in the sea only appear in stormy seas.

Even to the present day, in the North, priests say prayers to appease the spirits of those who have died by snow, and to prevent them from haunting people who are connected with them.

LEGEND TOLD BY A FISHERMAN ON LAKE BIWA AT ZEZE

Many years ago there was a *daimyō* who had constructed at the foot of the southern spur of Mount Hiei a castle, the ruins of which may still be seen just to the north of the military barracks of the Ninth Regiment in Otsu. The name of the *daimyō* was Akechi Mitsuhide, and it is his *hito dama* that we see now in wet weather on the lake. It is called the spirit of Akechi.

The reason of it is this. When Akechi Mitsuhide defended himself against the Toyotomi, he was closely invested; but his castle held out bravely, and could not be taken in spite of Toyotomi's greater forces. As time went on, the besiegers became exasperated, and prevailed upon a bad fisherman from Magisa village to tell where was the source of water which supplied Akechi's castle. The water having been cut off, the garrison had to capitulate, but not before Akechi and most of his men had committed suicide.

From that time, in rain or in rough weather, there has come from the castle a fireball, six inches in diameter or more. It comes to wreak vengeance on fishermen, and causes many wrecks, leading boats out of their course. Sometimes it comes almost into the boat. Once a fisherman struck it with a bamboo pole, breaking it up into many fiery bits; and on that occasion many boats were lost.

In full it is called "The Spider Fire of the Spirit of the Dead Akechi."

YOSOJI'S CAMELLIA TREE

In the reign of the Emperor Sanjō began a particularly unlucky time. It was about the year 1013 A.D. when Sanjō came to the throne—the first year of Chōwa. Plague broke out. Two years later the Royal Palace was burned down, and a war began with Korea, then known as "Shiragi."

In 1016 another fire broke out in the new Palace. A year later the Emperor gave up the throne, owing to blindness and for other causes. He handed over the reins of office to Prince Atsuhara, who was called the Emperor Go Ichijō, and came to the throne in the first year of the Kannin, about 1017 or 1018. The period during which the Emperor Go Ichijō reigned—about twenty years, up to 1036—was one of the worst in Japanese history. There were more wars, more fires, and worse plagues than ever. Things were in disorder generally, and even Kyoto was hardly safe to people of means, owing to the bands of brigands. In 1025 the most appalling outbreak of smallpox came; there was hardly a village or a town in Japan which escaped.

It is at this period that our story begins. Our heroine (if such she may be called) is no less a deity than the goddess of the mountain of Fuji, which nearly all the world has heard of, or seen depicted. Therefore, if the legend sounds stupid and childish, blame only my way of telling it (simply, as it was told to me), and think of the Great Mountain of Japan, as to which anything should be interesting; moreover, challenge others for a better. I have been able to find none myself.

During the terrible scourge of smallpox there was a village in Suruga Province called Kamiide, which still exists, but is of little importance. It suffered more badly than most other villages. Scarce an inhabitant escaped. A youth of sixteen or seventeen years was much tried. His mother was taken with the disease, and, his father being dead, the responsibility of the household fell on Yosoji—for such was his name.

Yosoji procured all the help he could for his mother, sparing nothing in the way of medicines and attendance; but his mother grew worse day by day, until at last her life was utterly despaired of. Having no other resource left to him, Yosoji resolved to consult a famous fortune-teller and magician, Kamo Yamakiko.

Kamo Yamakiko told Yosoji that there was but one chance that his mother could be cured, and that lay much with his own courage. "If," said the fortune-teller, "you will go to a small brook which flows from the southwestern side of Mount Fuji, and find a small shrine near its source, where Oki-naga-suku-neo* is worshiped, you may be able to cure your mother by bringing her water therefrom to drink. But I warn you that the place is full of dangers from wild beasts and other things, and that you may not return at all or even reach the place."

Yosoji, in no way discouraged, made his mind up that he would start on the following morning, and, thanking the fortune-teller, went home to prepare for an early start.

At three o'clock next morning he was off.

It was a long and rough walk, one which he had never taken before; but he trudged gaily on, being sound of limb and bent on an errand of deepest concern.

Towards midday Yosoji arrived at a place where three rough paths met, and was sorely puzzled which to take. While he was deliberating the figure of a beautiful girl clad in white came towards him through the forest. At first Yosoji felt inclined to run; but the figure called to him in silvery notes, saying:

"Do not go. I know what you are here for. You are a brave lad and a faithful son. I will be your guide to the stream, and—take my word for it—its waters will cure your mother. Follow me if you will, and have no fear, though the road is bad and dangerous."

The girl turned, and Yosoji followed in wonderment.

In silence the two went for fully four miles, always upwards and into deeper and more gloomy forests. At last a small shrine was reached, in front of which were two *torii,* and from a cleft of a rock gurgled a silvery stream, the clearness of which was such as Yosoji had never seen before.

"There," said the white-robed girl, "is the stream of which you are in search. Fill your gourd, and drink of it yourself, for the waters will prevent you catching the plague. Make haste, for it grows late, and it would not be well for you to be here at night. I shall guide you back to the place where I met you."

---

*The God of Long Breath.

Yosoji did as he was bid, drinking, and then filling the bottle to the brim.

Much faster did they return than they had come, for the way was all downhill. On reaching the meeting of the three paths Yosoji bowed low to his guide, and thanked her for her great kindness; and the girl told him again that it was her pleasure to help so dutiful a son.

"In three days you will want more water for your mother," said she, "and I shall be at the same place to be your guide again."

"May I not ask to whom I am indebted for this great kindness?" asked Yosoji.

"No: you must not ask, for I should not tell you," answered the girl. Bowing again, Yosoji proceeded on his way as fast as he could, wondering greatly.

On reaching home he found his mother worse. He gave her a cup of the water, and told her of his adventures. During the night Yosoji awoke as usual to attend to his mother's wants, and to give her another bowl of water. Next morning he found that she was decidedly better. During the day he gave her three more doses, and on the morning of the third day he set forth to keep his appointment with the fair lady in white, whom he found seated waiting for him on a rock at the meeting of the three paths.

"Your mother is better: I can see from your happy face," said she. "Now follow me as before, and make haste. Come again in three days, and I will meet you. It will take five trips in all, for the water must be taken fresh. You may give some to the sick villagers as well."

Five times did Yosoji take the trip. At the end of the fifth his mother was perfectly well, and most thankful for her restoration; besides which, most of the villagers who had not died were cured. Yosoji was the hero of the hour. Every one marveled, and wondered who the white-robed girl was; for, though they had heard of the shrine of Oki-naga-suku-neo, none of them knew where it was, and but few would have dared to go if they had known. Of course, all knew that Yosoji was indebted in the first place to the fortune-teller Kamo Yamakiko, to whom the whole village sent presents.

Yosoji was not easy in his mind. In spite of the good he had brought about, he thought to himself that he owed the whole of his success in finding and bringing the water to the village to his fair guide, and he did not feel that he had shown sufficient gratitude. Always he had hurried home as soon as he had got the precious water, bowing his thanks. That was all, and now he felt as if more were due. Surely prayers at the shrine were due, or something; and who was the lady in white? He must find out. Curiosity called upon him to do so. Thus Yosoji resolved to pay one more visit to the spring, and started early in the morning.

Now familiar with the road, he did not stop at the meeting of the three paths, but pursued his way directly to the shrine. It was the first time he had traveled the road alone, and in spite of himself he felt afraid, though he could not say why. Perhaps it was the oppressive gloom of the mysterious dark forest, overshadowed by the holy mountain of Fuji, which in itself was more mysterious still, and filled one both with superstitious and religious feelings and a feeling of awe as well. No one of any imagination can approach the mountain even today without having one or all of these emotions.

Yosoji, however, sped on, as fast as he could go, and arrived at the shrine of Oki-naga-suku-neo. He found that the stream had dried up. There was not a drop of water left. Yosoji flung himself upon his knees before the shrine and thanked the God of Long Breath that he had been the means of curing his mother and the surviving villagers. He prayed that his guide to the spring might reveal her presence, and that he might be enabled to meet her once more to thank her for her kindness. When he arose Yosoji saw his guide standing beside him, and bowed low. She was the first to speak.

"You must not come here," she said. "I have told you so before. It is a place of great danger for you. Your mother and the villagers are cured. There is no reason for you to come here more."

"I have come," answered Yosoji, "because I have not fully spoken my thanks, and because I wish to tell you how deeply grateful I am to you, as is my mother and as are the whole of our villagers. Moreover, they all as well as I wish to know to whom they are indebted for my guidance to the spring. Though Kamo Yama-kiko told me of the spring, I should never have found it but for your kindness, which has now extended over five weeks. Surely you will let us know to whom we are so much indebted, so that we may at least erect a shrine in our temple?"

"All that you ask is unnecessary. I am glad that you are grateful. I knew that one so truly filial as you must be so, and it is because of your filial piety and goodness that I guided you to this health-giving spring, which, as you see, is dry, having at present no further use. It is unnecessary that you should know who I am. We must now part: so farewell. End your life as you have begun it, and you shall be happy." The beautiful maiden swung a wild camellia branch over her head as if with a beckoning motion, and a cloud came down from the top of Mount Fuji, enveloping her at first in mist. It then arose, showing her figure to the weeping Yosoji, who now began to realize that he loved the departing figure, and that it was no less a figure than that of the great Goddess of Fujiyama. Yosoji fell on his knees and prayed to her, and the goddess, acknowledging his prayer, threw down the branch of wild camellia.

Yosoji carried it home, and planted it, caring for it with the utmost attention. The branch grew to a tree with marvellous rapidity, being over twenty feet high in two years. A shrine was built; people came to worship the tree; and it is said that the dewdrops from its leaves are a cure for all eye complaints.

Tales of Tōno

Tōno Monogatari [Tales of Tōno] is a collection of legends published in 1910 by Kunio Yanagita (1875–1962), the founder of folklore studies in Japan. Yanagita gave literary expression to legendary tales told to him by a country gentleman from the Tōno region of rural Iwate prefecture in northeastern Japan. The following selections illustrate characteristic themes of Japanese legends including stories of guardian spirits of the hearth, rich men who encounter fortune and misfortune, and evil foxes that have powers of transformation.

In every village there is always one old household which worships the deity Okunai-sama (the household deity that looks after the fate of the family). The image of this deity is carved from mulberry wood and has a face drawn on it. A hole is punched in the middle of a square piece of cloth and it is pulled down over the image to make the garment. On the fifteenth day of the New Year the immediate neighbors gather in this house to worship the deity.

There is also the deity Oshira-sama (an agricultural deity). The image of this deity is made in the same way and it is also worshiped when the villagers get together on the fifteenth day of the New Year. At this ceremony they sometimes put white powder on the face of the image.

There is always a tiny room of about twelve square feet in the old household. Those who sleep in this room at night always experience something strange. It's quite common for the pillow to get

Translation adapted from Kunio Yanagita, *The Legends of Tōno,* translated by Ronald A. Morse (Tokyo: The Japan Foundation, 1975), pp. 20–25, 30, 61–67.

turned over somehow. Sometimes the sleeping person is grabbed
and awakened or is shoved out of the room. No one is permitted to
sleep quietly there.

Good fortune comes to those who worship Okunai-sama. At
Kashiwazaki in Tsuchibuchi village there is a rich man named Abe
and the villagers refer to his house as "the house of rice fields."
One year this household was short of hands for the rice planting.
The sky warned of rain the next day and just as they were considering leaving some fields unplanted, all of a sudden a short boy came
up from somewhere. He offered to help work, so they let him work
as he pleased. At lunchtime they called to him to come and eat but
they could not find him. Later he reappeared and he worked busily
the whole day in the fields. Thus, they finished the planting on
that day. They did not know where the boy had come from, but in
the evening when they invited him to come and eat, he disappeared with the setting sun. When they returned home they found
the verandah covered with muddy little footprints that led into the
parlor and up to the altar for the Okunai-sama. Thinking "Well,
what next!" they opened the door of the altar and found the image
of the deity covered from the waist down with mud from the fields.

*   *   *

Among the older households there are quite a few houses that
have the spirit Zashikiwarashi (parlor child). At the oldest this deity is twelve or thirteen years old. From time to time it reveals itself
to people. At Iide in Tsuchibuchi village Kanjūrō Imabuchi's
daughter, who goes to a girls' high school, recently returned home
for vacation. One day in the dark corridor, all of a sudden, she
bumped into Zashikiwarashi and was badly shocked. Zashikiwarashi was definitely a male child.

At Yamaguchi in the same village the mother of Mr. Sasaki
was sewing alone one day when she heard the sound of paper rus-
tling in the next room. That room was only for the master of the
house, but he was in Tokyo. Thinking it was strange, she opened
the wooden door and looked in, but no one was there. After having been seated a short time, again there was the sound of someone
sniffing. She concluded that it must be Zashikiwarashi. It had been

rumored for some time that Zashikiwarashi resided in this house. The house that this deity lives in is said to become rich and prestigious.

* * *

Zashikiwarashi can also be a girl child. It has been traditionally said that there are two girl deities in the house of Magozaemon Yamaguchi, also an old house in Yamaguchi. One year a certain man from the village was on his way back from town and near Tomeba bridge he met two lovely girls whom he had never seen before. They were walking pensively toward him.

"Where did you come from?" he asked.

"We have come from Magozaemon's in Yamaguchi," they replied.

"Where are you headed now?" he inquired.

"To a certain house in another village," was the reply. That certain household in a somewhat distant village is now wealthy and the people live well. Hearing this the man conjectured that Magozaemon was headed for ruin, and not too long after that, twenty or so people in the family died in one day from mushroom poisoning. Only one seven-year-old girl did not die. She merely grew old without having any children, and recently died of an illness.

Magozaemon was at home one day when he heard the servants discussing whether or not they should eat some unusual mushrooms that had grown around a pear tree. Magozaemon, the master of his household, suggested that it would be best not to eat them, but one manservant said, "No matter what kind of mushrooms they are, if you put them into a water bucket and mix in hemp seeds there is no chance of poisoning." Everyone agreed with this, and the whole family ate them. The seven-year-old girl was outside on this day absorbed in playing. The fact that she forgot to come home for lunch saved her.

After the sudden death of the master, and while people were still at a loss over what to do, relatives from far and near came and took all the household goods, even the soybean paste. They said that they had loaned money to the family earlier or had some kind of agreement. This was the family of a rich man, one of the first to establish the village, but in a single morning no trace of it was left.

Before this calamity there were various omens. One day when the men were taking out the hay with their pitchforks, they found a large snake. The master said not to kill it, but they did not listen and beat it to death. After this there were numerous snakes under the hay and when they wiggled out, the men, partially for amusement, killed them all. Finally, needing a place to throw them they dug a hole, buried them and then made a mound. These snakes are said to have filled any number of straw baskets.

Magozaemon, the man mentioned above, was quite a scholar. He had Japanese and Chinese books sent from Kyoto and was usually absorbed in reading. He was somewhat eccentric. One day, he decided to find out how to get on good terms with the fox in order to make his house wealthy. First, he built an Inari (fox deity) shrine in his garden and then went himself to Kyoto to obtain the highest order of fox deity.* After that, every day without fail, he offered, with his own hands, a piece of the fox's favorite fried bean curd at the shrine and worshiped. Gradually the fox got used to him and did not run away when he approached. It is said he could reach out and touch the fox on the head. The keeper of the village's Yakushi (Buddha of Healing) temple would joke and say: "Nothing is offered to our Buddha, but it gives more benefits than Magozaemon's deity."

*　*　*

A variety of birds live in the mountains, but the one with the lonliest voice is the *otto* (husband) bird. It sings on summer nights. It is said that pack drivers and others coming over the pass from the seashore at Ozuchi hear this bird off in the bottom of the valley.

Once there was the daughter of a rich man, who was intimate with the son of another rich man. While they were off wandering in the mountains one day, the young man disappeared. Into the evening and until late at night, the girl walked around looking for

---

*Inari shrines are dedicated to the gods of harvests. It is said the head Inari shrine in Kyoto was the highest in the ranking system of premodern Japan. However, there is a popular view that Inari is the fox deity. Hence, the fox has the highest rank. [Ed.]

him, but to no avail. It is said she eventually became the *otto* bird. The bird's song, *"otto-n, otto-n,"* means "my husband, my husband." Its voice gradually grows hoarse and sounds quite pathetic.

* * *

To go to Kashiwazaki from Yamaguchi one has to go around the base of Mount Atago. Along the way there are rice fields and then pine trees. From the spot where one can see the houses of the people of Kashiwazaki, there are thickets of bushes and small trees.

There is a small shrine on the top of Mount Atago, and a path for worshipers which goes through the woods. There is a sacred Shinto gate and about twenty or thirty old cedar trees at the entrance to the mountain. Next to this there is a vacant shrine. In front of the shrine there is a stone monument with the words "mountain deity" carved into it. It has been said since olden times that this is the spot where the "mountain deity" first appeared.

A youth from Wano had some business in Kashiwazaki, and in the evening, when passing by the shrine, he saw a tall man coming down from the top of Mount Atago. Wondering who it could be, the youth approached and looked at the person's face, which appeared above a cluster of trees. At the bend in the road the two met unexpectedly. The tall man, unsuspecting, was quite surprised. The face looking at the youth was bright red, had radiant eyes, and indeed contained an expression of surprise. The youth knew it was the "mountain deity" and he ran off to Kashiwazaki without ever looking back.

* * *

There is a man in the town of Tōno who is knowledgeable about the mountains. At one time he was in charge of the falcons of Baron Nambu. The people in the town call this man by the nickname Torigozen, which means "Bird Keeper." He knows the shape and location of every tree and rock on Mount Hayachine and Mount Rokkoushi. When he was old he went gathering mushrooms with a companion who was an excellent swimmer. The companion had the reputation of being able to go into the water with some straw and a mallet, and to come out with straw sandals made.

These two men went to the hill, Mukēyama, which is across the Saru-ga-ishi River from the town of Tōno. From there they went into the mountains just a little higher up than the spot with the unusual rocks. This spot is known as Tsuzukiishi in Ayaori village. The two men separated and Torigozen went still a little higher up the mountain. The light of the autumn sky lingered just above the western hills, as it does around four o'clock in the afternoon. Suddenly, in the shadow of a huge rock, he came across a red-faced man and woman standing and talking. They watched Torigozen approach, and then stretched out their hands as if to press him back or restrain him. But he went on regardless, and the woman seemed to cling to the man's chest. From the way they looked, Torigozen did not think they were humans. Being a playful type, for fun, he drew out the long knife at his side and struck at them. The red-complexioned man raised his leg as if he were going to kick, and that is the last thing Torigozen remembered.

The companion looked around for Torigozen, and he was found at the bottom of the valley, unconscious. He received care and was taken home. Torigozen told all of the details of the day and how he had never before experienced such a thing. He said, "I might have died then. Don't tell anyone else about this." He was sick for about three days and died. Family members thought his manner of death somewhat strange and went to consult with the itinerant priest named Kenkō-in. He told them that because Torigozen had disturbed the place where the "mountain deities" were playing, he had been cursed and died. This man was an acquaintance of Mr. Inō and others. The incident took place over ten years ago.

*   *   *

The wife of Kikuzō Kikuchi of Wano comes from Hashino, which is on the other side of Fuefuki-tōge (flute-blowing pass). While she was back in her native village her son, who was five or six years old, took sick. It was past noon when Kikuzō got over Fuefuki-tōge, and arrived at the village to bring his wife home.

This was a well-known ridge of Mount Rokkoushi, and the mountain path was thick with trees. Especially in the area going down to Kurihashi from Tōno, there were steep cliffs on both sides of the path. The sunlight was hidden by the cliff and it was getting dark when someone called out "Kikuzō!" from behind. He turned around and saw someone looking down from the top of the cliff. His face was red and his eyes were bright and radiant—just as in the previous tale. The man said, "Your child is already dead!" When Kikuzō heard these words, before he could be afraid, he thought, "Oh! It must be so!" The form on top of the cliff disappeared quickly. Kikuzō and his wife hurried home throughout the night, but the child was, as he had feared, already dead. This happened four or five years ago.

*   *   *

This same Kikuzō had reason to visit his sister's house in Kashiwazaki. When he left her house he put into his bosom some rice cakes that had been left over. Just as he passed the woods at the base of Mount Atago, he met his good friend Tōshichi of Zōtsubo, who was quite a drinker. They were still in the woods, but there were some grassy areas. Tōshichi smiled and pointing to a grassy spot said, "How about wrestling here a bit?" Kikuzō thought it a good idea and they spent some time wrestling on the grass. But Tōshichi seemed weak, and so light as to be easily grappled with and thrown. It was such fun that they did it three times. Then Tōshichi said, "I'm no match for you today. I'd better be going." They parted. After Kikuzō had gone several yards, he noticed that his rice cakes were gone. He went back to the spot where they had wrestled and looked around, but they were not there.

For the first time he thought, "I wonder if that was a fox." Since he was ashamed of what others would say, he didn't mention it to anyone. Four or five days later he went to a wine dealer and met Tōshichi. Kikuzō told him of his experience and Tōshichi said, "I wrestled with you? I was at the coast that day." At last it was clear that Kikuzō had wrestled with a fox. Kikuzō kept it a secret, but last year during the New Year's holiday, when everyone was drinking, the topic of foxes came up. He revealed the tale of what he had, in fact, experienced . . . and was really laughed at.

The Nariai
Kannon

"The Nariai Kannon" is one of more than a thousand religious stories and folktales included in the *Konjaku monogatari shū*. The collection was compiled in the present form some time around A.D. 1100. It includes tales by authors who seem to have been inspired by stories from India and China as well as those of Japan. The richness of the collection is seen in its variety of subjects and styles, and depth of human observation. In the following tale, Kannon, who is worshiped in Japan as a goddess of mercy, miraculously provides a starving monk with food.

In Tango, in the old days, there was a mountain temple named Nariai. A miraculous, wonder-working Kannon was enshrined there. It was called Nariai because of the following incident.

In those days, a poor Buddhist disciple was in seclusion in the temple, absorbed in his devotions. The temple was on the top of a high mountain where the snow was deeper than anywhere else and a loud wind raged through the pine forest. It was midwinter; the mountain path was closed by the snow and not a soul passed by.

The food that the monk had brought with him was all gone, but the snow was too deep for him to go down to the village to beg for more. Nor were there plants to eat. The monk could bear his hunger at first, but after ten days without food he could no longer stand. He spread a torn straw raincoat in the southeast corner of the main hall and lay down on it. He did not have enough energy to build a fire to keep off the cold wind that blew mercilessly

"Nariai Kannon," in *Nihon no gūwa*, edited by Naoaki Ichinose (Tokyo: Hōbunkan, 1960), pp. 170–175. Translated for this book by Hiroko Kataoka.

through the holes in the torn paper of the sliding doors. As he listened to the sound of the blizzard raging through the woods his fear increased. At last the monk lost even the energy to chant sutras and pray to the Buddha. All he could do was to wait for starvation.

The monk appealed to the Kannon of the temple, saying, "Hail, Kannon! I hear that you will answer the prayers of those who have invoked your hallowed name only once. That I who have for so long revered and placed faith in your miraculous virtues should be allowed to die in your very presence is truly cruel. It is not as if I were seeking prestige or riches. All I ask for is enough food to get me through just one day."

As he prayed with fervor, to his great surprise he saw through a broken temple window a large black object lying on the snow. Looking closely, the monk saw that it was a wild boar which must have been brought down by a wolf. Truly this must be the mercy of Kannon! The monk was about to cut into the boar when it occurred to him that as one who had long devoted himself to the Buddhist path he could hardly on this night break the prohibition against eating animal flesh. Is it not said that all living things are mothers and fathers from previous existences? Even if one is dying of starvation it will not do to eat the flesh of one's parents. It is written that those who eat the flesh of living animals are those who utterly destroy the source of Buddhahood. And there is no doubt that after death those who have eaten such flesh fall into the path of evil. This must be the reason why all beasts run away at the sight of man, and why the Buddhas and Buddhist saints keep their distance from those who eat meat. Oh, to think I was on the verge of committing such a heinous offense!

Thus the monk reflected, over and over again. And yet, with food there in front of his eyes, his hunger only increased. Could it be that firm faith cannot control instinct after all? Saying, "Oh, it makes no difference. The torments of the afterlife cannot compare with the starvation of today," the monk drew out a knife, cut a piece of meat from the thigh of the boar, boiled it, and ate it. Shamefully he indulged himself. It was overwhelmingly delicious. Every delicacy he had ever tasted paled by comparison. Even his sense of repletion following such extreme hunger was of an exceptional quality. At the same time, however, he was filled with remorse. His conscience smote him for his sin, and he wailed and lamented.

Eventually the snow melted away, and even in the deep mountains there was a faint suggestion of spring. One day the monk sensed the approach of villagers.

"I wonder what became of the monk who was cloistered here?"

"Not a soul could get through with all that snow."

"Having been here for so long I bet he was completely without food." The voices of the villagers and the sound of their footsteps came closer and closer.

The monk was worried to death. He would have to deceive the villagers so they would not discover that he had eaten the boar. And yet there was still a piece of meat in the pot! The more he panicked the more difficult it became for him to decide what to do. While the monk was still in a frenzy, the villagers came pouring in.

"We're glad to see you safe!"

It's a miracle you were able to make it through the winter," exclaimed the villagers while they looked around the room. They saw the pot with a piece of cypress in it. It was evident that the monk had boiled and eaten it.

"Granted you were out of food, but imagine being able to eat a piece of wood."

"You've had a rough time of it."

While the villagers voiced their sympathy, they happened to look at the image of the Kannon. They noticed that a piece had been torn from each of the Kannon's thighs.

"Well, the monk must have cut them and eaten them, but still it is all very strange," they thought. "Surely," the villagers exclaimed, "if you had wanted to eat wood you could have torn some from one of the temple pillars, but what do you mean by taking a piece from the sacred image? It's a sacrilege!"

The monk himself was most surprised at their remarks and looked at the Kannon. It was just as the villagers had said.

"Then it was an incarnation of Kannon that I ate—thinking it was boar's meat! Surely it could only have been the Kannon's loving spirit that would save such a wretched monk as I." Choked with tears of gratitude, the monk confessed what he had done. The villagers were moved to tears at the divine grace of the Kannon.

Once again the monk faced the image of Kannon and prayed fervently: "If all this is true, won't you please return to your original form." While all looked on, both of the Kannon's thighs returned to their original form. Everyone was overcome with tears of joy.

This is why the temple is called Nariai, a temple of healing.

The Jizō with the Bamboo Hats

This folktale comes from the eastern island of Kyushu. A Jizō is a Buddhist deity who is portrayed in Japan as a guardian of children and pregnant women and capable of saving souls on their way to one of the Buddhist hells.

Once upon a time lived an honest old man and woman. They were very poor. Every day they put together sacks of charcoal and took them to town to sell. With the money they earned they bought their rice. Thus, from day to day, they managed to eke out an existence.

At the end of the year, by working hard, the old man had put together many sacks. "My dear, I'll use these and go get some things for the New Year." So saying, he went off in a heavy snowstorm to sell the sacks in town.

On the way, six images of Jizō stood huddled together in a field like good friends. The old man bowed to them saying, "My dear Jizō, thank you for allowing me to pass this way each day." He noticed that snow had piled high on their heads. "Oh, my dear Jizō, you must be awfully cold," said the old man. He continued on his way, yet he could not help feeling sorry for them.

Once in town he sold all the sacks of charcoal. "There's no reason why I have to buy rice," he thought. "I'd rather buy some-

---

"Kasa Jizō," in *Nihon mukashibanashi hyakusen*, edited by Kōji Inada and Kazuko Inada (Tokyo: Sanseidō, 1977), pp. 384–386. Translated for this book by Hiroko Kataoka.

thing warm for the Jizō." So the old man bought six woven bamboo hats.

On his way home, the old man stopped to wipe the snow off the head of each Jizō and place a hat on top of it. "My dear Jizō, you'll be warm now," he said, and then returned home.

"Did you buy anything?" his wife asked.

"No. Nothing."

"This is New Year's Eve, and you didn't buy even one fish? What are we going to do?"

"Well, you know the Jizō we always pass on the way to town? Their heads were covered with snow. They looked so cold that I felt sorry for them and spent all the money I earned today to buy bamboo hats for their heads. I'm glad to know that the Jizō will be warm from now on. My dear, let's make do with rice gruel tonight."

"Ah, you did a wonderful thing. We don't need rice cakes. We can greet the New Year with gruel."

Thus the two ate gruel, pickles, and hot water. And they went to bed early.

Toward midnight they were awakened by shouts: "Yo-ho, Yo-ho!" "On this cold and snowy New Year's Eve someone seems to be pulling something heavy and shouting 'Yo-ho,' " the husband said. They slid open the door, but no one was there. Thinking they must not have heard anything after all, they got back under the covers. They were just warming up when there came a "Yo-ho!" from somewhere close by. Opening the door and staring out they saw six Jizō with bamboo hats shouldering huge bags of rice. These they deposited under the eaves of the old man's house.

"Such a blessing! You shouldn't have done it," they exclaimed, clasping their hands and bowing in reverence. But by then the Jizō were no more to be seen.

Three Tales
from Uji

The following three stories are included in *A Collection of Tales from Uji,* an anthology of about two hundred short tales probably compiled about 1213–1219. Some of the tales like "How a Sparrow Repaid Its Debt of Gratitude" are believed to have been recorded from tales popular among the Japanese people at the time. Others like "How the Priestly Nobleman from Mikawa Retired from the World" and "About the Holy Man in the Province of Shinano" are an attempt to popularize Buddhist teachings.

HOW A SPARROW REPAID ITS DEBT OF GRATITUDE

Long ago, one fine day in spring, a woman of about sixty was sitting cleansing herself of lice when she saw a boy pick up a stone and throw it at one of the sparrows which were hopping around in the garden. The stone broke the bird's leg, and as it floundered about, wildly flapping its wings, a crow came swooping down on it. "Oh, the poor thing," cried the woman, "the crow will get it," and snatching it up, she revived it with her breath and gave it something to eat. At night, she placed it for safety in a little bucket. Next morning, when she gave it some rice and also a medicinal powder made from ground copper, her children and grandchildren ridiculed her. "Just look," they jeered, "Grannie's taken to keeping sparrows in her old age."

Reprinted from D. E. Mills (trans.), *A Collection of Tales from Uji,* Cambridge Oriental Publications No. 15 (Cambridge, England, 1970), pp. 209–214, 227–229, 286–291, by permission of Cambridge University Press. Copyright 1970.

For several months she tended it, till in time it was hopping about again, and though it was only a sparrow, it was deeply grateful to her for nursing it back to health. Whenever she left the house on the slightest errand, the woman would ask someone to look after the sparrow and feed it. The family ridiculed her and wanted to know whatever she was keeping a sparrow for, but she would reply, "Never you mind! I just feel sorry for it." She kept it till it could fly again, then, confident that there was no longer any risk of its being caught by a crow, she went outside and held it up on her hand to see if it would fly away. Off it went with a flap of its wings. Everyone laughed at the woman because she missed her sparrow so much. "For so long now I've been used to shutting it up at night and feeding it in the morning," she said, "and oh dear, now it's flown away! I wonder if it will ever come back."

About three weeks later, she suddenly heard a sparrow chirruping away near her house, and wondering if all this chirruping meant that her sparrow had come back, she went out to see, and found that it had. "Well I never!" she exclaimed. "What a wonderful thing for it to remember me and come back!" The sparrow took one look at the woman's face, then it seemed to drop some tiny object out of its mouth and flew away. "Whatever can it be, this thing the sparrow has dropped?" she exclaimed, and going up to it, she found it was a single calabash seed. "It must have had some reason for bringing this," she said, and she picked it up and kept it. Her children laughed at her and said, "There's a fine thing to do, getting something from a sparrow and treating it as if you'd got a fortune!" "All the same," she told them, "I'm going to plant it and see what happens"; which she did. When autumn came, the seed had produced an enormous crop of calabashes, much larger and more plentiful than usual. Delighted, the woman gave some to her neighbors, and however many she picked, the supply was inexhaustible. The children who had laughed at her were now eating the fruit from morning to night, while everyone in the village received a share. In the end, the woman picked out seven or eight especially big ones to make into gourds, and hung them up in the house.

After several months, she inspected them and found that they were ready. As she took them down to cut openings in them, she thought they seemed rather heavy, which was mysterious. But when she cut one open, she found it full to the brim. Wondering whatever could be inside it, she began emptying it out—and found it full of white rice! In utter amazement, she poured all the rice into a large vessel, only to discover that the gourd immediately refilled itself. "Obviously some miracle has taken place—it must be the sparrow's doing," she exclaimed, bewildered but very happy. She put that gourd away out of sight before she examined the rest of them, but they all proved to be crammed full of rice, just like the first one. Whenever she took rice from the gourds, there was always far more than she could possibly use, so that she became extremely rich. The people in the neighboring villages were astonished to see how prosperous she had become, and were filled with envy at her incredible good fortune.

Now the children of the woman who lived next door said to their mother, "You and that woman next door are the same sort of people, but just look where she's got to! Why haven't you ever managed to do any good for us?" Their criticism stung the woman into going to see her neighbor. "Well, well, however did you manage this business?" she asked. "I've heard some talk about it being something to do with a sparrow, but I'm not really sure, so would you tell how it all came about, please?" "Well, it all began when a sparrow dropped a calabash seed and I planted it," said the other woman, rather vaguely. But when her neighbor pressed her to explain the whole story in detail, she felt she ought not to be petty and keep it to herself, so she explained how there had been a sparrow with a broken leg that she had nursed back to health, and how it must have been so grateful that it had brought her a calabash seed, which she had planted; and that was how she had come to be wealthy. "Will you give me one of the seeds?" she was asked, but this she refused to do. "I'll give you some of the rice that was in the gourds," she said, "but I can't give you a seed. I can't possibly let those go." The neighbor now began to keep a sharp lookout in case she too might find a sparrow with a broken leg to tend. But there were no such sparrows to be found. Every morning as she looked out, there would be sparrows hopping around pecking at any grains of rice that happened to be lying about outside the back door—and one day she picked up some stones and threw them in the hope of hitting one. Since she had several throws and there was such a flock of birds, she naturally managed to hit one, and as it lay on the ground, unable to fly away, she went up to it in great excitement and hit it again, to make sure that its leg was broken. Then she picked it up and took it indoors, where she fed it and treated it with medicine. "Why, if a single sparrow brought my neighbor all that wealth," she thought to herself, "I should be much richer still if I had several of them. I should get a lot more credit from my children than she did from hers." So she scattered some rice in the doorway and sat watching; then when a group of sparrows gathered to peck at it, she threw several stones at them, injuring three. "That will do," she thought, and putting the three sparrows with broken legs into a bucket, she fed them a medicinal powder made from ground copper. Some months later, feeling very pleased with herself now that they had all recovered, she took them outdoors and they all flew away. In her own estimation she had acted with great kindness. But the sparrows bitterly resented having had their legs broken and being kept in captivity for months.

Ten days went by, and to the woman's great joy the sparrows returned. As she was staring at them to see if they had anything in their mouths, they each dropped a calabash seed and flew off. "It's worked," she thought exultantly, and picking up the seeds, she planted them in three places. In no time, much faster than ordinary ones, they had grown into huge plants, though none of them had borne much fruit—not more than seven or eight calabashes. She beamed with pleasure as she looked at them. "You complained that I had never managed to do any good for you," she said to her children, "but now I'll do better than that woman next door," and the family very much hoped that she would. Since there were only a few calabashes, she did not eat any herself or let anyone else eat any, in the hope of getting more rice from them. Her children grumbled, "The woman next door ate some of hers and gave some to her neighbors. And we've got three seeds, which is more than she had, so there ought to be something for ourselves and the neighbors to eat." Feeling that perhaps they were right, the woman gave some away to the neighbors, while she cooked a number of the fruit for herself and her family to eat. The calabashes tasted terribly bitter, however; they were just like the *kihada** fruit that people use as a medicine, and made everyone feel quite nauseated. Every single person who had eaten any, including the woman herself and her children, was sick. The neighbors were furious and came round in a very ugly mood, demanding to know what it was she had given them. "It's shocking," they said. "Even people who only got a whiff of the things felt as if they were on their last legs with sickness and nausea." The woman and her children, meanwhile, were sprawled out half-unconscious and vomiting all over the place, so that there was little point in the neighbors' complaining, and they went away. In two or three days, everyone had recovered, and the woman came to the conclusion that the peculiar things which had happened must have been the outcome of being overhasty and eating the calabashes which should have given rice. She therefore hung the rest of the fruit up in store. After some months, when she felt they would be ready, she went into the storeroom armed with buckets to hold the rice. Her toothless mouth grinning from ear to ear with happiness, she held the buckets up to the gourds and went to pour out the contents of the fruit—but what emerged was a stream of things like horse-flies, bees, centipedes, lizards and snakes, which attacked and stung her, not only on her face but all over her body. Yet she felt no pain, and thought that it was rice pouring over her, for she shouted, "Wait a moment, my sparrows. Let me get it a little at a time." Out of the seven or eight gourds came a vast horde of venomous creatures which stung the children and their mother—the latter so badly that she died. The sparrows had resented having their legs broken and had persuaded swarms of insects and reptiles to enter the gourds; whereas the sparrow next door had been grateful because when it had broken its leg it had been saved from a crow and nursed back to health.

So you see, you should never be jealous of other people.

---

*An Amur cork tree. Its yellow bark can be used for dyeing. In Asia its fruit is used to treat burns and cardiac problems. [Ed.]

HOW THE PRIESTLY NOBLEMAN FROM MIKAWA RETIRED
FROM THE WORLD

While the Priestly Nobleman from Mikawa* was still a layman, he fell in love with a young and beautiful girl and abandoned his first wife, taking this girl with him as his new wife when
he went down to his province of Mikawa. After a long illness, the
girl's beauty faded and she died, but so great was his grief that he
did not have her buried, and lay night and day talking to her dead
body and kissing it. Not until a foul smell began to issue from her
mouth did he feel repelled, and then he tearfully had her buried.

From that time on he realized the sadness of this world.
Meanwhile, at the Festival of the Wind† held in Mikawa, he saw a
wild boar being cut up as a living sacrifice, and he resolved to quit
this province. When someone presented him with a live pheasant
which he had caught, the Governor said, "Let us cook this pheasant alive before we eat it. I should like to see if it tastes any better
that way," and one of his retainers, a stupid man who was desper-
ately anxious to please his master, chimed in to say, "What a fine
idea, sir! It's sure to taste better." The more sensitive of his retainers were disgusted.

The Governor ordered the men to pluck the bird alive while
he watched. At first it kept flapping its wings, but then they held
it down and began to pluck as fast as they could go; tears of blood‡
started from the bird's eyes, and with fluttering eyelids it looked
from one man to the next. So horrible was the sight that some of
the men moved away, unable to bear it. But others only cried,
"Hark at it screeching!" and laughed with pleasure, plucking away
more cruelly than ever. When the plucking was finished, the Gov-

---

*Mikawa no nyūdō, i.e., Ōe Sadamoto, 962–1034, who entered the priest-
hood under the name of Jakushō in 986 and died in China. Nyūdō is commonly
translated "Lay Priest," but as the opening of this story shows, this use of the
word "lay" is misleading. The term is used simply of a person (it was on the whole
restricted to the nobility, hence the Reischauer translation "Priestly High Court
Noble") who takes holy orders without becoming a shukke, i.e., leaving home
and going into a temple. [He is referred to as the Governor in this story.]

†A ceremony of prayer for favorable winds, either at harvest time or for purposes of navigation.

‡A common expression for tears shed in pain or desperation.

ernor had the men slice the bird up. With every cut of the knife, the blood came spurting out, but they kept wiping it away and continued slicing up the bird until it finally died, uttering horrible nerve-racking cries. When they had finished cutting it up, the Governor ordered them to roast it and see how it tasted. Having done so, they told him, "It was really delicious, much better than when it's killed first before being cut up and roasted." As he watched them and listened to them, tears streamed down his face and he groaned aloud—much to the surprise of the men who had been telling him how tasty the bird was. That very same day, he left the Governor's mansion and went up to the capital, where he entered the priesthood. The sole purpose of this strange experiment he had made was to strengthen his resolve, now that religious faith had stirred within him.

Once, while begging for food, he visited a certain house where he was given a magnificent meal on a mat spread in the garden. As he sat down on the mat to begin his meal, he noticed that the blinds were rolled up, and on looking at the well-dressed lady who was sitting inside, he found it was his first wife, who he had divorced. "You there, beggar! How I've longed to see you come to this!" she said, looking him straight in the eye. But the priest gave no sign of being embarrassed or hurt; he said simply, "My humble thanks, madam," and after making a hearty meal, took his leave.

How rare are men of such a nature! Once he had developed a strong faith, not even such an experience could wound him.

ABOUT THE HOLY MAN IN THE PROVINCE OF SHINANO

Long ago, there was a priest who lived in the province of Shinano. Having entered religion in such a remote country place, he had not been properly ordained, and felt he would like to go up to the capital* and take his vows at the Tōdai-ji. Somehow he managed to arrange a visit and thus he was finally ordained.

Now he had intended to return to his native province, but he

---

*"Capital" means "the general area of the country in which the capital is situated" (roughly the same as *kamigata*) or perhaps refers to "the southern capital," Nara.

did not relish the thought of going back to such a pagan locality
and he decided to stay where he was. He prayed before the Buddha
at the Tōdai-ji that he might find some place where he could live
in peace practicing his rites, and looking all around, he espied a
mountain that was just visible away to the southwest. "That is
where I'll live and practice my devotions," he decided, and he
moved there. Deep in the heart of the mountain country, he lived
a life of most sublime religious devotion and found himself as a result of his prayers the possessor of a small Buddhist image—one of
the god Bishamon—about the size that is kept in a small altar-
cupboard.

He built a small chapel to house it and continued his devotions zealously, year after year. Now at the foot of this mountain
there lived a low-class but very rich man to whose house the hermit's bowl would fly regularly, always returning loaded with food.
One day, when he had opened the storehouse and was taking out
some goods, this bowl came flying up to ask for alms as usual, but
the rich man said, "Oh, here's that bowl again! It's just too greedy
for words!" and he threw it into the corner of the storehouse, un-
willing to put himself out to fill it. The bowl lay waiting, but when
the man had finished dealing with his goods, he went away and
locked the door behind him, forgetting the bowl and leaving it
empty inside the storehouse. After a while, the building began for
no apparent reason to rock violently, and to the astonishment of
those who were watching, it lurched to and fro and rose about a
foot off the ground. "What on earth is happening?" everyone
shrieked in amazement. "Ah, yes," said someone. "We forgot to
bring that bowl out. Perhaps that's what's causing it." Just then,
the bowl emerged from inside the storehouse, and the building,
borne upon the bowl, rose higher and higher, ten or twenty feet in
the air, and began to fly away, leaving the bewildered onlookers
shouting and arguing about what had happened. As for the owner
of the storehouse, there was nothing he could do, and he set off,
accompanied by all his neighbors, to follow the storehouse and see
where it went. On and on they saw it fly, until it came to the
mountain where this holy man practiced his rites, in the province
of Kawachi; there it came to earth with a bump, right beside
his hut.

This was more puzzling than ever. But something had to be done, so the rich man went up to the holy man's hut and told him of the strange thing that had happened. "The bowl always used to come regularly and I would send it away full. But today I was so busy that I put it into the storehouse and forgot to take it out when I locked up. The storehouse began lurching violently, then it flew through the air and came down here. Please let me have it back." "That certainly is strange," said the hermit, "but since the storehouse has flown here to me, I cannot return it to you. I haven't got such a place here, and it will be handy to keep things in. But you may take all its contents." "But how can I have anything taken back at such short notice?" said the rich man. "There are five thousand bushels of rice piled up in it." "That is easy," said the hermit. "I will transport them for you." He loaded a bale of rice onto the bowl and sent it flying off, whereupon the remaining bales followed on behind like a skein of geese or a flock of sparrows. The rich man watched in amazement and felt such reverence for the holy man that he said, "Do not send it all just now. Keep a thousand or fifteen hundred bushels of rice for your own use." "No, I cannot do that," replied the holy man. "What can I do with it if you leave it here?" "Then let me give you at least as much as you can use, say, fifty or a hundred." "But I shan't want that much," said the hermit, and he saw to it that the bales were all deposited back at their owner's house.

The hermit continued to live this life of devout religious observances. Now it happened that about this time the Engi Emperor became seriously ill and despite the multitude of remedies that were tried—prayers of all kinds, incantations and sutra readings— he showed no sign of recovery. Then someone informed him, "There is a holy man at Shigi* in the province of Kawachi who has for years past lived a life of religious devotion in total seclusion. He is a very saintly man, blessed with the power to work miracles. He can make his begging bowl fly through the air, and without lifting a finger himself, he performs all kinds of extraordinary feats. If

---

*Shigi actually was, as the *Konjaku* and the *Shigisan engi* versions of this story say, in Yamato, but so near the border of Kawachi that the tradition recorded in *Uji shūi* and *Kohon* places it in that province.

Your Majesty sends for him to say prayers, then you will surely recover." "Let us try him, then," said the Emperor, and he dispatched one of his archivists to fetch the hermit.

When the messenger arrived, he found that the holy man did indeed look most wonderfully saintly. He explained that he had come to convey an Imperial summons to the hermit to present himself at Court forthwith. The holy man asked why he was being summoned, and showed no inclination to budge. The messenger described the circumstances of the Emperor's serious illness and asked him to pray for his recovery. "I can do that here," said the hermit, "without going to the Palace." "But in that case, even if the Emperor recovered, how should we know that it was through your prayers?" "What does it matter whether the Emperor knows or does not know whose prayers have made him well? All that matters is that he should recover." "But surely it will be desirable to have some sign as to which of all the many prayers said has been successful," persisted the messenger. "Very well, then," replied the holy man. "When I pray for His Majesty, I shall send a Sword Guardian Spirit. If he should see this spirit in a dream or in some other vision, then he will know that it comes from me; the spirit will be wearing a robe made of swords plaited together. But I cannot go to the capital myself." The Imperial messenger returned and made his report. Three days later, at about noon, the Emperor was feeling a little drowsy when he suddenly noticed something glittering brightly, and on looking to see what it was, he decided that it must be the Sword Guardian Spirit of which the hermit had spoken. At once, he began to feel brighter, all trace of discomfort left him and he found himself completely recovered. There was universal rejoicing, and everyone agreed what a wonderful miracle-worker the holy man was.

The Emperor himself was deeply impressed by his magical powers and sent a messenger to offer him high rank in the priesthood, or a grant of land for his temple. But in reply to the Emperor's message, the holy man merely said, "I have no desire for high rank. And if a place such as this were to receive a grant of land, it would only mean that there would be an Intendant or some other official appointed, and then far from benefiting me, it would be a nuisance and tempt me to sinful thoughts of worldly things. I am happy to remain as I am." And there the matter rested.

Now this hermit had an elder sister, who worried about what might have happened to him, since nothing had been heard of him for so many years after he had gone up to the capital to be ordained. She went to the capital herself to search for him, and inquired at the Tōdai-ji and the Yamashina-dera whether they had any priest living there whose name was Mōren Koin. But she found no one who knew him, and despaired of finding him. Uncertain what to do, but determined not to go home until she discovered what had become of her brother, she spent the whole of that night praying before the Great Buddha at the Tōdai-ji, and begging him to reveal to her Mōren's whereabouts. Having dropped off to sleep, she had a dream in which the Buddha told her, "The priest you are looking for is living on a mountain to the southwest of here. Go and look for him where you see a trail of cloud over a mountain." She woke from her dream to find that it was nearly daybreak, and sat watching eagerly for the dawn to come. At last the gray light of dawn appeared, and as she looked out to the southwest, she could faintly make out the mountain, with a trail of purple cloud hanging above it. Joyfully making her way towards it, she found what she had expected—there was a chapel, for instance—and going up to a building which seemed to be occupied, she called out, "Moren Koin, are you there?" "Who is that?" he replied, and came outside—to find that it was his sister from Shinano! "What a surprise!" he said. "What has brought you here to see me?" She told him what had happened, and adding, "How you must have felt the cold! I have brought this for you to wear," she produced a present for him. It turned out to be a coat made of specially stout yarn, thick and closely woven and very hard-wearing. The hermit was delighted with his gift and put it on at once. Till then, his only clothing had consisted of one garment—and that made of paper! Now, as it was very cold, he wore his new coat underneath the other and felt very warm and comfortable. And so he continued his devotions for many years, and his sister the nun, instead of returning to her native province, stayed with him practicing her devotions, too.

For many years the hermit continued to wear this coat constantly, till in the end it was worn to rags. The storehouse that had been carried there on the bowl was called "The Flying Storehouse." The ragged remnants of the coat were stored in it and indeed are still there. People lucky enough to obtain even a tiny fragment of these rags kept it as a charm. The storehouse, too, still stands, though it is now very dilapidated. Anyone who secured so much as a tiny fragment of wood from it as a charm, and people who fashioned their piece of wood from the storehouse into a figure of Bishamon, never failed to become rich. And so as the word spread, other people tried to find contacts that would help them to buy a piece of the wood from the storehouse. Shigi is thus a place where the most wonderful miracles are worked, and even today it is full of pilgrims from morning to night. The figure of Bishamon there is said to be the very one that the holy man Mōren conjured up by his prayers.

Evening Addresses
of Sage Ninomiya

Ninomiya Sontoku (1787–1856) was an agricultural reformer and moralist. A man of peasant origins himself, he wanted to improve the lot of the Japanese peasantry. In sermons delivered to groups of commoners Ninomiya Sontoku exhorted his listeners to diligence, frugality, and hard work in return for the blessings bestowed on humankind by heaven and one's family. The following excerpts are from sermons written down from memory by one of his disciples.

TEACHING BY PERSONAL EXAMPLE

With the support of the sage a certain Confucian scholar of commonplace character was teaching Confucianism to a group of young men. One day he indulged in excessive drinking while on a visit to a neighboring village and lying at full length on the wayside behaved disgracefully to the disgust of all passersby. One of his pupils, who found him in this condition, refused to attend his lectures the following day.

Angry at this, the scholar waited on the sage and said: "I admit my behavior was anything but decent, but what I lecture on is a book written by a sage. Is it right for one to give up his teaching for the simple reason that I have disgraced myself? Pray admonish the young man, so that he may resume his study."

Reprinted from Ninomiya Sontoku, *Sage Ninomiya's Evening Talks,* translated by Isoh Yamagata, reprint ed. (Westport, Conn.: Greenwood Press, 1970), pp. 26–28, 29–33, 43–44, 54–59, 81–84.

In reply, the sage said: "Don't be angry. To explain by a parable, supposing I have here some rice and after boiling I put it into an extremely filthy vessel and present it to you to eat. Would you then take it? I think not. The rice is clean, but when the vessel containing it is filthy nobody will eat it. It will then serve only as food for dogs. Your learning is exactly like it. Originally it came from the brains and minds of saintly men, but when it is presented through the filthy mouth of yours young men refuse to listen to what you speak. Can we say they are unreasonable?"

SINCERITY AND PRACTICE

The keynote of my teaching is nothing more or less than sincerity and practice. Accordingly it may be extended even to birds, beasts, insects, fish, and plants. Much more is it so with men. Consequently it does not place much value on talent, wisdom, and eloquence. With these things one can win over men but cannot do the same with birds, beasts, and plants. Possibly birds and beasts, which possess instincts, may be deceived, but on no account can plants be. As my teaching stresses sincerity and practice, if acted upon, it makes all plants grow and prosper, no matter be it rice, wheat, vegetables, orchids, or chrysanthemums. Neither the greatest talent and wisdom nor the best eloquence can make plants grow and prosper. Accordingly my teaching does not place much value on talent, wisdom, or eloquence, but stresses sincerity and practice. An old saying likens sincerity with a divine being, but it is not wrong to say God is sincerity. You should always bear in mind that unless you are sincere and practice virtues, however wise and learned you may be, you can achieve no real success.

A PILL THAT DISPELS ANY DISEASE

For a long time I have been thinking about the question: What does Shintoism teach, what are its weak points and what its strong points? I have been thinking of these matters in regard to Confucianism and Buddhism too. And I have come to the conclusion that each of these doctrines has its own merits as well as defects. I have composed a short poem expressing my regret, which runs as follows:

Doctrines are scaffolding poles cast aside,
Some are too long, others too short,
There's none that suits my purpose.

Now to mention what each of these doctrines chiefly aims at, Shintoism shows the way of founding a state, Confucianism that of governing it, and Buddhism that of ruling one's mind. I do not put undue value on what is high-toned. Nor do I discard what is familiar and lowly. In framing my teaching, I have adopted the essence of each of these three doctrines. By essence I mean what is useful to mankind. By adopting what is useful and rejecting what is not, I have built up a teaching, which I have called the teaching of returning virtue for virtue and is the best in this world. Jokingly I call my teaching the peerless pill containing the essences of Shintoism, Confucianism, and Buddhism. Its virtues are so extensive that they cannot be enumerated. Use it for the administration of a country: it will cure it of all diseases leading to decline and fall. Use it for the management of a household: it will cure it of all diseases causing poverty and misery. When one who has waste land takes it, reclamation will be accomplished. When one who is heavily in debt takes it, repayment of the debt will be made, and when one who is troubled with lack of capital takes it, capital will come to him. One who has no house will get it if he takes it and one in want of farming tools will be supplied with them if he takes it. Take it and other troubles that make one unhappy such as poverty, extravagance, dissipation, abandonment, and laziness will disappear.

Asked by a disciple of the quantities of the essences of the three doctrines he infused in preparing his pill, the sage replied: "One spoonful of Shintoism, and half a spoonful of Confucianism and Buddhism each." Hearing this, another disciple drew a diagram showing the respective quantities the sage mentioned and showing it to him asked: "Is your pill like this?" "Oh, no," laughed the master, "There are no such pills as this which is just a collection of things. A pill worthy of the name is made up of various medicines, which have been so well mixed up that one cannot distinguish one component from others. Otherwise when you put it into the mouth it will irritate the tongue and when it goes down into the belly you will feel unpleasant. In preparing a good pill you must mix up its ingredients so well that none can know what they are."

ALL LIVING THINGS ARE GODS AND BUDDHAS

All living things in this world, human beings included of course, beasts, birds, worms and insects, fishes and plants, may be said to be scions of Heaven. For no human power, without the aid of the creative power of Heaven and Earth, can grow and raise even river-worms, gnats, and plants. Human beings are at the head of all creation, so that man is called the master of all living things. The proof that he is such is that he rules over beasts, birds, insects, and plants and may kill or keep them alive without being condemned therefor. Man's power is great indeed, but fundamentally man is not quite different from animals and plants. All being descendants of Heaven, Buddhism teaches that they are all Buddhas. Our country being one of gods, one may say all of them are gods. But it is generally considered that while we are alive we are men and after death become Buddhas. As we are Buddhas even while we are alive, we continue to be Buddhas after we die. There can be no reason that while living we are men and when dead Buddhas. There can be no reason that after death mackerels become dried bonitoes. There is no tree which is a pine tree while standing in the woods, but which turns into a cedar tree when it is felled. Thus as we are Buddhas or gods while alive, we become Buddhas or gods after we die. Great men are often honored as gods after their death, but as they were gods while alive, they become gods after death. Isn't this logic quite clear? Gods and Buddhas are different in names only, but are the same in reality. The names differ, be-

cause the countries differ. It is with this idea that I have composed
two short poems as follows:

> Even plants and trees are gods:
>   Know then the whereabouts of
>   life after death.

> Even plants and trees are living Buddhas:
>   Know then the whereabouts of
>   life after death.

DO YOUR BEST AND LEAVE THE REST TO HEAVEN

The way of Heaven is natural. Though the way of man is in
compliance with that of Heaven it is partly artificial. Men should
do all that is prescribed in the way of man and then leave the rest
to the order of the way of Heaven. Do not complain of the unkind-
ness of the way of Heaven without doing all that is prescribed in
that of man. In accordance with the way of Heaven, dead leaves accumulate in the yard. They are insentient and pile up day after day
and night after night. It is at variance with the way of man not to
sweep them away. But after sweeping them away, one finds them
falling from trees afresh. It is foolish for one to worry one's mind
about them and rise with a broom in hand every time a dead leaf
falls upon the ground, for doing so is no better than being put to
work by rubbish. It is in accordance with the way of Heaven that
dead leaves fall from trees. Sweep them away once every morning
in accordance with the way of man: that is enough. If dead leaves
accumulate again, take no notice of them. Do not make yourself a
servant of insentient dead leaves. But do not neglect to do what is
prescribed in the way of man and do not leave the dead leaves un-
attended as they pile up. Such is the way of man. Teach well even
those who are foolish or wicked. If they do not follow your counsel,
do not worry your mind on that account. Even if they do not listen
to you, do not give them up as hopeless, but teach them again and
again. Never be angry even if they turn a deaf ear to your teaching.
It is unkind of you to forsake them even if they do not listen to

you. It is unwise to be angry if they do not accept your advice. A
virtuous man hates to be unkind and unwise. You should try to
make your virtue perfect by being mindful of both kindness and
wisdom.

ROOT OF GOOD AND EVIL

It is very difficult to determine what is good and what is evil.
Fundamentally there is neither good nor evil. As we regard one
thing as good, another thing comes to be considered as evil. This
sorting of good from evil is man's work and is a feature of the way
of man. Accordingly apart from man, there is neither good nor
evil. In other words because man exists, good and evil come into
being. For this reason, though man considers reclamation of waste
land as good and devastation of cultivated fields as bad, wild boars
and deer will regard the former as evil and the latter as good. Society condemns stealing as evil, but among thieves it may be considered as good, they regarding those preventing it as evildoers.
Thus it is difficult to determine what is good and what is evil. To
comprehend this truth plainly, it is expedient to consider the matter of proximity and distance. Suppose we have here two posts, one
having the word "far" and another the word "near" inscribed on
it. You are then told to erect one at a spot far from you and another
at a spot near you. You will then quickly understand how this matter of proximity and distance stands. I have a verse of my composi-
tion saying:

> Looking out over the place,
> There is neither proximity nor distance:
> It depends upon the position
>   the viewer occupies.

If I were to say in the above there is neither good nor evil instead of
saying there is neither proximity nor distance, people cannot comprehend the meaning of the poem because good or evil is a matter
immediately affecting personal interest, but the matter of proximity and distance being not so, people will easily understand what I

mean. . . . In fact whether anything is far away or near is determined according to the position one occupies and when one's position is unsettled there is neither proximity nor distance. A man
who says Osaka is far away is probably an inhabitant of the Kwanto
district, and another who says the Kwanto district is far away lives
in all likelihood somewhere near Kyoto. Fortune and misfortune,
good and evil, right and wrong, gain and loss are all like this matter of proximity and distance. Fortune and misfortune are one; so
are good and evil, gain and loss. All being one, if one regards half
of it as good, the other half is sure to be evil. To desire the latter to
be good too is to desire what is impossible. The joy of birth is inseparable from the sorrow of death. It is the same as the certain fall
of a blooming flower or the withering of sprouting grass. A parable
recorded in one of the Buddhist sutras illustrates this point. It says
that a beautiful woman called at a certain house. Asked who she
was by the master of the house, the woman said that she was the
goddess of good fortune and that wherever she went happiness,
wealth, and every other good thing followed her footsteps. Highly
pleased, the master begged her to step into his house. Thereupon
the fair visitor said that she had a companion who would surely
come soon after and asked whether he was willing to open the
doors of his house for her. As soon as he agreed to do so, another
woman appeared, who was extremely ugly. Asked who she was, she
replied that she was the goddess of misfortune and wherever she
went miseries, calamities, and every other evil thing accompanied
her. Upon hearing this, the master of the house was very angry and
commanded her to retire in a hurry. The ugly visitor then said that
the goddess of good fortune who came before her was her sister,
with whom she was inseparable. If he desired her sister to stay in
his house he must ask her to stay too, but if he desired her to leave
he must allow her sister to leave too. After thinking for awhile the
man decided that both women should go and so the two women
left the house together. This is a parable illustrating the truth of
the certainty of death coming to a living thing and that of parting
taking place to those who meet. Not to mention life and death, so
it is with fortune and misfortune, good and evil, gain and loss. Essentially misfortune is at one with fortune, both being of the same

stock, as it is the case with good and evil, which are brothers. So it is also the case with all things. When your house is near the place where you work, you are glad that it is so near, but if fire breaks out at a place which is far away from your house, you are glad that it did not occur near your house. From this homely illustration you will see how the matter stands.

WEALTH AND POVERTY

Wealth and poverty are not far apart, the disparity between the two being only slight. Whether one attains wealth or is reduced to poverty depends upon his preparedness. A poor man works to-day or during the current year to dispose of the task he should have done yesterday or during the preceding year. Accordingly he struggles all through his lifetime to no avail. On the other hand a wealthy man works today or during the current year to prepare himself for the needs of tomorrow or the coming year, so that he is at ease and free and succeeds in whatever thing he undertakes. Whereas when they have no *sake* to enjoy or no rice to eat today, many people drink the beverage or eat the cereal by borrowing. This is the cause that drives them to poverty. If one gathers faggots today to boil rice with the next morning or makes ropes this night to tie fences with the next day, he can be at his ease. But in the case of a poor man, he wants to boil his rice this evening with faggots he may gather the next day or tie fences with ropes today he may make the next day. On this account, though he struggles, he fails to succeed. Therefore I often say, it is usual with a poor man, who desires to mow grass but possesses no sickle, to borrow it from a neighbor, but this unpreparedness is the cause of his poverty. If he has no sickle, he should first of all work as a day laborer, and after buying a sickle with the wage he has earned he should set himself to the task of mowing grass. This way rests on the basis of the Great Way prescribed by gods on the day of Creation and therefore there is nothing unmanly or mean in it. It is indeed in conformity with the spirits of the gods who descended upon this land from heaven to found this Empire of ours. Accordingly one who possesses this mentality attains wealth, but one who lacks it can never be well off.

SOUND ADVICE TO AN ERRING MAN

There lived in the town of Sakura-machi* a mat-maker, Genkichi by name, who was patronized by the sage. Though he was a clever speaker and a talented man, he was always in needy circumstances, because he was excessively fond of drinking in addition to being lazy. One year-end, he called on the sage and asked for the loan of some glutinous rice in order to have it made into *mochi*.† The sage said to the man:

> It is wrong of a man like you, who neglects his occupation all through the year and spends whatever money he happens to have on drinking, to desire to eat *mochi* on New Year's Day like decent people who have worked hard during the past year. Neither does New Year come by accident, nor rice can be obtained by accident. A New Year comes after some 360 days and nights have come and gone, while rice is obtained after being sown in spring, freed from weeds in summer, and reaped in autumn. As you have never sown in spring, removed weeds in summer, and reaped in autumn, it is quite natural that you have no rice now. So you have no right to eat *mochi* though it is New Year's Day. If I lend some to you, how can you return it to me? If you cannot, you will make yourself a criminal. If you desire to eat *mochi* on New Year's Day, you should put an end to your indolent habit, cease drinking, go to the woods to gather fallen leaves, and make manure of them. You till land next spring, sow seeds of rice in it, and make them grow with the manure you have made. Obtain rice in this way and eat *mochi* on New Year's Day of the year after next. Meanwhile go without *mochi*, but eat the fruit of repentance.

Speaking in this wise, the sage admonished the man carefully and sympathetically. Genkichi was thoroughly convinced of his mistake. Showing sincere repentance on his face he said that he was quite wrong to think of eating *mochi* on New Year's Day as do de-

---

*A town in the province of Shimotsuke (present prefecture of Tochigi), where the sage lived and worked for many years engaged in the restoration of a ruined fief.
†Rice cake often eaten at the New Year's celebrations. [Ed.]

cent people, who have worked hard during the year, while he lived
without engaging in his occupation with diligence and spending all
he had on drinking. He would eat no rice cake on coming New
Year's Day, but eat the fruit of repentance. He would change his
life at once, stop drinking altogether, and take up his occupation in
earnest on the second day of the New Year, cherishing hope that he
would be able to have *mochi* at the end of the coming year like
other people and eat it on New Year's Day of the year after next.
He thanked the sage cordially for the kind advice given him and
bidding goodbye quite crestfallen he was about to make his exit
through the gate. The sage called him back and asked whether he
was really impressed and reformed by his teaching. Genkichi replied that he was deeply impressed and that never forgetting what
he was told, he would stop drinking and wholeheartedly apply
himself to his occupation. Thereupon the sage gave him one bag-
ful of glutinous rice and one *ryo* of gold in addition to some radishes and potatoes. Afterward Genkichi was a changed man and all
through the rest of his life he was well off and happy.

   This is one instance of countless cases in which the sage led er-
ring people to the right path.

A Sermon
by Hosoi Heishū

The following sermon was delivered by Hosoi Heishū (1728–1801) to a crowd of commoners in the city of Nagoya in 1783. In sermons such as this one the values of the warrior class were translated into popular terms for the peasants, artisans, and merchants of the commoner class. Those values included loyalty and obedience to one's lord, filial piety toward parents, self-discipline, diligence and adherence to duty, and frugality in daily life.

I would like to talk to you today about the meaning of learning. Please listen carefully to what I have to say. Learning is the perception of reason; it is through reason that we know the difference between good and evil. We can achieve reason by studying the Classics. I myself have come to understand reason from books and I give talks to lords on its meanings.

The number of books in the world is staggering. All of you here, men and women alike, whether you are warriors, artisans, or merchants, are far too busy to study the Classics on your own. You couldn't possibly read them all, and it would take me a long time, months in fact, just to summarize them for you. I certainly couldn't do it in a day or two.

I can make you understand far more easily by telling you a few stories. Learning is not something that can be found only in books;

Reprinted with minor changes and omission of technical footnotes, from Michiko Y. Aoki and Margaret B. Dardess, "The Popularization of Samurai Values: A Sermon by Hosoi Heishū," *Monumenta Nipponica* 31, no. 4 (Winter 1976), pp. 400–413, with permission from *Monumenta Nipponica*.

you can find it in your daily lives as well. Everything around you contains great teachings if you will only look for them.

Of all creatures in the universe man is the most blessed. He alone is good at heart, and his goodness comes from *makoto* [sincerity]*. Because of *makoto* man is born free from evil. An example of *makoto* is the relationship between mother and child. A mother cherishes her child. If she leaves the child with another woman while she goes to the toilet the child will cry for her, and no amount of comforting will console him. The child will only stop crying when the mother returns. He will be happy then even though she scolds him for crying. The child is innocent; his only desire is to be close to his mother. Correspondingly the mother loves her child and is happy. Their feelings for each other are an expression of *makoto*. Human beings must never lose such innocence and purity for without it we will become evil.

The lessons of nature are all around us and teach us about *makoto*. In every year there are four seasons. Spring is warm; summer is hot; autumn is cool; winter is cold. It has been that way for millions of years. While there is some variation—such as an occasional cold day in spring or summer—the general pattern remains the same. Spring weather makes the seeds sprout. Summer brings thunderstorms and along with them cicadas and mosquitoes. The sun rises in the east; the moon waxes and wanes. Everything follows the laws of nature that emanate from *makoto*.

Makoto also underlies all human relationships. We want to make other people happy. We receive a visitor warmly even when we do not know why he has come, and he, in turn, greets us and expresses concern for our well-being. That is beautiful conduct; it accords with the code of human conduct that stems from *makoto*.

A feeling of good fellowship grows up among travelers even though they have never met before. When food and shelter are scarce, a traveler will share what he has with his fellow travelers. He will not eat alone and let the others go hungry. This, too, is an ex-

---

Makoto was the central ethical concept of the Shinto revival in the eighteenth century. It connotes sincerity, devotion, a childlike innocence, truth, or reality.

pression of *makoto*. Guided by *makoto* we save each other from starvation. If a friend loses sight of *makoto* and comes to you in rage, try not to respond in kind. Instead, treat him with the kindness and sincerity of *makoto*, and he will be calm and meek.

In all our relations with other people it is essential to keep *makoto* in mind. Remember this: if a person loses *makoto*, his mind will become inhabited by evil spirits. We humans are superior to other animals. We should learn from the examples of *makoto*, and not succumb to evil spirits.

There are, it is true, ignorant people who by sheer chance avoid making mistakes. Without realizing it they live according to *makoto*. Yet their lives are surrounded by pitfalls. To live in ignorance of *makoto* is like walking along a bad road in the dark without a lantern. Because they cannot see what is ahead of them they are in danger of slipping on debris and stumbling into a ditch. But those who do understand the lessons of *makoto* are safe from all harm. They are like men who carry brightly burning torches to guide them through the darkness.

In summary, all things in the universe are regulated by the laws of nature derived from *makoto*. It is important for us to understand these teachings and remember them.

The foundation of all human relationships was laid down by our ancestral gods, Izanagi and Izanami. Those two gods gave birth to many deities and from their descendants human beings were born. We can see from this creation story that marriage between a husband and wife is the most fundamental of all human relationships. A couple produces children, and then they in turn give birth to children. Relationships between grandparents and grandchildren, uncles and nephews, and nieces, all grow out of the original union of the husband and wife. Because their relationship is the basis of all these other relationships, it is vitally important that a husband and wife be guided by *makoto*. A husband loves his wife and she in turn respects him. The husband goes out to work and the wife stays home to take care of the house. Responsibility for fulfilling social obligations toward the outside world belongs to the husband, and it is he who gives gifts to the appropriate people when the occasion demands.

Suppose some member of a friend's family is going to be married. The husband wants to give the family a wedding gift, and he thinks about giving material for an *obi* or a roll of silk cloth. At times like these he'll probably consult his wife. If the wife understands her husband's social obligations she will realize that, although it will be hard on the family budget to give a gift, it is important to maintain a good relationship with the friend's family. When a wife is understanding, her husband will not feel worried about giving the gift. But if the wife refuses to cooperate and remains indifferent and aloof, the husband will be uneasy. He will hesitate to fulfill his obligations.

Now it is one thing if the wife's attitude stems from frugality, but that is seldom the case. In general, because relations with the outside world are a man's responsibility, men try to live up to their duties and obligations, while women do not understand them at all. If the wife's real concern is for the family budget, she can economize on her own clothing and cosmetics, rather than on social obligations. Women seldom do that.

When I was young, women in this province of Owari were very thrifty. When I went to Edo after studying here in Nagoya I was astonished at the extravagance of the women there. Now that I have returned to my home province, I find things greatly changed. Here, too, women have become overly extravagant. Their clothing is far too elaborate; they dress like princesses. They wear fancy ornaments in their hair—and not just one but several! A woman should wear a comb to keep her hair in place, and one comb is enough for anyone. In my younger days, women were not like that at all. Of course, I'm not saying you women should be like the women of the old days. It is quite all right to use a little hair oil from the store when you put your hair up.

But I have wandered off the subject a bit. My point is that women should try to understand their husbands' obligations and struggles. The husband earns money by the sweat of his brow, and he has to work very hard just to support his family. Only an ignorant and selfish wife could fail to appreciate his efforts. Such a woman is blind to her husband's anguish. She indulges herself with expensive clothes instead of helping her husband meet his social obligations.

There is no need for women to be extravagant in their dress. By nature, males are better looking than females anyway. Take birds, for example. A cock has far prettier feathers than a hen. Male birds, in general, are more beautiful than female birds, and the same is true of humans. Men are simply better looking than women. They are born that way and women should accept it. Consider how ugly a woman would look if she did not use cosmetics and shaved her head or dressed up in men's clothing. She would certainly not look as nice as a man does.

No one needs more than what is essential. If a plain silk outfit is sufficient for your needs, wear it. You do not need to buy silk crepe. If cotton clothing will do, wear that. You do not have to wear silk. If you are careful and thrifty and save as much as you can, you will not go hungry in the future. Your old age will be peaceful and happy.

Think about the example set by our superiors. All of us have three noble masters. The highest is the emperor, the next is the shogun, and the third and closest to us is the lord of this province. I know that our lord is not poor. You know that, too. He does not have to scrimp on his spending.

But he is very careful with his money because he wants to set a good example for you. Look at my own clothes. I go to see my lord in the very same clothes that I am wearing now. They are made of cotton, not of silk. I know how important he considers it to set an example of thrift for the people. He makes me feel very humble indeed, and so I wear rough cotton clothing.

Now that you know how important your lord considers your welfare, you should not indulge yourself by buying lots of things. I don't believe that any one of you could be extravagant if you consider your lord's concern for you.

Criminals are punished in this province as they are elsewhere. Arsonists are burned alive, and thieves are beheaded. The lord does not like to take such actions and he pities those he executes, but he has no choice if he is to maintain order in the province. If he were too lenient with criminals, it would encourage others to become criminals. So, too, a father must discipline a child who has done something wrong, even though it hurts the father to do so. If the father does not do his duty, his other children will follow the bad example set by the naughty child. When our lord must punish a criminal, he feels just as a father does toward his own child.

All wrongdoing is uncovered sooner or later. You may think you will get away with it if you break into a storehouse in disguise, but you'll end up getting caught because heaven is watching you. No evil in the world can be concealed forever. The gods know when a crime has been committed. Buddha and the gods are invisible, but they are always with us, even now. We are born with *makoto,* but evil spirits may lead us astray. It is very important to keep our minds straight. If our minds remained as straight as they were when we were born, there would be no wicked people. It is when our minds become twisted that evil spirits rise up to corrupt us. A person who breaks into a storehouse does so because he has lost sight of *makoto.*

The character for "thrift" really means to eliminate luxury, to keep things simple, and to reduce one's affairs to the bare essentials and manage them with care. The character for "modest" or "simple" means to reduce things to manageable proportions.

We humans need three basic things: food, clothing, and shelter. Our bodies must be nourished, clothed, and protected if we are to survive even for one day. Thanks to our lord we all have food to eat, clothes to wear, and a place to live. We owe him a debt of gratitude for that. We can show our appreciation in return by obeying the laws of the land so as to spare him the grief our misconduct would cause him. Parents and children, brothers and sisters, all have a code of behavior to observe. Let us remember to follow that code and the laws of the domain throughout our lives. Only then will we be able to enter paradise in the other world when we die.

All parents truly want to raise their children to be filial. In order to do so parents must discipline their children. This is especially necessary in the rearing of girls. Girls and boys are not raised in the same way. In general, girls are more protected than boys. Parents expect their daughters to grow up and lead a sheltered life of home and marriage. So they do not send the daughters out to learn the ways of the world. Instead, they try to shield them from it, and in doing this they sometimes spoil their daughters.

There is a saying that it is the lot of girls to be obedient. When she is young, a girl must obey her parents. When she is married, she must obey her husband. When she grows old, she must obey her sons. These are the three obligations of a woman and, like it or not, it is a fact of life. You must be careful to prepare your daughters to fulfill their obligations.

But for the present I want to discuss the education of boys. Boys mature by mingling with people outside of their homes. While girls are kept at home, boys are encouraged to go out. When a father needs someone to run an errand, he sends his son to do it. This is true even in the poorest families. Because they are encouraged to go out and play, boys often meet with other boys, whereas girls seldom even meet people outside of their families. If one boy wants a toy belonging to another child, he will try to take it away from him, while the boy with the toy will fight to keep it. If a grownup sees the fight, he will probably break it up and decide to punish the one who started it. The boy who tried to grab the toy will cry when he is disciplined, but he will understand what he has done wrong. Boys are exposed to social restraints by situations such as this, and by the time they reach adulthood they can distinguish between good and bad. Parents send their sons out into the real world at an early age because they believe the world is the best place for a boy to learn about society.

The parents' attitude toward their daughters is just the opposite. Because they want their daughters to be nice and docile, the parents keep them apart from the world, and speak more gently to the girls than to the boys. Their overprotection spoils the girls and the girls take advantage of their parents. They tend to sleep late in the morning because of their parents' leniency. When parents are too nice to their daughters, the girls tend to become thoughtless. This spoiling causes them great difficulty when they later marry and move in with their husbands' families.

After marrying, a girl cannot behave as she did in her parents' home. She must live up to the expectations of her mother-in-law.

After all, she is in someone else's house and she must be careful not to offend anyone. She had better get up early in the morning, clean the house, greet her in-laws, and give appropriate instructions to the servants. Only then will she be accepted into her new household. Only then will she live in harmony with her husband's family. If a spoiled girl continues to behave as she did at home, she will soon be at odds with her mother-in-law. They are likely to start fighting and the girl may eventually find herself divorced. There are many such cases. Is it really the mother-in-law who is unreasonable? Although she does not realize it, it is the girl who is at fault. She is too spoiled.

Happiness in marriage is rather unpredictable. A very beautiful woman may be happy with an ugly fellow. A very handsome man such as Narihira may marry an ugly woman and be happy. Marriage is an institution designed by our parents. Even if your parents choose a husband or wife for you who is ugly or of low birth, you must obey their wishes and marry that person. It is for your parents to decide whether your spouse is good or bad for you. You must never marry someone of your own choice against the wishes of your parents. That would be unfilial conduct. If you disregard your parents' views, you're no better than an animal!

All human relations must be based on harmony. This applies not only to the members of a family but to all of society. Each member of a family—father, son, son-in-law, daughter-in-law—has individual needs and desires. But nothing can be gained if each one insists on having his own way without compromise. I'm not saying that such individual wishes are necessarily bad, only that every person has a place in society and if we are to fulfill our roles we must try to achieve harmony.

A stringed instrument like the *samisen* exemplifies harmony. A *samisen* has three strings and each makes a different sound. The first string makes a low and heavy sound. The second is a little higher and lighter. The third is very high and light. Each makes sounds of a different quality from the others. But when the strings are in tune, they achieve a beautiful three-toned harmony. We humans can do the same.

There is a saying about the difference between men and women. "A man finds his spirit in a sword; a woman finds her spirit in a mirror." A man has his sword always by his side. He is expected to have a cause. If his cause is challenged, his honor depends upon his defending it with his sword even to the death. That is why we say a man finds his spirit in his sword. A woman is expected to be open and honest. Her mirror will reflect the true state of her mind. No amount of makeup will cover up animosity or insincerity; if a woman lacks sincerity, her mirror will tell her. She should look in her mirror to see if her mind is correct, and if she finds ugliness there, she must reform herself. That is why we say a woman finds her spirit in a mirror.

I have been telling you how important it is for us to have *makoto* in order to live a correct life. Wherever *makoto* exists, it naturally gives rise to virtuous behavior. Let me illustrate my point with a story about a filial girl.

There was once a wealthy family in Hitachi province that supplied a certain village with its headman generation after generation. In time the family's fortune declined and the family became poor. Nevertheless, the family was proud of its long lineage of village headmen, and the present head of the family still served in that capacity. That particular headman had a daughter who was about twelve years old. She knew about her family's money troubles and offered to find a job to help support them.

"Father, I know that hard times have befallen the family and I can no longer sit back and do nothing about it. Please let me find a position as a servant. I realize that I am young and cannot earn very much, but I will do the best I can to help the family."

The girl's parents were moved by her offer, but they could not bring themselves to accept it. After all, she was their only child, and they could not bear the thought of being separated from her. The father said to his daughter:

"My child, I appreciate your good intentions, and it is very kind of you to make such an offer. But you are our only child. Even though we are very poor, your mother and I would rather die than live without you. I cannot let you leave us. Please give up the idea of becoming a servant in someone else's house."

The daughter was determined to help her family. In spite of

what her father said, she continued to plead with him until he finally gave in.

"Well, daughter, if you are that determined, I cannot refuse. You have my blessing. But where do you intend to find work? You don't know anyone who can give you a job, do you?"

"Yes, Father, I do. I am counting on my aunt in Edo to find a job for me."

In the end the father reluctantly agreed to the scheme and sent the girl off to her aunt. When she arrived at the aunt's house in Edo, the girl told her that she wanted to find work and asked her help. The aunt agreed and promised to find a job for her. She introduced her to her friends and finally found a place for her as a maid in the household of a *hatamoto*.* Having secured the position for the girl, the aunt then took her on a sightseeing tour of the city. She took her to a busy shopping district where they passed a store that catered mainly to women customers. Among the goods in the store were children's toy masks, including a mask of the devil *tengu,* and one of an ugly man. There was also a mask of a woman. When the girl saw it, she begged her aunt to buy it for her. The aunt was surprised since the masks were playthings for children.

"You are still a child at heart, aren't you? What use can you possibly have for such a toy now that you are a grown girl and about to become a servant?"

Then the aunt relented.

"Well, after all you are from the country. Everything probably looks glamorous to you. I will buy it for you."

The girl was delighted with the mask. She put it in her powder box and cherished it. Soon after, she moved into the *hatamoto* household and everything was new to her. As a country girl she knew very little of life in Edo. The other servants found her manner very odd. Each morning she would get up and close herself in her room for a long time. At first the other servants thought that she was fixing her hair.

---

*A *hatamoto* or bannerman at the time of this story was a member of a class of *samurai* who were often employed as upper-level bureaucrats.[Ed.]

"After all, she is a country girl. It probably takes her a long time to make herself look nice."

But they were wrong. When she came out, her hair was not particularly well dressed. In fact, she looked rather untidy. Day after day the servants would watch the girl shut herself up in her room and spend most of the morning there. They became more and more curious until one morning they peeped into her room. There was the girl sitting in front of her mirror wearing the mask of a woman and sobbing.

"Why on earth is she doing such a thing?" said one.

"Odd behavior, isn't it?" said another.

"There must be something the matter with her!" exclaimed a third.

The news spread quickly to the other servants and they all came to look at the girl. Everyone agreed that she was crazy. The senior maids went to the head servant and told her of the girl's strange behavior. They urged that the girl be dismissed, but the head servant disagreed.

"The girl is very new here. Everything is strange to her. You must be patient and kind. I want you to take care of her."

The senior maids went back to work but with some hope that the girl's behavior would improve. Several days passed, but the girl remained the same. Every morning she went to her room and shut herself in. She put on the mask and wept. Finally the maids could stand it no longer.

"This is ridiculous! How silly of us to let her go on like that day after day. We must do something."

They mulled the problem over among themselves. As you know, the maids could not openly scold the girl since the head servant had asked them to be kind to her. They devised a mischievous scheme instead. They bought a devil mask, secretly put it in the girl's powder box, and took away the mask of the woman. The next morning, when the girl opened the box, she was horrified. You see, she didn't know that the other servants had switched the masks.

"What has happened! The old woman mask has turned into a mask of a devil!" she cried. "I wanted the mask because it looked like my mother. Because I was sold into this household I could not return to my parents. I put on the mask and looked in the mirror to remind myself of my mother. Oh, now I see the image of a wretched devil! This must be a sign that something terrible has happened to my mother at home. What can it be? Are my parents all right?"

Terribly worried about her parents, the girl could no longer contain herself. Still holding the devil mask she rushed out of the house. Everyone in the *hatamoto* household was alarmed. After all, the girl's home was a long way off and they were afraid that she did not know her way. A search party was hastily organized and sent out, but to no avail.

Meanwhile, the girl hurried toward her home province of Hitachi. She had only a vague idea of the direction she should take, but she rushed on anyway. She was still far from home when night came on. There was no inn or house on the road. When it finally grew dark she could not tell whether she was walking on the road or in a rice field. She stumbled into a ditch, scratching her feet. Still she went on, and at last she saw a light in the distance.

"Ah, that must be a house ahead where I see the light. I can make it that far and find a place to rest."

When she reached the light, however, she saw a group of villainous-looking young men gambling at cards. They all looked like *sumō** wrestlers. Because it was summer, they wore only loincloths and sat by the fire to keep the mosquitoes away. The girl was speechless. She tried to run, but it was too late. They had already seen her.

The men were equally startled by the sudden appearance of a young girl walking alone after dark.

"What on earth is a young girl like you doing here at this hour? Where are you going? You have no business being out this late. How silly can you get?"

The girl told them her whole story and begged them to let her stay with them. One man suggested that she watch the fire and keep the mosquitoes away. Another gathered green grass and told her to pile it on the fire. The girl tried to do exactly as she was told

---

Sumō is a Japanese style of wrestling. [Ed.]

to make the smoke drive away the mosquitoes, but they kept coming back. The gamblers grew impatient and one of them hit her.

"You stupid girl," he shouted. "Don't you know how to
smoke out mosquitoes?"

The others joined in berating her. They, too, hit her. The girl
was desperate. "If I don't do something they will kill me," she
thought. What could she do? Suddenly she had a bright idea. She
put on the devil mask. The gamblers were suspicious of the girl's
story in the first place. When they saw the change in her, they fell
back.

"She has turned into a devil!" they cried and ran off into the
darkness.

Free from danger, the girl immediately set off for home. She
was in such a hurry that she tripped over something and fell. She
picked it up and without stopping to look at it ran on with no idea
of which way she was going. As dawn appeared she finally found
the right direction and made her way to her home province. As
soon as she saw her village, she ran toward her home as fast as her
legs could carry her.

"Mother, Father, where are you?"

She found her parents sitting in the kitchen. They looked
downcast.

"What has happened to you?" she asked. "Yesterday I suddenly had a feeling that something awful had happened to you
and I decided to come home. I did not even stop to ask my lord for
permission to leave. Are you ill or injured?"

"Oh, my dearest daughter. I am so happy that you have come
home!" exclaimed the father. "This must be a blessing from heav-
en. We thought you were gone forever."

Tears came into everyone's eyes and they were all too choked
with emotion to speak for a while. When they had stopped crying,
the father said:

"As you know, our family has suffered ill fortune for some
time. It has been so bad that even you, our precious daughter, have
had to go to work. Even though we were very poor, I could not neglect my responsibility as a village headman. For generations some-

one from our family has had the honor of serving as village headman, and I was determined not to let that honor pass out of our
family, no matter how poor I was. Now even greater misfortune has
befallen us. As headman I am responsible for collecting taxes from
the people in this village. They came to exactly fifty *ryo* in gold
cash. I finished the collection the day before yesterday, one day before they were due. On that very night the tax money was stolen. I
couldn't tell the villagers about the theft. I was afraid they would
suspect me of stealing the money for my own needs. Your mother
and I kept it to ourselves and thought about the course we should
take. We have considered disappearing somewhere or committing
suicide. That is the reason you find us in such low spirits."

The daughter could hardly bear to hear the story.

"Oh, what trouble we are in! No wonder I found that terrible
thing in my powder box!"

The girl told her parents about her mask which turned from a
woman into a devil, and about her meeting with the villainous
gamblers in loincloths. Finally she described her narrow escape
from death at the hands of the ruffians. Then she showed her parents the thing she had picked up on her way home. It looked like a
purse.

"This is truly the blessing of heaven! You have found my
purse with the stolen tax collection in it," cried the father. "I can't
believe it! I never dreamed that the money would be recovered.
This is truly the work of heaven! My dearest child, your filial piety
has been rewarded. What a rare thing this is. Now let us take the
money to the authorities right away. You have restored the money
and saved our lives."

Now you see how this girl's *makoto* caused her to act virtuous-
ly. Virtue naturally arises from *makoto*. If you keep filial piety fore-
most in your mind, you will protect others from danger as well as
yourself. Filial piety is a virtue. The girl in my story had *makoto*,
and *makoto* gave rise to her filial piety. So great was her filial feeling that it moved the gods to look on her with favor. Therefore, if
you preserve *makoto* and keep your heart pure, you will naturally
act with virtue. If you are virtuous, your life will be peaceful and
happy.

The Buddha Tree

The Buddha Tree is a novel by Fumio Niwa (b 1904) that was first published serially in 1955–1956. The author, the son of a hereditary priest, drew on his own personal recollection to portray aspects of contemporary Buddhism in Japan. In this selection, the priest of the novel, Soshu of the Butsuoji temple, visits the home of a factory worker and a communist, Yosuke Tachi.

Punctual to the minute, Father Soshu entered the house of Yosuke Tachi, one of his parishioners. The little single-storey house consisted of only three rooms, one behind the other, with an earthen passage running along one side; kitchen, lavatory, and storeroom were in an outhouse. A tiny strip of soil served for a garden. Tachi's neighbors were a *senbei*-seller* on one side and a teacher of Japanese dressmaking, who taught about twenty pupils in his two-storey house, on the other.

Soshu was shown to the middle of the three rooms. Tachi had been working in the garden, but the moment Soshu arrived he washed his hands and came to join him. He was still in his working clothes, black trousers and a jacket buttoned up to the neck.

"It's good of you to come."

Tachi was a slightly built man of fifty, with a lean, taut-looking face, and white hair which he kept cut short in workman's style.

Reprinted from Fumio Niwa, *The Buddha Tree,* translated by Kenneth Strong (London: Peter Owen, Ltd., 1966), pp. 50–55.
*A seller of Japanese crackers.

"I suppose you've taken a day off from the factory today?"

"Just the afternoon, that's all." It was the twenty-third anni-versary of his father's death—Whenever I'm with this man I feel I'm in debt to him somehow. . . . I wonder why, thought Soshu. At twelve Tachi had left school to take a job in a porcelain factory, in order to help support his family, and had worked there ever since. During and since the war he had served continuously as Chairman of the union which the workers in the factory, of whom there were about three hundred, had formed before the war. Yet there was nothing of the belligerent or fanatical union leader about him; he was pleasant and friendly, and one would not have taken him for anything other than an ordinary worker. Popular with his fellow workers, he was respected and trusted by the management. People were always surprised at his lively intelligence and remark-able fund of knowledge, which enabled him on occasion to carry on a theoretical argument for hours on end.

While his wife was serving tea, Tachi opened the family shrine which was kept behind the sliding doors of the cupboard, lit the candles, and began to burn incense. A devout and wholly sincere believer, one would say. "Perhaps it's his being a Communist, one of the chief Communists in Tan'ami, that makes me feel not quite easy with him," Soshu thought. There were a great many types of people in his congregation, but Yosuke Tachi gave him the impres-sion of being different in kind from all the others. This was partly due to Soshu's ignorance of Communism, and if he felt constraint in Tachi's presence, it was largely because he never knew what Tachi—a materialist, presumably—thought about the spiritual truths with which Buddhism was concerned.

After burning incense, Tachi sat before the shrine in silence, his hands clasped in reverence to the dead, then bowed to Soshu as the latter put on a ceremonial stole marked with the Butsuoji crest. Tachi's son, his only child, had not yet come back from school. As always, the house was quiet and tidy.

Soshu turned to face the shrine. Holding his rosary so that the single big bead was uppermost and the tassel hung down over the back of his left hand, he placed his hands together in the attitude of worship. Behind him Yosuke and his wife murmured a *nem-*

butsu. What did these services with the long scripture readings mean to Tachi, as a Communist Party member? He would ask him some day, Soshu thought.

Two accounts are given of the meaning and purpose of such services. According to the first, the relatives ask the priest to come and read the sutras for the benefit of the deceased. For this service —reading the sutras in the prescribed manner—the priest receives money offering from the family. The absolute purity of body, mouth, and mind which is required of a priest on such occasions is not easy to attain, and Soshu was painfully aware that his life was a continual negation of this threefold demand. Especially since Renko had left him, his sense of guilt had become almost unbearable. At Butsuoji he bowed each day before the statue of Amida and the portrait of Shinran, to all appearances still the saintly priest. But on his visits to members of the congregation, he felt as if his very body was foul, exuding corruption.

The efficacy of the scripture readings is held to increase according to the rank and standing of the priest who performs them. Soshu still belonged to the lowest rank.

He began with the Three Sutras of the Pure Land Sect. Altogether the readings took about two hours. Usually there would be a pause in the middle, while the priest rested and sipped a little tea to keep his voice fresh. Yosuke Tachi and his wife sat listening till the end, Yosuke without once relaxing his erect, formal posture. The first of the Three Sutras, The Book of Eternal Life According to Buddha, is a translation from the Sanscrit original made by Sogi, Tenjiku Sanzo, and Kosogai. It is always intoned, in the manner peculiar to the reading of the Buddhist sutras, and to Tachi, therefore, sitting behind Soshu, it was wholly unintelligible. To have to listen quietly for two hours must have been a considerable physical strain, but Tachi did not seem to find it difficult.

The curious doctrine that the efficacy of scripture reading varies with the rank of the priest-reader is said to be derived from the theory of *jiriki eko.* According to this belief, one seventh of the merit acquired by a memorial service of sutra readings accrues to the soul of the dead for whom the service is held, the other six sevenths to the mourning relatives—on the analogy, perhaps, of the practice, common in ancient times, of pilfering en route sums of money dispatched to an exile, so that the exile himself received only a small fraction of the original amount. The 7:1 proportion is purely arbitrary.

The other interpretation of these services is that they are expressions of gratitude to Amida Buddha for his mercy. There is no suggestion of acquiring merit for oneself by holding the service. The anniversaries of the death of a relative are regarded simply as occasions for deepening one's faith and giving thanks to Buddha for his infinite grace; and on these days, if the souls of the dead should chance to have fallen into the River of the Three Ways, Amida in his compassion will send his glorious light to shine upon them and help them in their distress. This salvation does not depend upon the merit of the reader of the sutras, or of whoever pays the offering to the temple for the service. It is wholly due to the grace of Amida.

The *nembutsu* which Yosuke and his wife, sitting behind Soshu, murmured from time to time were like a refrain to the long intoning. Soshu had a fine voice, merely to listen to which was a sensuous pleasure, however incomprehensible the words themselves might be; a perfect instrument for intoning the scriptures.

A truck rumbled past along the old highway. Recognizing the priest's voice as he came home from school, Yosuke's son tiptoed into the room and sat down between his parents. Even passersby on the road outside could hear Soshu. In this room Tachi and his fellow workers would often spend all night discussing union business, yet nothing about the normal appearance of the room suggested that it was used for such a purpose. The sliding doors, with their paper panels, may have been old; but the house always had an atmosphere of order and cleanliness that harmonized perfectly with the intoning of the scriptures. Tachi's neighbors, who would hear both the union discussions and the sutra readings, felt the latter suited the house far better than the former.

After the Three Sutras, Soshu began the Monruige scripture, Tachi and his wife joining in as he did so. Soshu himself, of course, knew the text by heart, and so did they, having recited it, in Tachi's case at least, at regular intervals for twenty years or more. Nowadays fewer and fewer of the members of the Butsuoji congregation who lived in the commercial part of Tan'ami could remember the scriptures well enough to recite them together with Soshu; but in the farming households even the children knew them still. Tachi and his wife joined in again, though rather uncertainly, in the final hymns after the scripture. Their son sang, too. In the same way, Ryokun at Butsuoji had learnt the Monruige and the Buddhist hymns from hearing them repeated night after night, sitting on his grandmother's knee. "A shop-boy living near a temple learns to chant a sutra," one of the Japanese alphabet cards says; and the boys had learnt sutras and scriptures such as these long before they were old enough to know what religion is—the more readily because of their simple musical settings, which are used to make chanting in unison easier.

"He looketh in mercy on all that call upon His Name, in every corner of the earth; He turneth not His people away, but watcheth over them with loving care. Let us worship Him, the Lord Amida is His name. . . ."

Finally, Soshu read from one of the Senshuji religious commentaries. His copy, which was paper-covered and bound with cotton thread in the old style, had been used by generations of Butsuoji priests; the cover was torn, and the faint smell of incense that clung to the pages made the book itself seem somehow holy. As the text was short, Soshu would often read it on his regular monthly visits to members of the congregation, when it was usual to choose a short sutra, too, such as the Amida-Sutra. The first section was by Abbott Gyoshu.

"Hear first the teaching of the holy Saint, our founder. Revere the laws of the Emperor and respect the Shogunate; obey the decrees of the governors of provinces, and of the lords of manors; perform faithfully your allotted part in public works; be unswerving in loyalty to your lord, fail not in duty to your parents. He that would escape the snares of the world, let him honor all Buddhas and Bodhisattvas, all spiritual beings; let him not speak evil of other ways there may be to salvation. What is the way to peace? Hear

now the teaching of our master. To call on Amida with one's whole
soul, casting upon Him and the power of His Original Vow* all our
fear of death and the hereafter; to repeat His holy name of Amida
in unwavering faith by day and by night, as long as our lives shall
last; this is the true peace of the soul. Amen. Amen. . . ."

Ridiculously out-of-date the words must seem to a layman
nowadays—especially when he is a Communist. . . . Soshu had
never read from this particular book at Tachi's house before. Such
words and style may have been current in Gyoshu's time, but
"laws of the Emperor," "Shogunates," and "governors and lords
of manors" meant nothing in twentieth-century Japan. To go on
woodenly reading the same text generation after generation as the
priests of Senshuji and all its subordinate temples did—such tradi-
tionalism was absurdly remote from real life, Soshu felt. It was one
thing to preserve a text like this for its historical significance; but to
recite it to members of a temple congregation, let alone to this particular member, was ludicrously inappropriate. When he reached
the twenty-fifth chapter, Soshu moved a little to the left, so that he
was no longer directly in front of the shrine, bent his head slightly,
raised the book reverently to his forehead, and began to read
again, holding the book now with both hands just below the level
of his eyes:

"If we look earnestly upon the shifting vicissitudes of the
world, whose sleeve will not be filled with tears? If a man ponder
in silence this floating life of ours, sorrow will be engraved upon
his heart. Is it not written in the sutra, 'All the manifold changes
of Karma are but the passing phases of a dream'?" These, too,
were the words of Abbott Gyoshu. "Ever-recurring are the seasons
of the year, endless the passing of men through the cycle of birth
and death. Truly all creatures, animate and inanimate, are bound
by this law. He who sports with flowers on a spring morning, at
evening he is laid low, as the north wind withers the pampas-grass;
he who views with delight the autumn moon, at dawn he is hidden

---

*The Vow in which Amida is said to have declared that he would not accept
enlightenment for himself unless he could be sure that all sentient beings would
be saved by faith in him.

from sight in the clouds. . . . Ah, the sadness of things! For no
man is his desire fulfilled: the tree would be still, but the wind
never ceases; the father stays not in this world for his son to cherish
him. . . ."

Tachi and his wife and son listened with bowed heads. Soshu
turned to face them when he had finished reading, and after Tachi
had thanked him formally for performing the rite, began to take
off his stole. Mrs. Tachi went to prepare a meal for him. In all the
households of the temple congregation, it was customary to invite
and entertain all the relatives to these memorial services, which are
held on the seventh, thirteenth, seventeenth, and twenty-third anniversary of the death of a member of the family. On this occasion,
the twenty-third anniversary of his father's death, Tachi had invited no one outside the immediate family; but even so, there was no
question of omitting the meal that was always offered to the offi-
ciating priest. Soshu merely tasted the food briefly, for politeness'
sake. Afterwards, as was the custom with families living near Butsuoji, the dishes would be taken, just as they were, to the temple,
an unexpected treat for the priest's family—yet not so unexpected
either, since with two hundred or so families in the parish, one
such meal would be brought to Butsuoji practically every week.
Formerly the meal offered to the priest had been more lavish, and
not strictly vegetarian. Even *sake* had been served sometimes. In
those days Soshu had taken off his priest's gown and sat down in
his plain white robe to take the meal in the house where he had
held the service.

The Prophet
Of Tabuse

The Prophet of Tabuse is the official biography of Sayo Kitamura (1900–
1967), founder of the Dancing Religion *(Odoru shūkyō)*. According to
her biographer Sayo Kitamura believed that a Shinto deity entered her
body and spoke to her, giving divine guidance. In the following selection
she explains the atomic bomb and the occupation of Japan as a divine act
intended to cleanse Japan of evildoers. The religion she founded is known
to most Japanese as the Dancing Religion because body movements accompanied by chanting are part of the devotional service.

On the 8th of May, 1945, the war in Europe at last came to an end.
The defense of Japan was becoming more and more difficult. On
June 27, God in Her body ordered the Foundress, who had been
suffering from diarrhea for the previous ten days, to go to the fields
in front of Her house and stool. She obeyed and excreted a yellow
stool just like that of a baby. God in Her body explained, "I have
cleansed Your dirty human stomach and now You have become
God's baby."

On the night of the 20th of July, She had several attacks of
diarrhea and when She recovered, She was informed by God in
Her body, "Osayo, by this Your baby stomach has been cleansed,
and You have become an Angel seventeen years old."

Prior to this attack of diarrhea, arrangements for delivering

Reprinted from *The Prophet of Tabuse: A Translation of* Seisho (Tabuse,
Yamaguchi Prefecture, 1954), pp. 51–61. *Seisho* ["Book of Life" or "Bible"],
edited by Tenshō Kōtaijingūkyō Honbu, was published by Tokyo Bunka Kenkyū-
jo, Tokyo, 1951.

Her first sermon at Her house had been made. The date had been set for July 22, and invitations had been sent to all Her acquaintances and to the persons whom She had met in Yanai in June, as well as to the neighbors. In those days people feared military defeat and were uneasy day and night. About fifty men and women came early in the morning of the appointed day, hoping to meet the Foundress in person and to obtain comfort.

The Foundress, dressed in black trousers and a white blouse, entered the room where the people awaited Her. Her smiling face was shining and was in sharp contrast to the weary faces of the war sufferers. She then preached in songs and in words with a silvery sweet voice. She also exhibited an ecstasy dance by Herself. The audience was sitting in a circle with the Foundress in the center. Her bashful and childish behavior and gestures were exactly like those of a girl seventeen years of age, just as God in Her body had intimated. All the members of the audience were magnetized, and they listened earnestly to Her teachings, forgetting all of their worries and troubles. At the end She said, "This is only an experimental performance, and as token of My appreciation for your presence I will give you a talisman which will guard you from the disasters of air raids."

Those people who assembled there on that occasion never forgot these words. At noon a luncheon was served. In the afternoon the size of the audience increased as people came from the neighboring villages and towns to hear the Foundress' sermons. Through Her songs the Foundress disclosed the faults of many attendants. Some people were praised because of their merits, some were severely chastised, and others were given parental advice. The songs varied according to circumstances and depending on the character of each individual. The congregation wondered and was amazed at Her superhuman power and knowledge, because She penetrated into the bottom of their hearts, revealing their personal secrets. Consequently, they realized that the Foundress was not an ordinary mortal. Her sermons were not just sentences, inert and lifeless; they had a living meaning, and they contained no discrepancies or contradictions. The people acknowledged Her doctrines, but they still felt that the teachings had no direct bearing upon their actual daily lives. Therefore, they could not immediately make up their minds to put the teachings into practice.

At the end the Foundress said, "On the 12th of August I shall announce great news to you. On the 22nd of August a Divine Wind will blow. Turn on your radios on the 12th of August."

They wondered what kind of news it would be but the Foundress did not comment any further.

Her sermon came to an end, but She did not distribute the expected talismans that would guard the audience from bombs. The people anxiously asked the Foundress for the talismans. She laughed and replied, "I didn't mean a paper talisman. A thousand sheets of paper talismans are useless. You must remove the dirt from your souls, and then I shall give you the genuine spiritual talisman to take back to your homes. It is the One in My body that decides where a bomb will be dropped and whether or not it will explode. Therefore, do as I tell you and follow the teachings I have given you; then the bombs will never fall. The one in My body said, 'I have not created a Heaven where bombs would fall!' "

When they heard this teaching, some realized their mistakes and were afraid. Some were disappointed, and others could not understand the sermon's true meaning. They returned to their homes as the lengthy summer day was turning into night, and in their hearts there was comfort and new hope. Since this was the first day She had preached at Her house, the date later became a most important memorial day for the followers. After the first sermon, the Foundress no longer went into town as before but preached Her sermons in Her house, since the number of followers had increased.

Mrs. Honjo, who lives in the city of Tokuyama, was among those present on July 22. She requested the Foundress to come to her house in Tokuyama some day and deliver Her sermons.

The Foundress replied, "The One in My body says that I shall be very busy and not a minute can be spared in August. This month may be all right. What would you say to My coming on the 27th?"

"If only You would come. I don't mind when it will be."

"I shall come, then, but before I go, I shall drive the maggots from Tokuyama City by scouring it with bombs, incendiary shells, and machine-gun bullets. Please tell your people so."

At midnight on July 26, the air raid which the Foundress had foretold devastated the city. As soon as the sirens began to screech, a heavy attack was opened by some one hundred and twenty American planes, and the greater part of Tokuyama City was enveloped in flames. Soon after, countless bodies of the dead and wounded lay on the streets. It was a terrible cleaning of the city—a thorough cleaning.

The long, horrible night was over. The next day, the 27th, was the day the Foundress had promised to call on Mrs. Honjo in Tokuyama. The city had been completely changed in appearance during the night and all over the city the buildings were still smouldering. People were homeless, some had lost their families and relatives, and others who seemed to have lost their souls wandered aimlessly about. At Tabuse Station the railway clerk refused to issue a ticket to Tokuyama because the city had been severely bombed during the night, and had been so ravaged by fire that it would be useless to attempt a trip into the city. But the Foundress insisted that the house where She was going had not been bombed or burned.

"If you insist, I'll issue a ticket as far as Kushigahama, the station before Tokuyama."

The Foundress got off the train at Kushigahama Station and walked to Tokuyama and Honjo's house, passing through the ruins of the great fire. Honjo's house was safe. Several bombs had dropped near it, but none had exploded. Having been saved from the disaster, Mrs. Honjo thanked the Foundress sincerely. The Foundress arrived just as Mrs. Honjo was cleaning the mess in her house. This was the first time the Foundress had called on Mrs. Honjo, but nobody had guided Her, nor had She asked the way. She arrived without getting lost after a three-mile walk. The Foundress said to Mrs. Honjo, who came rushing to the entrance to welcome Her, "Honjo, I showed you the entrance of Hell last night, didn't I? That was Hell. Make up your mind. Just now I had a cordial reception with your husband's former wife who appeared together with five other spirits."

The Foundress handed a small bag of rice and sweet potatoes

to Mrs. Honjo, and said, "I have blessed them with prayer. All of you eat this together so that you may go ahead on the Heavenly Road in peace."

As Mr. Honjo appeared to greet the Foundress, She pointed to Mrs. Honjo and said to him, "Your real wife is this one. By virtue of this one's sincerity your family has been saved. The former wife I saw a little while ago was better looking and more slender than your present wife but was vain and had a hysterical disposition. She died from tuberculosis. Isn't that so? She is not yet saved. She haunts you from time to time, which is proof that she has not yet been converted."

And then with songs and words She pointed out the virtues, the weak points, and prophesied the fate of each member of the Honjo family. To the eldest daughter, who was married to Lieutenant General Shirogane, She said, "Shirogane has sound ideas on patriotism and on religion. I can hardly say you are a beautiful woman, but you are fortunate because he believes that you are the best wife in the world. I will return him to you as a common man with no rank. I guarantee ninety-nine percent, but the remaining one percent depends on your sincerity." She continued, "Honjo's sons are all in the Army now, but I will return them safely. They will come back without uniforms."

The Foundress stayed that night at Mrs. Honjo's residence and returned to Tabuse the next morning, realizing that the seeds of God had been sown in the Tokuyama area.

August of that year will never be forgotten by the Japanese people, nor for that matter by the world. The atomic bomb which was dropped on Hiroshima City on the 6th of August became the immediate cause of Japan's unconditional surrender, with 200,000 people either killed outright or wounded, and with 100,000 homes destroyed at a single blow.

Mrs. Fujimoto, one of the earnest followers living in a nearby village, rushed to the Foundress with the news of the atomic bombardment. The Foundress, who was eating gruel-rice at that moment, replied, "Calm down and keep quiet. The atomic bomb is now eating gruel-rice right here."

On August 8, the Foundress was told to sew a snow-white

dress and to prepare a set of white bedding, and when these were ready She was told to wear the dress and to sleep alone before the altar on the night of the 11th. On the 10th She had another attack of diarrhea and was told at the time that She had been made an Angel twenty-five years old. The night of August 11 came, and She did as She had been told. After sleeping about thirty minutes, She was awakened, and God in Her body said, "With the midnight bell of the 11th, You will be made the Only Daughter of Tensho-Kotai-Jingu. Now You have been given Divine Sight by means of which You can view the whole world at a glance. What I have hithertofore referred to as 'Tobyo,' or 'Controller of the Mouth,' or 'Guiding God,' is the same Deity as Tensho-Kotai-Jingu."

Thereafter the whole universe could be seen by the Foundress —the world of phenomena, the spiritual world, including the eternal Hell, to say nothing of all varieties of fish, insects, animals, and ghosts in the human world as well as in the Celestial World. Explanations were provided for each one of these visions. For three days the kaleidoscopic views continued, making Her wonder if She had to see these things all the time to the point of nervous exhaustion. In response to Her wondering, God in Her body said, "Osayo, say it is enough."

When She replied affirmatively, God in Her body added, "Osayo, from now on I will show You only what is necessary."

Thereafter only necessary things were shown Her, like the abbreviated scenes in a news film. Thus, on midnight of August 11, She was definitely adopted as the Only Daughter of the Absolute God of the Universe. God in Her body explained that, "The Male God Kotai-Jin, who descended into Your body on November 27 last year, and the Female God Amaterasu Meokami who descended on August 11, have united together as one God, making Your body a temple, and thus forming the 'Trinity'!"

The past three years had been long and difficult. On the 12th of August, She had begun Her religious practice; and thereafter She had never once failed to take Her daily cold bath of penance, and had followed God's instructions earnestly, overcoming all kinds of persecutions and hardships.

The 12th of August, a day of deep significance, having come round the third time, God made Her the true Redeemer and began the sacred task of building up God's Kingdom on this earth. On that very day, Japan's surrender to the Allied Powers was decided.

On August 14, 1945, the Foundress saw a man in a white shirt sitting on the stoop of the room where She used to deliver sermons. The God in Her body said to Her, "I brought this man in."

She said to the man, "You came to see Me, so come on in."

The man replied, "I came from Hirao Police Station to tell You to come to the Station personally before 12 o'clock bringing Your personal seal with You."

"Don't be silly, how can I go there before 12 o'clock? It is already 10:30. I shall be there about 2:30. Tell your men not to go elsewhere but to be there at that hour to meet Me."

"Sure, we shall all be there," said the man as he went away.

When the Foundress got ready and left Her house for the Hirao Police Station, She noticed that Hikari City, the site of a naval arsenal not very far from Tabuse, was under a heavy air raid, and that flights of B-29's circled several times above Tabuse before turning toward the target.

Several air raid wardens, dressed in uniform, were shouting, "Take shelter, take shelter!"

At that time the Foundress, wearing a white blouse and carrying a parasol, was riding Her bicycle. Some guards stopped Her and inquired who She was.

"It is I," She replied in a loud voice, and as they recognized Her they did not detain Her any longer. She said to them, "What are you doing there? If it were cold, it might be good to wear an anti-air raid cotton hood, but why in this heat! I have never put on such a thing in My life. The place where I am is Paradise, and God did not create a Paradise that would be destroyed by bombs. All attempts to guard against bombs are useless unless you make your place a Paradise, no matter where you are."

Great columns of gray smoke had risen up in the southwestern sky. Someone asked Her, "Is that Hikari City?"

She also thought that it must be Hikari City, but Her mouth involuntarily said, "That cannot be Hikari."

"Then what place is it?" All the bystanders looked at Her in amazement.

"The place that is burning is where there is no godliness!" She exclaimed.

Keeping the guards at bay, She rode Her bicycle toward the police station, and as soon as She entered the station She was interviewed by the chief of the Special Service Section. Other members of the station focused their gazes upon Her and listened with close attention.

"Have You ever delivered speeches in public at the Town Office?"

"Yes," replied the Foundress.

"Is it true You said that next year will be the first year of a new epoch? Because You said this, the people of the town are much perturbed and interpret the statement as meaning that Japan will lose the war. We have suffered inconveniences as a consequence of Your preachings. Please don't say such things again."

"But there is Someone in My body Who said on the first morning of this year, 'God once entrusted His world into the hands of humans, but they have ruined it, and therefore it is natural that God retrieve and reform it. The degenerated human era will have ended upon the completion of 2,605 years; God's World will commence next year and will last for 2,300 years. Nevertheless, this does not mean losing the war. No, absolutely not. Japan will become the spiritual leader of the world. However, the present Japanese are such maggot beggars that they are unworthy of this responsibility. Let the bombs and shells fall to exterminate the maggots in this country!' "

"That might be understandable to persons of your knowledge, but ignorant people would interpret it as a warning that the war will be lost. The national structure will remain unchanged forever," said the policeman.

"Did I say that the Japanese national structure will be changed? I am merely announcing the renewal of the present era.

The national constitution means the national body politic. There is
no need to conquer other countries. Japan Proper is big enough.
Clean out the maggots masked with human faces. Although you
are short, see what will happen when you add others' legs to yours;
you won't be able to walk a step."

The chief of police clicked his heels and said with nervousness,
"I am advising You as a police officer. I want You to stop making
such speeches."

"If you say not to, I will do so," replied the Foundress, "but if
next year does witness the beginning of a new era, will you take off
your hat and come to apologize to me?"

"Sure, we will. That will be all. You may go now," said the officers.

"Don't be ridiculous! You told Me to bring My seal, so show
Me to what document I should affix it. You summoned Me in this
heat; therefore, make the trip worth My while. You are paid to protect the people, and I would like an explanation of how you are
protecting them," said the Foundress.

Satisfied with these remarks, She left the police station and returned home.

At noon the next day, the Emperor broadcast to the people
the news of the unconditional surrender.

On the 16th the Foundress attended a gathering which had
been planned by the Women's Association of Tabuse in order to
hear Her sermons. She sang the following sermon:

> Awake, you maggot beggars!
>   Awake, you traitor beggars!
> The Door of Heaven has now opened
>   For the pious souls to enter.
>
> The war, fought for eight long years,
>   Was designed by His wish
> To reveal the true human road
>   And to convert all people to His Kingdom.
>
> They have spoiled His Land
>   With egoism, with selfishness, and

With the delusion that honesty is disadvantageous.
　　But, at last, this age of corruption has ended.

God descends, subjugates, and controls
　　The degraded human world with His Hand,
And changes it into His most wonderful
　　And amazing Celestial Kingdom.

Cultivate a patriotic spirit
　　And pray for victory.
But if your prayers are selfish,
　　God will take no notice of them.

Do not expect selfish prayers to be answered,
　　But endeavor instead to be reborn as His child.
Only His children will survive
　　And enjoy Celestial Bliss forever.

The present condition of Japan
　　Is caused by maggot beggars
Who have fallen down from God's Kingdom
　　And lost their way in darkness.

Her singing voice reverberated through the entire hall and the
people listened in silence to Her sermon, because they were impressed with Her strong faith.

It was a complete surprise to the Japanese people in general to
learn of an unconditional surrender, because they had been thoroughly indoctrinated in the belief that the Divine Country, Japan,
could never be defeated, and further, that in the darkest hours
they could rely upon a Divine Wind to save the country. The news
was very hard to believe, and it took quite some time for most Japanese to realize that the nation had unconditionally surrendered.
In view of these circumstances, God in Her body explained as follows: "This surrender does not mean the loss of the war. This is but
the end of fighting between maggots. The war will be carried on by
Me from now on against evil spirits. Return to a true human state
as soon as possible because it is the only way to win the war. Pray
and pray, for this war can be won by prayer."

The people could not grasp the real significance of these words, but they felt a certain hope in their hearts.

On August 20, Mrs. Machida came to see the Foundress. While pounding on the floor she wailed, "God, God, the American soldiers will land in our country if You do not arrange for the Divine Wind."

The Foundress replied forcefully, "By the end of next February (lunar year) at the latest I will celebrate the establishment of God's Era. If you want to rely on a Divine Wind, create it yourself."

After the 22nd of August, Japanese airplanes were seen no longer in the skies and American planes flew over the whole of Japan at will.

On the 30th of August General MacArthur, the Supreme Commander of Allied Powers, landed from Manila at Atsuki airfield. As soon as the occupying forces landed in Japan, American soldiers were seen everywhere, and now the people of Japan were forced to realize that an unconditional surrender had actually been made. They lost their confidence and could no longer rely on belief in the infallibility of the Emperor, which had previously been their source of spiritual and moral guidance. Thus there was much consternation and deep meditation began.

The Foundress proclaimed: "The collapsing human world has ceased to exist as of August 15 of the 2,605th year of Jimmu's Era. Your beggars' world is now nothing, and will remain so for eternity. The death knell of the maggots' world is the herald of God's Kingdom. Daybreak, daybreak, God's Kingdom has dawned! There is no foolish God in Heaven Who will expunge the country of Japan. Return to a human state without delay. Differences of race, nationality, and color are not justifiable causes for enmity. God's enemies are those who do not meet His Will. The war between Sacred God and Evil Spirits has now begun. You are mistaken if you think that this disaster would never have befallen us if Tojo had not been Premier. Just as cold blasts will always blow in winter, we would have suffered no matter who was the head of the State. Because of this war, the Kingdom of God will be created on earth."

At the end of September the Foundress spoke of the Divine Wind: "The other name for MacArthur is the 'Messenger of Divinity'. He was sent to Japan as an agent of the Divine Wind. Those well-dressed gentlemen with combed hair and moustaches who gave no thought to the poor are terrible, shameful beggars. The police who chased after thieves were worse than the criminals. The members of the Diet were high-handed criminals, and the Cabinet Ministers were even worse. Who put them in jail? Nobody but MacArthur—Is this not the work of a good Divine Wind?"

During the period of national prostration following defeat, the number of social crimes increased and the moral and spiritual lepers showed their true colors. Most of the people pursued their own selfish interests, and the country was thoroughly demoralized. On the other hand, thoughtful people were anxious to devise means of reconstructing Japan because their hearts suffered with the agony of defeat.

In this setting of demoralization the Foundress boldly and repeatedly said, "Beggars of a defeated nation, wake up as soon as you can! Then you will be in the Kingdom of God. If you do not awaken, you will always be in the beggars' world, and if you are in this condition don't shout to God for help. God will not come down to the beggars' world to help people who are crying for His mercy. Clean your souls with your own endeavor until you are acceptable in the eyes of God; then you will be able to get into the Kingdom of God. You people who are living at this time can never rest in peace unless you find the road to survival for your descendants. And when your country becomes again independent and real world peace is established, you will not then be sorry to die. Thus you can be real followers of God."

Part 2

THE FAMILY

Few societies have been as conscious of the family as an ideal and a kinship unit as have the Japanese throughout their history. The family was the most important social unit in premodern Japan, and even in the modern period Japanese society cannot be fully understood without giving it deep consideration. Until the end of World War II the schools and the media repeatedly stated, by official government policy, the ideals of the Japanese family system. The family was the embodiment of traditional Japanese virtues and a training ground for loyalty to the state. In theory the state was an extension of the family with the emperor as family head. The ideal was a single unbroken line in every family, including both living and dead members. The chief function of living members was to care for ancestors and preserve the prosperity and continuity of the family line. From 1890 through 1945 schoolchildren read daily the Imperial Rescript on Education, which included the declaration: "Ye, Our subjects, be filial to your parents and affectionate to your brothers and sisters; as husbands and wives be harmonious."

Under the traditional family system, especially when fortune and property were involved, the main family inherited the major share of the family holdings and accepted responsibility for needy members. The main family consisted of all those who lived together and shared in the family's social and economic life. A typical main family included a man, his wife, unmarried brothers and sisters, the eldest son and his wife and children, and unmarried sons and daughters. The family could also include adopted members and others who lived with it and contributed to its economic functioning in some way. The head of the household was responsible for controlling family members, providing for them materially, and offering moral guidance. He arranged the marriages of his children and unmarried brothers and sisters. Succession to the headship usually passed to the eldest male direct descendant on the death or retirement of a former head. In instances where no adult male descendant existed, a widow could be the head until she married and her husband replaced her. If a family did not have a male heir, it could adopt a son as a way of ensuring the continuity of the family line. The heir was generally adopted as a young man —often at the time of his marriage to a daughter of the house. Frequently the adopted son was the younger son of a family of equal or slightly higher social position than the family into which he was adopted. In the absence of any child, a child of either sex might be adopted. An adopted male would eventually become head of the family; an adopted female would marry someone who would succeed the head. In the selection "On Becoming an Adoptee," a man describes his initial feelings of ambivalence upon receiving an offer of adoption and marriage from a wealthy family. In order to enjoy the advantages of being the first son of his new family, he would have to give up his own family name and heritage. His loyalty and allegiance would belong to his new family.

Daughters and younger sons belonged to a family until they grew up and married. On her marriage a daughter, like an adopted child, became a member of her husband's family and was expected to transfer her loyalty to her new family. With permission of the main family, a younger son could marry and start a branch family of his own. Theoretically a main family could have many branches and the branches in turn could have more branches, all of them subordinate to the main family. In fact, however, only prosperous families had branches, and only a branch family that had some economic connection with the main family maintained close ties with it. The branch family usually lived apart from the main family, but it shared the same ancestry and typically followed the occupation of the main family. A merchant family might turn over some part of the family business to the branch family, for example, or assist it in establishing itself in business in another location.

The family in the selection from *The Makioka Sisters* is an old and established one from the merchant class of the commercial city of Osaka, and the story takes place in the decade just preceding World War II. The central problem of the story is the arrangement of a marriage for the third daughter, Yukiko. Since there were no Makioka sons, the husband of the oldest daughter became head of the main family on the death of the father. The second sister invited Yukiko to live with her family so that Yukiko might have more opportunities to see candidates for a husband. Ordinarily, unmarried sisters live with the oldest sister's family. In the selection offered here, the family meets with a prospective groom for Yukiko. Prior to the meeting each side has thoroughly investigated the background of the other. In addition to the practical considerations involved in the arrangement of a marriage, it is evident from this story that the wishes of the couple are taken into account. Yukiko has refused several suitable matches because she did not like the man.

In families where there is little property and no social standing to consider, marriage arrangements are less involved than those portrayed in *The Makioka Sisters*. In rural communities young couples, particularly those from poor families, have greater freedom of choice in selecting their spouses than their counterparts in propertied families. Adoption, too, is more the concern of families with wealth, property, and position to maintain than it is of the poor.

Traditionally, family relationships were governed by a set of principles directing behavior and the organization of the family. Yet the family in prewar Japan, like families in any society, were bound by ties of affection as well as by principle. A young bride did not break all emotional bonds with her own family even though her duties lay with her husband's family. Although marriages were often arranged by the family, husbands and wives could grow to love each other. In theory the central relationship in the traditional family was between the parents and their children; a man took a wife so that she would serve his parents and bear his children. Emotional ties between husband and wife were condoned so long as they did not disturb other family relationships.

Extramarital affairs were permitted the husband in the traditional family as long as he did not allow them to disrupt the family.

In *The Love Suicides at Amijima,* an eighteenth-century play, a paper merchant's love for a prostitute causes him to neglect his family business and his responsibilities to the household. He squanders the family's resources including his wife's dowry. In the selection presented here, the wife's family intervenes with the intention of either forcing the merchant to fulfill his family obligations or taking back their daughter and dissolving the marriage.

The selection from *The Sound of the Mountain* also involves an extramarital affair, this time in a contemporary setting, and again the family intervenes. A war widow has conceived a child out of wedlock. Despite the urgings of her lover's father she is determined to have the child because she has no other family. Her lover's father, as the head of his household, visits the woman and asks her to have an abortion because, he argues, the child will not have a father or family. The son's affair has clearly disrupted his family life and his wife has had an abortion because of it. The old man's sadness shows his concern not only for the welfare of his family but also for the grandchild who will be related by blood but not be a part of his family.

The selections from the autobiography of Motoko Hani concern the family of an unusual Japanese woman. A precocious child, she was determined to be well educated in the Meiji period, when not many women received more than a few years of formal education. Her grandfather helps her. In her family, as in *The Sound of the Mountain,* the grandfather acts as family head. Her father was adopted into the family upon marrying her mother and was expelled from it when the grandfather feared that his behavior would disgrace the family. Motoko Hani and her mother remain part of the mother's family after the divorce. She tells of her two marriages, the first to a dissolute man she has chosen on her own and married only with the reluctant consent of her grandfather and the second to a fellow journalist and educator with whom she founded a school and a magazine, *The Woman's Friend.* Motoko Hani's autobiography shows that Japanese society is sufficiently flexible to allow a talented and ambitious woman to achieve professional success and a nontraditional marriage and family life as well.

Since World War II the principles and ties of the traditional family have been weakened by social change. Large companies provide the security and welfare services that were formerly the responsibility of the family. Younger sons often move to urban areas and ties with the main family weaken. A son who moves to the city has no responsibility to his family in the country and, moreover, is unlikely to appeal to the main family for financial assistance. In many instances the urban branch families become richer than the main families, further weakening the power of the main family over the branch. Traditionally, older members of a family were cared for by the oldest child in their home. With greater numbers of Japanese living in small houses or apartments in urban areas, however, it has become increasingly difficult to care for aging relatives. In the *Housewife and Woman* selection, the husband's resentment toward his invalid father who lives with him exemplifies this problem. His wife concludes that aging parents should not live with their children. Responsibility for their care, she says, should be taken over by society as a whole.

The role of women in postwar Japan, as in other modern industrial societies, is changing. Increasing numbers of women are working, and some continue to work after marriage or return to work once their children are in school. In *Housewife and Woman*, the conflict between the woman's desire to work and her traditional role as full-time housewife and mother illustrates the increasing opportunities for women outside the home and the reexamination of their role in society.

Postwar society and the tendency of Japanese, particularly in urban areas, to live in small nuclear family units means that relatives often are not close at hand to offer aid and advice when children are born. Traditionally, advice on childrearing was passed down verbally from older women to younger. Today, when grandmothers may be far away, new mothers often turn to books on child care for guidance when earlier generations of women would have looked to their relatives. Dr. Michio Matsuda's books on child care are very popular, and he is rapidly gaining the fame in Japan that Dr. Spock has had in the United States. Dr. Matsuda calls upon Japanese women to follow traditional child care methods rather than borrow Western practices. These Japanese practices often encourage a close mutual dependency between mother and child. In the excerpts presented here, Dr. Matsuda recommends physical contact with the child and advises mothers to follow the traditional practice of carrying their babies on their backs and nursing them whenever they cry. Mothers should sit with their babies until they fall asleep. The traditional Japanese methods, according to Dr. Matsuda, put great emphasis on the psychological needs of the child and recognize his idiosyncrasies.

In an increasingly urban Japan, the traditional family system is giving way to a new order. The nuclear family composed of husband, wife, and children is the basic social unit in Japan today, particularly among white-collar workers. Real authority in running the household usually lies with the wife; the husband is away from home at his company or with fellow employees much of the time. Nevertheless loyalty to the family remains strong. Most people would like, if possible, to continue their family line although few follow the old practices of adoption. There is often a strong sentimental attachment to the ancestral home and to the ideal of family solidarity. "Grandfather Sōhachi" illustrates this attachment to family tradition. The writer Ryōtarō Shiba clearly feels a strong bond with an eccentric grandfather who died before he was born. He tells of a trip to a temple to see a memorial tablet to his grandfather.

Love Suicides
at Amijima

The following selection is the second act of *The Love Suicides at Amijima*, a play written for the puppet theater *(bunraku)* by Chikamatsu Monzaemon (1653–1725). First performed in 1721, the play is a domestic tragedy about a paper merchant named Jihei who is torn by his love for a prostitute and his need for his wife. Here he pleads with his father-in-law not to take his wife away and promises to reform. He lacks the moral courage to renounce the prostitute, however, and ultimately the situation leads to the breakup of his family and his double suicide with his mistress.

Scene: The house and shop of Kamiya Jihei.
Time: Ten days later.

Narrator: The busy street that runs straight to Tenjin Bridge,* named for the god of Temma, bringer of good fortune, is known as the Street Before the Kami,† and here a paper shop does business under the name Kamiya Jihei. The paper is honestly sold, the shop well situated; it is a long-established firm, and customers come thick as raindrops.

Outside crowds pass in the street, on their way to the Ten

Reprinted from D. Keene (trans.), *Major Plays of Chikamatsu* (New York: Columbia University Press, 1961), pp. 403–414, by permission of the publisher.
*The reference is to Temma Tenjin, the name as a deity of Sugawara no Michizane.
†A play on the words *kami* (god) and *kami* (paper).

Nights service, while inside the husband dozes in the *kotatsu*,*
shielded from drafts by a screen at his pillow. His wife Osan keeps
solitary, anxious watch over shop and house.

Osan: The days are so short—it's dinnertime already, but
Tama still hasn't returned from her errand to Ichinokawa.† I wonder what can be keeping her. That scamp Sangorō isn't back either.
The wind is freezing. I'm sure the children will both be cold. He
doesn't even realize that it's time for Osue to be nursed. Heaven
preserve me from ever becoming such a fool! What an infuriating
creature!

Narrator: She speaks to herself.

Kantarō: Mama, I've come back all by myself.

Narrator: Her son, the older child, runs up to the house.

Osan: Kantarō—is that you? What's happened to Osue and
Sangorō?

Kantarō: They're playing by the shrine. Osue wanted her
milk and she was bawling her head off.

Osan: I was sure she would. Oh—your hands and feet are fro-
zen stiff as nails! Go and warm yourself at the *kotatsu*. Your father's sleeping there. What am I to do with that idiot?

Narrator: She runs out impatiently to the shop just as Sangorō
shuffles back, alone.

Osan: Come here, you fool! Where have you left Osue?

Sangorō: You know, I must've lost her somewhere. Maybe
somebody's picked her up. Should I go back for her?

Osan: How could you? If any harm has come to my precious
child, I'll beat you to death!

Narrator: But even as she screams at him, the maid Tama returns with Osue on her back.

Tama: The poor child—I found her in tears at the corner. Sangorō, when you're supposed to look after the child, do it properly.

Osan: You poor dear. You must want your milk.

---

*A source of heat in which a charcoal burner is placed under a low, quilt-
covered table.

†Ichinokawa was the site of a large vegetable market near the north end of
Tenjin Bridge.

Narrator: She joins the others by the *kotatsu* and suckles the child.

Osan: Tama—give that fool a taste of something that he'll remember!*

Narrator: Sangorō shakes his head.

Sangorō: No, thanks, I gave each of the children two tangerines just a while ago at the shrine, and I tasted five myself.

Narrator: Fool though he is, bad puns come from him nimbly enough, and the others can only smile despite themselves.

Tama: Oh—I've become so involved with this half-wit that I almost forgot to tell you, ma'am, that Mr. Magoemon and his aunt† are on their way here from the west.

Osan: Oh dear! I'll have to wake Jihei in that case. *(To Jihei.)* Please get up. Mother and Magoemon are coming. They'll be upset again if you let them see you, a businessman, sleeping in the afternoon, with the day so short as it is.

Jihei: All right.

Narrator: He struggles to a sitting position and, with his abacus in one hand, pulls his account book to him with the other.

Jihei: Two into ten goes five, three into nine goes three, three into six goes two, seven times eight is fifty-six.

Narrator: His fifty-six-year-old aunt enters with Magoemon.

Jihei: Magoemon, aunt. How good of you. Please come in. I was in the midst of some urgent calculations. Four nines make thirty-six *momme*. Three sixes make eighteen *fun*. That's two *momme* less two *fun*.‡ Kantarō! Osue! Granny and Uncle have come! Bring the tobacco tray! One times three makes three. Osan, serve the tea!

Narrator: He jabbers away.

Aunt: We haven't come for tea or tobacco. Osan, you're young I know, but you're the mother of two children, and your excessive forbearance does you no credit. A man's dissipation can always be traced to his wife's carelessness. Remember, it's not only

---

*A pun on the two meanings of *kurawasu*: "to cause to eat" and "to beat."
†Magoemon's (and Jihei's) aunt, but Osan's mother.
‡Meaningless calculations. Twenty *fun* made two *momme*.

the man who's disgraced when he goes bankrupt and his marriage breaks up. You'd do well to take notice of what's going on and assert yourself a bit more.

Magoemon: It's foolish to hope for any results, aunt. The scoundrel even deceives me, his elder brother. Why should he take to heart criticism from his wife? Jihei—you played me for a fool. After showing me how you returned Koharu's pledges, here you are, not ten days later, redeeming her! What does this mean? I suppose your urgent calculations are of Koharu's debts! I've had enough!

Narrator: He snatches away the abacus and flings it clattering into the hallway.

Jihei: You're making an enormous fuss without any cause. I haven't crossed the threshold since the time I saw you except to go twice to the wholesalers in Imabashi and once to the Tenjin Shrine. I haven't even thought of Koharu, much less redeemed her.

Aunt: None of your evasions! Last evening at the Ten Nights service I heard the people in the congregation gossiping. Everybody was talking about the great patron from Temma who'd fallen in love with a prostitute named Koharu from the Kinokuni House in Sonezaki. They said he'd driven away her other guests and was going to ransom her in the next couple of days. There was all kinds of gossip about the abundance of money and fools even in these days of high prices.

My husband Gozaemon has been hearing about Koharu constantly, and he's sure that her great patron from Temma must be you, Jihei. He told me, "He's your nephew, but for me he's a stranger, and my daughter's happiness is my chief concern. Once he ransoms the prostitute he'll no doubt sell his wife to a brothel. I intend to take her back before he starts selling her clothes."

He was halfway out of the house before I could restrain him. "Don't get so excited. We can settle this calmly. First we must make sure whether or not the rumors are true."

That's why Magoemon and I are here now. He was telling me a while ago that the Jihei of today was not the Jihei of yesterday— that you'd broken all connections with Sonezaki and completely reformed. But now I hear that you've had a relapse. What disease can this be?

Your father was my brother. When the poor man was on his deathbed, he lifted his head from the pillow and begged me to look after you, as my son-in-law and nephew. I've never forgotten those last words, but your perversity has made a mockery of his request!

Narrator: She collapses in tears of resentment. Jihei claps his hands in sudden recognition.

Jihei: I have it! The Koharu everybody's gossiping about is the same Koharu, but the great patron who's to redeem her is a different man. The other day, as my brother can tell you, Tahei—they call him the Lone Wolf because he hasn't any family or relations—started a fight and was trampled on. He gets all the money he needs from his home town, and he's been trying for a long time to redeem Koharu. I've always prevented him, but I'm sure he's decided that now is his chance. I have nothing to do with it.

Narrator: Osan brightens at his words.

Osan: No matter how forbearing I might be—even if I were an angel—you don't suppose I'd encourage my husband to redeem a prostitute! In this instance at any rate there's not a word of untruth in what my husband has said. I'll be a witness to that, Mother.

Narrator: Husband's and wife's words tally perfectly.

Aunt: Then it's true?

Narrator: The aunt and nephew clap their hands with relief.

Magoemon: Well, I'm happy it's over, anyway. To make us feel doubly reassured, will you write an affidavit which will dispel any doubts your stubborn uncle may have?

Jihei: Certainly. I'll write a thousand if you like.

Magoemon: Splendid! I happen to have bought this on the way here.

Narrator: Magoemon takes from the fold of his *kimono* a sheet of oath-paper from Kumano, the sacred characters formed by flocks of crows.* Instead of vows of eternal love, Jihei now signs under penalty of Heaven's wrath an oath that he will sever all ties and affections with Koharu. "If I should lie, may Bonten and Tai-

---

*The charms issued by the Shinto shrine at Kumano were printed on the face with six Chinese characters, the strokes of which were in the shape of crows. The reverse side of these charms was used for writing oaths.

shaku above, and the Four Great Kings below, afflict me!"* So the
text runs, and to it is appended the names of many Buddhas and
gods. He signs his name, Kamiya Jihei, in bold characters, im-
prints the oath with a seal of blood, and proffers it.

Osan: It's a great relief to me too. Mother, I have you and Magoemon to thank. Jihei and I have had two children, but this is his
firmest pledge of affection. I hope you share my joy.

Aunt: Indeed we do. I'm sure that Jihei will settle down and
his business will improve, now that he's in this frame of mind. It's
been entirely for his sake and for love of the grandchildren that
we've intervened. Come, Magoemon, let's be on our way. I'm anxious to set my husband's mind at ease.—It's become chilly here.
See that the children don't catch cold.—This too we owe to the
Buddha of the Ten Nights. I'll say a prayer of thanks before I go.
Hail, Amida Buddha!

Narrator: She leaves, her heart innocent as Buddha's. Jihei is
perfunctory even about seeing them to the door. Hardly have they
crossed the threshold than he slumps down again at the *kotatsu*.
He pulls the checked quilting over his head.

Osan: You still haven't forgotten Sonezaki, have you?

Narrator: She goes up to him in disgust and tears away the
quilting. He is weeping; a waterfall of tears streams along the pillow, deep enough to bear him afloat. She tugs him upright and
props his body against the *kotatsu* frame. She stares into his face.

Osan: You're acting outrageously, Jihei. You shouldn't have
signed that oath if you felt so reluctant to leave her. The year before last, on the middle day of the Boar of the tenth moon,† we lit
the first fire in the *kotatsu* and celebrated by sleeping here together, pillow to pillow. Ever since then—did some demon or snake
creep into my bosom that night?—for two whole years I've been
condemned to keep watch over an empty nest. I thought that tonight at least, thanks to Mother and Magoemon, we'd share sweet

---

*A formal oath. Bonten (Brahma) and Taishaku (Sakra), though Hindu
gods, were considered to be protective deities of Buddhist law. The four Deva
kings served under Sakra and were also protectors of Buddhism.

†It was customary to light the first fire of the winter on this day, which would
generally be toward the end of November in the Western calendar.

words in bed as husbands and wives do, but my pleasure didn't last long. How cruel of you, how utterly heartless! Go ahead, cry your eyes out, if you're so attached to her. Your tears will flow into Shijimi River and Koharu, no doubt, will ladle them out and drink them! You're ignoble, inhuman.

Narrator: She embraces his knees and throws herself over him, moaning in supplication. Jihei wipes his eyes.

Jihei: If tears of grief flowed from the eyes and tears of anger from the ears, I could show my heart without saying a word. But my tears all pour in the same way from my eyes, and there's no difference in their color. It's not surprising that you can't tell what's in my heart. I have not a shred of attachment left for that vampire in human skin, but I bear a grudge against Tahei. He has all the money he wants, no wife or children. He's schemed again and again to redeem her, but Koharu refused to give in, at least until I broke with her. She told me time and again, "You have nothing to worry about. I'll never let myself be redeemed by Tahei, not even if my ties with you are ended and I can no longer stay by your side. If my master is induced by Tahei's money to deliver me to him, I'll kill myself in a way that'll do you credit!" But think—not ten days have passed since I broke with her, and she's to be redeemed by Tahei! That rotten whore! That animal! No, I haven't a trace of affection left for her, but I can just hear how Tahei will be boasting. He'll spread the word around Osaka that my business has come to a standstill and I'm hard pressed for money. I'll meet with contemptuous stares from the wholesalers. I'll be dishonored. My heart is broken and my body burns with shame. What a disgrace! How maddening! I've passed the stage of shedding hot tears, tears of blood, sticky tears—my tears now are of molten iron!

Narrator: He collapses with weeping. Osan pales with alarm.

Osan: If that's the situation, poor Koharu will surely kill herself.

Jihei: You're too well bred, despite your intelligence, to understand her likes! What makes you suppose that faithless creature would kill herself? Far from it—she's probably taking *moxa* treatments and medicine to prolong her life!

Osan: No, that's not true. I was determined never to tell you so long as I lived, but I'm afraid of the crime I'd be committing if I concealed the facts and let her die with my knowledge. I will reveal my great secret. There is not a grain of deceit in Koharu. It was I who schemed to end the relations between you. I could see signs that you were drifting towards suicide. I felt so unhappy that I wrote a letter, begging her as one woman to another to break with you, though I knew how painful it would be. I asked her to save your life. The letter must have moved her. She answered that she would give you up, though you were more precious than life itself, because she could not shirk her duty to me. I've kept her letter with me ever since—it's been like a protective charm. Could such a noble-hearted woman violate her promise and brazenly marry Tahei? When a woman—I no less than another—has given herself completely to a man, she does not change. I'm sure she'll kill herself. I'm sure of it. Ahhh—what a dreadful thing to have happened! Save her, please.

Narrator: Her voice rises in agitation. Her husband is thrown into a turmoil.

Jihei: There was a letter in an unknown woman's hand among the written oaths she surrendered to my brother. It must have been from you. If that's the case, Koharu will surely commit suicide.

Osan: Alas! I'd be failing in the obligations I owe her as another woman if I allowed her to die. Please go to her at once. Don't let her kill herself.

Narrator: Clinging to her husband, she melts in tears.

Jihei: But what can I possibly do? It'd take half the amount of her ransom in earnest money merely to keep her out of Tahei's clutches. I can't save Koharu's life without administering a dose of 750 *momme* in New Silver. How could I raise that much money in my present financial straits? Even if I crush my body to powder, where will the money come from?

Osan: Don't exaggerate the difficulties. If that's all you need, it's simple enough.

Narrator: She goes to the wardrobe, and opening a small drawer takes out a bag fastened with cords of twisted silk. She unhesitantly tears it open and throws down a packet which Jihei retrieves.

Jihei: What's this? Money? Four hundred *momme* in New Silver? How in the world—

Narrator: He stares astonished at this money he never put there.

Osan: I'll tell you later where this money came from. I've scraped it together to pay the bill for Iwakuni paper that falls due the day after tomorrow. We'll have to ask Magoemon to help us keep the business from betraying its insolvency. But Koharu comes first. The packet contains 400 *momme.* That leaves 350 *momme* to raise.

Narrator: She unlocks a large drawer. From the wardrobe lightly fly kite-colored Hachijō silks;* a Kyoto crepe *kimono* lined in pale brown, insubstantial as her husband's life which flickers today and may vanish tomorrow; a padded *kimono* of Osue's, a flaming scarlet inside and out—Osan flushes with pain to part with it; Kantarō's sleeveless, unlined jacket—if she pawns this, he'll be cold this winter. Next comes a garment of striped Gunnai silk lined in pale blue and never worn, and then her best formal costume—heavy black silk dyed with her family crest, an ivy leaf in a ring. They say that those joined by marriage ties can even go naked at home, though outside the house clothes make the man: she snatches up even her husband's finery, a silken cloak, making fifteen articles in all.

Osan: The very least the pawnshop can offer is 350 *momme* in New Silver.

Narrator: Her face glows as though she already held the money she needs; she hides in the one bundle her husband's shame and her own obligation, and puts her love in besides.

Osan: It doesn't matter if the children and I have nothing to wear. My husband's reputation concerns me more. Ransom Koharu. Save her. Assert your honor before Tahei.

Narrator: But Jihei's eyes remain downcast all the while, and he is silently weeping.

---

*Hachijō silks were woven with a warp of brown and a woof of yellow thread to give a color like that of the bird called the kite. "Kite" also suggests that the material flies out of the cupboard.

Jihei: Yes, I can pay the earnest money and keep her out of Tahei's hands. But once I've redeemed her, I'll either have to maintain her in a separate establishment or bring her here. Then what will become of you?

Narrator: Osan is at a loss to answer.

Osan: Yes, what shall I do? Shall I become your children's nurse or the cook? Or perhaps the retired mistress of the house?

Narrator: She falls to the floor with a cry of woe.

Jihei: That would be too selfish. I'd be afraid to accept such generosity. Even if the punishment for my crimes against my parents, against Heaven, against the gods and the Buddhas fails to strike me, the punishment for my crimes against my wife alone will be sufficient to destroy all hope for the future life. Forgive me, I beg you.

Narrator: He joins his hands in tearful entreaty.

Osan: Why should you bow before me? I don't deserve it. I'd be glad to rip the nails from my fingers and toes, to do anything which might serve my husband. I've been pawning my clothes for some time in order to scrape together the money for the paper wholesalers' bills. My wardrobe is empty, but I don't regret it in the least. But it's too late now to talk of such things. Hurry, change your cloak and go to her with a smile.

Narrator: He puts on an under *kimono* of Gunnai silk, a robe of heavy black silk, and a striped cloak. His sash of figured damask holds a dirk of middle length worked in gold: Buddha surely knows that tonight it will be stained with Koharu's blood.

Jihei: Sangorō! Come here!

Narrator: Jihei loads the bundle on the servant's back, intending to take him along. Then he firmly thrusts the wallet next to his skin and starts towards the gate.

Voice: Is Jihei at home?

Narrator: A man enters, removing his fur cap. They see—good heavens!—that it is Gozaemon.

Osan and Jihei: Ahhh—how fortunate that you should come at this moment!

Narrator: Husband and wife are upset and confused. Gozaemon snatches away Sangorō's bundle and sits heavily. His voice is sharp.

Gozaemon: Stay where you are, harlot!—My esteemed son-in-law, what a rare pleasure to see you dressed in your finest attire, with a dirk and a silken cloak! Ahhh—that's how a gentleman of means spends his money! No one would take you for a paper dealer. Are you perchance on your way to the New Quarter? What commendable perseverance! You have no need for your wife, I take it.—Give her a divorce. I've come to take her home with me.

Narrator: He speaks needles and his voice is bitter. Jihei has not a word to reply.

Osan: How kind of you, Father, to walk here on such a cold day. Do have a cup of tea.

Narrator: Offering the teacup serves as an excuse for edging closer.

Osan: Mother and Magoemon came here a while ago, and they told my husband how much they disapproved of his visits to the New Quarter. Jihei was in tears and he wrote out an oath swearing he had reformed. He gave it to Mother. Haven't you seen it yet?

Gozaemon: His written oath? Do you mean this?

Narrator: He takes the paper from his *kimono.*

Gozaemon: Libertines scatter vows and oaths wherever they go, as if they were monthly statements of accounts. I thought there was something peculiar about this oath, and now that I am here I can see I was right. Do you still swear to Bonten and Taishaku? Instead of such nonsense, write out a bill of divorcement!

Narrator: He rips the oath to shreds and throws down the pieces. Husband and wife exchange looks of alarm, stunned into silence. Jihei touches his hands to the floor and bows his head.

Jihei: Your anger is justified. If I were still my former self, I would try to offer explanations, but today I appeal entirely to your generosity. Please let me stay with Osan, I promise that even if I become a beggar or an outcast and must sustain life with the scraps that fall from other people's chopsticks, I will hold Osan in high honor and protect her from every harsh and bitter experience. I feel so deeply indebted to Osan that I cannot divorce her. You will understand that this is true as time passes and I show you how I apply myself to my work and restore my fortune. Until then please shut your eyes and allow us to remain together.

Narrator: Tears of blood stream from his eyes and his face is pressed to the matting in contrition.

Gozaemon: The wife of an outcast! That's all the worse. Write the bill of divorcement at once! I will verify and seal the furniture and clothes Osan brought in her dowry.

Narrator: He goes to the wardrobe. Osan is alarmed.

Osan: My clothes are all here. There's no need to examine them.

Narrator: She runs up to forestall him, but Gozaemon pushes her aside and jerks open a drawer.

Gozaemon: What does this mean?

Narrator: He opens another drawer: it too is empty. He pulls out every last drawer, but not so much as a foot of patchwork cloth is to be seen. He tears open the wicker hampers, long boxes, and clothes chests.

Gozaemon: Stripped bare, are they?

Narrator: His eyes set in fury. Jihei and Osan huddle under the striped *kotatsu* quilts, ready to sink into the fire with humiliation.

Gozaemon: This bundle looks suspicious.

Narrator: He unties the knots and dumps out the contents.

Gozaemon: As I thought! You were sending these to the pawnshop, I take it. Jihei—you'd strip the skin from your wife's and your children's bodies to squander the money on your whore! Dirty thief! You're my wife's nephew, but an utter stranger to me, and I'm under no obligation to suffer for your sake. I'll explain to Magoemon what has happened and ask him to make good whatever inroads you've already made on Osan's belongings. But first, the bill of divorcement!

Narrator: Even if Jihei could escape through seven padlocked doors, eight thicknesses of chains, and a hundred girdling walls, he could not evade so stringent a demand.

Jihei: I won't use a brush to write the bill of divorcement. Here's what I'll do instead! Good-bye, Osan.

Narrator: He lays his hand on his dirk, but Osan clings to him.

Osan: Father—Jihei admits that he's done wrong and he's apologized in every way. You press your advantage too hard. Jihei may be a stranger, but his children are your grandchildren. Have you no affection for them? I will not accept a bill of divorcement.

Narrator: She embraces her husband and raises her voice in tears.

Gozaemon: Very well. I won't insist on it. Come with me, woman.

Narrator: He pulls her to her feet.

Osan: No, I won't go. What bitterness makes you expose to such shame a man and wife who still love each other? I will not suffer it.

Narrator: She pleads with him, weeping, but he pays her no heed.

Gozaemon: Is there some greater shame? I'll shout it through the town!

Narrator: He pulls her up, but she shakes free. Caught by the wrist she totters forward when—alas!—her toes brush against her sleeping children. They open their eyes.

Children: Mother dear, why is Grandfather, the bad man, taking you away? Whom will we sleep beside now?

Narrator: They call out after her.

Osan: My poor dears! You've never spent a night away from Mother's side since you were born. Sleep tonight beside your father. *(To Jihei.)* Please don't forget to give the children their tonic before breakfast.—Oh, my heart is broken!

Narrator: These are her parting words. She leaves her children behind, abandoned as in the woods; the twin-trunked bamboo of conjugal love is sundered forever.

The Makioka
Sisters

In the traditional Japanese family, marriages are arranged for the prestige and well-being of the families involved. The personal choice of the couple is usually taken into account, though, as this selection indicates. A marriage is usually worked out between the parents or guardians of both parties through the mediation of a go-between. The following excerpt, the first two chapters of *The Makioka Sisters*, a novel by Jun'ichirō Tanizaki (1886–1965), illustrates the way in which a typical marriage proposal begins and the considerations involved. The story takes place in the late 1930s and early 1940s.

1

"Would you do this please, Koi-san?"

Seeing in the mirror that Taeko had come up behind her, Sachiko stopped powdering her back and held out the puff to her sister. Her eyes were still on the mirror, appraising the face as if it belonged to someone else. The long under-*kimono*, pulled high at the throat, stood out stiffly behind to reveal her back and shoulders.

"And where is Yukiko?"

"She is watching Etsuko practice," said Taeko. Both sisters spoke in the quiet, unhurried Osaka dialect. Taeko was the youn-

Reprinted from Jun'ichirō Tanizaki, *The Makioka Sisters*, translated by Edward Seidensticker (New York and London, 1957), pp. 3–11, by permission of Alfred A. Knopf, Inc., and Martin Secker & Warburg, Ltd.

gest in the family, and in Osaka the youngest girl is always "Koi-san," "small daughter."

They could hear the piano downstairs. Yukiko had finished dressing early, and young Etsuko always wanted someone beside her when she practiced. She never objected when her mother went out, provided that Yukiko was left to keep her company. Today, with her mother and Yukiko and Taeko all dressing to go out, she was rebellious. She very grudgingly gave her permission when they promised that Yukiko at least would start back as soon as the concert was over—it began at two—and would be with Etsuko for dinner.

"Koi-san, we have another prospect for Yukiko."

"Oh?"

The bright puff moved from Sachiko's neck down over her back and shoulders. Sachiko was by no means round-shouldered, and yet the rich, swelling flesh of the neck and back somehow gave a suggestion of a stoop. The warm glow of the skin in the clear autumn sunlight made it hard to believe that she was in her thirties.

"It came through Itani."

"Oh?"

"The man works in an office, M.B. Chemical Industries, Itani says."

"And is he well off?"

"He makes a hundred seventy or eighty *yen* a month, possibly two hundred fifty with bonuses."

"M.B. Chemical Industries—a French company?"

"How clever of you. How did you know?"

"Oh, I know that much."

Taeko, the youngest, was in fact far better informed on such matters than her sisters. There was a suggestion occasionally that she took advantage of their ignorance to speak with a condescension more appropriate in someone older.

"I had never heard of M.B. Chemical Industries. The head office is in Paris, Itani says. It seems to be very large."

"They have a big building on the Bund in Kobe. Have you never noticed it?"

"That is the place. That is where he works."

"Does he know French?"

"It seems so. He graduated from the French department of the Osaka Language Academy, and he spent some time in Paris—not a great deal, though. He makes a hundred *yen* a month teaching French at night."

"Does he have property?"

"Very little. He still has the family house in the country—his mother is living there—and a house and lot in Kobe. And nothing more. The Kobe house is very small, and he bought it on installments. And so you see there is not much to boast of."

"He has no rent to pay, though. He can live as though he had more than four hundred a month."

"How do you think he would be for Yukiko? He has only his mother to worry about, and she never comes to Kobe. He is past forty, but he has never been married."

"Why not, if he is past forty?"

"He has never found anyone refined enough for him, Itani says."

"Very odd. You should have him investigated."

"And she says he is most enthusiastic about Yukiko."

"You sent her picture?"

"I left a picture with Itani, and she sent it without telling me. She says he is very pleased."

"Do you have a picture of him?"

The practicing went on below. It did not seem likely that Yukiko would interrupt them.

"Look in the top drawer on the right." Puckering her lips as though she were about to kiss the mirror, Sachiko took up her lipstick. "Did you find it?"

"Here it is. You have shown it to Yukiko?"

"Yes."

"And?"

"As usual, she said almost nothing. What do you think, Koi-san?"

"Very plain. Or maybe just a little better than plain. A middling office worker, you can tell at a glance."

"But he is just that after all. Why should it surprise you?"

"There may be one advantage. He can teach Yukiko French."

Satisfied in a general way with her face, Sachiko began to unwrap a *kimono.*

"I almost forgot." She looked up. "I feel a little short on 'B.' Would you tell Yukiko, please?"

Beri-beri was in the air of this Kobe-Osaka district, and every year from summer into autumn the whole family—Sachiko and her husband and sisters and Etsuko, who had just started school—came down with it. The vitamin injection had become a family institution. They no longer went to a doctor, but instead kept a supply of concentrated vitamins on hand and ministered to each other with complete unconcern. A suggestion of sluggishness was immediately attributed to a shortage of Vitamin B, and, although they had forgotten who coined the expression, "short on 'B' " never had to be explained.

The piano practice was finished. Tacko called from the head of the stairs, and one of the maids came out. "Could you have an injection ready for Mrs. Makioka, please?"

2

Mrs. Itani ("Itani" everyone called her) had a beauty shop near the Oriental Hotel in Kobe, and Sachiko and her sisters were among the steady customers. Knowing that Itani was fond of arranging marriages, Sachiko had once spoken to her of Yukiko's problem, and had left a photograph to be shown to likely prospects. Recently, when Sachiko went for a wave-set, Itani took advantage of a few spare minutes to invite her out for a cup of tea. In the lobby of the Oriental Hotel, Sachiko first heard Itani's story.

It had been wrong not to speak to Sachiko first, Itani knew, but she had been afraid that if they frittered away their time they would miss a good opportunity. She had heard of this possible husband for Miss Yukiko, and had sent him the photograph—only that, nothing more—possibly a month and a half before. She heard nothing from the man, and had almost forgotten about him

when she learned that he was apparently busy investigating Yukiko's background. He had found out all about the Makioka family,
even the main branch in Osaka.

(Sachiko was the second daughter. Her older sister, Tsuruko,
kept the "main" house in Osaka.)

. . . And he went on to investigate Miss Yukiko herself. He
went to her school, and to her calligraphy teacher, and to the
woman who instructed her in the tea ceremony. He found out
everything. He even heard about that newspaper affair, and he
went around to the newspaper office to see whether it had been
misreported. It seemed clear to Itani that he was well enough satisfied with the results of the investigation, but, to make quite sure,
she had told him he ought to meet Miss Yukiko face to face and see
for himself whether she was the sort of girl that the newspaper article had made her seem. Itani was sure she had convinced him. He
was very modest and retiring, she said, and protested that he did
not belong in a class with the Makioka family, and had very little
hope of finding such a splendid bride, and if, by some chance, a
marriage could be arranged, he would hate to see Miss Yukiko try
to live on his miserable salary. But since there might just be a
chance, he hoped Itani would at least mention his name. Itani had
heard that his ancestors down to his grandfather had been leading
retainers to a minor *daimyo* (lord) on the Japan Sea, and that even
now a part of the family estate remained. As far as the family was
concerned, then, it would not seem to be separated by any great
distance from the Makiokas. Did Sachiko not agree? The Makiokas
were an old family, of course, and probably everyone in Osaka had
heard of them at one time or another. But still—Sachiko would
have to forgive her for saying so—they could not live on their old
glory forever. They would only find that Miss Yukiko had finally
missed her chance. Why not compromise, while there was time, on
someone not too outrageously inappropriate? Itani admitted that
the salary was not large, but then the man was only forty, and it
was not at all impossible that he would come to make more. And it
was not as if he were working for a Japanese company. He had time
to himself, and with more teaching at night he was sure he would
have no trouble making four hundred and more. He would be able

to afford at least a maid, there was no doubt about that. And as for the man himself, Itani's brother had known him since they were very young, and had given him the highest recommendation. Although it would be perfectly ideal if the Makiokas were to conduct their own investigation, there seemed no doubt that his only reason for not marrying earlier was that he had not found anyone to his taste. Since he had been to Paris and was past forty, it would be hard to guarantee that he had quite left women alone, but when Itani met him she said to herself: "Here's an honest, hardworking man, not a bit the sort to play around with women." It was reasonable enough for such a well-behaved man to insist on an elegant, refined girl, but for some reason—maybe as a reaction from his visit to Paris—he insisted further that he would have only a pure Japanese beauty—gentle, quiet, graceful, able to wear Japanese clothes. It did not matter how she looked in foreign clothes. He wanted a pretty face too, of course, but more than anything he wanted pretty hands and feet. To Itani, Miss Yukiko seemed the perfect answer.

Such was her story.

Itani supported her husband, bedridden with palsy, and, after putting her brother through medical school, had this spring sent her daughter to Tokyo to enter Japan Women's University. Sound and practical, she was quicker by far than most women, but her way of saying exactly what was on her mind without frills and circumlocutions was so completely unladylike that one sometimes wondered how she kept her customers. And yet there was nothing artificial about this directness—one felt only that the truth had to be told—and Itani stirred up little resentment. The torrent of words poured on as through a broken dam. Sachiko could not help thinking that the woman was really too forward, but, given the spirited Itani's resemblance to a man used to being obeyed, it was clear that this was her way of being friendly and helpful. A still more powerful consideration, however, was the argument itself, which had no cracks. Sachiko felt as if she had been pinned to the floor. She would speak to her sister in Osaka, then, she said, and perhaps they could do a little investigating themselves. There the matter ended.

Some, it would appear, looked for deep and subtle reasons to explain the fact that Yukiko, the third of the four sisters, had passed the marriageable age and reached thirty without a husband. There was in fact no "deep" reason worth the name. Or, if a reason had to be found, perhaps it was that Tsuruko in the main house and Sachiko and Yukiko herself all remembered the luxury of their father's last years and the dignity of the Makioka name—in a word, they were thralls to the family name, to the fact that they were members of an old and once-important family. In their hopes of finding Yukiko a worthy husband, they had refused the proposals that in earlier years had showered upon them. Not one seemed quite what they wanted. Presently the world grew tired of their rebuffs, and people no longer mentioned likely candidates. Meanwhile the family fortunes were declining. There was no doubt, then, that Itani was being kind when she urged Sachiko to "forget the past." The best days for the Makiokas had lasted perhaps into the mid-twenties. Their prosperity lived now only in the mind of the Osakan who knew the old days well. Indeed even in the mid-twenties, extravagance and bad management were having their effect on the family business. The first of a series of crises had overtaken them then. Soon afterwards Sachiko's father died, the business was cut back, and the shop in Semba, the heart of old Osaka—a shop that boasted a history from the middle of the last century and the days of the Shogunate—had to be sold. Sachiko and Yukiko found it hard to forget how it had been while their father lived. Before the shop was torn down to make way for a more modern building, they could not pass the solid earthen front and look in through the shop windows at the dusky interior without a twinge of sorrow.

There were four daughters and no sons in the family. When the father went into retirement, Tsuruko's husband, who had taken the Makioka name, became active head of the family. Sachiko, too, married, and her husband also took the Makioka name. When Yukiko came of age, however, she unhappily no longer had a father to make a good match for her, and she did not get along well with her brother-in-law, Tatsuo, the new head of the family. Tatsuo, the son of a banker, had worked in a bank before he became the Makioka heir—indeed even afterwards he left the management of the shop largely to his foster father and the chief clerk. Upon the father's death, Tatsuo pushed aside the protests of his sisters-in-law and the rest of the family, who thought that something could still be salvaged, and let the old shop pass into the hands of a man who had once been a family retainer. Tatsuo himself went back to his old bank. Quite the opposite of Sachiko's father, who had been a rather ostentatious spender, Tatsuo was austere and retired almost to the point of timidity. Such being his nature, he concluded that rather than try to manage an unfamiliar business heavily in debt, he ought to take the safer course and let the shop go, and that he had thus fulfilled his duty to the Makioka family—had in fact chosen that course precisely because he worried so about his duties as family heir. To Yukiko, however, drawn as she was to the past, there was something very unsatisfactory about this brother-in-law, and she was sure that from his grave her father too was reproaching Tatsuo. It was in this crisis, shortly after the father's death, that Tatsuo became most enthusiastic about finding a husband for Yukiko. The candidate in question was the heir of a wealthy family and executive of a bank in Toyohashi, not far from Nagoya. Since that bank and Tatsuo's were correspondents, Tatsuo knew all he needed to know about the man's character and finances. The social position of the Saigusa family of Toyohashi was unassailable, indeed a little too high for what the Makioka family had become. The man himself was admirable in every respect, and presently a meeting with Yukiko was arranged. Thereupon Yukiko objected, and was not to be moved. There was nothing she really found fault with in the man's appearance and manner, she said, but he was so countrified. Although he was no doubt as admirable as Tatsuo said, one could see that he was quite unintelligent. He had fallen ill on graduating from middle school, it was said, and had been unable to go farther, but Yukiko could not help suspecting that dullness somehow figured in the matter. Herself graduated from a ladies' seminary with honors in English, Yukiko knew that she would be quite unable to respect the man. And besides, no matter how sizable a fortune he was heir to, and no matter how secure a future he could offer, the thought of living in a provincial city like

Toyohashi was unbearably dreary. Yukiko had Sachiko's support—
surely, said Sachiko, they could not think of sending the poor girl
off to such a place. Although Tatsuo for his part admitted that
Yukiko was not unintellectual, he had concluded that, for a thoroughly Japanese girl whose reserve was extreme, a quiet, secure life
in a provincial city, free from needless excitement, would be ideal,
and it had not occurred to him that the lady herself might object.
But the shy, introverted Yukiko, unable though she was to open
her mouth before strangers, had a hard core that was difficult to
reconcile with her apparent docility. Tatsuo discovered that his
sister-in-law was sometimes not as submissive as she might be.

As for Yukiko, it would have been well if she had made her
position clear at once. Instead she persisted in giving vague answers
that could be taken to mean almost anything, and when the crucial
moment came it was not to Tatsuo or her older sister that she revealed her feelings, but rather to Sachiko. That was perhaps in part
because she found it hard to speak to the almost too enthusiastic
Tatsuo, but it was one of Yukiko's shortcomings that she seldom
said enough to make herself understood. Tatsuo had concluded
that Yukiko was not hostile to the proposal, and the prospective
bridegroom became even more enthusiastic after the meeting; he
made it known that he must have Yukiko and no one else. The negotiations had advanced to a point, then, from which it was virtu-
ally impossible to withdraw gracefully; but once Yukiko said "No,"
her older sister and Tatsuo could take turns at talking themselves
hoarse and still have no hope of moving her. She said "No" to the
end. Tatsuo had been especially pleased with the proposed match
because he was sure it was one of which his dead father-in-law
would have approved, and his disappointment was therefore great.
What upset him most of all was the fact that one of the executives
in his bank had acted as go-between. Poor Tatsuo wondered what
he could possibly say to the man. If Yukiko had reasonable objec-
tions, of course, it would be another matter, but this searching out
of minor faults—the fellow did not have an intelligent face, she
said—and giving them as reasons for airily dismissing a proposal of
a sort not likely to come again: it could only be explained by Yukiko's willfulness. Or, if one chose to harbor such suspicions, it was

not impossible to conclude that she had acted deliberately to embarrass her brother-in-law.

Tatsuo had apparently learned his lesson. When someone came with a proposal, he listened carefully. He no longer went out himself in search of a husband for Yukiko, however, and he tried whenever possible to avoid putting himself forward in marriage negotiations.

The Sound
of the Mountain

In an honor-conscious society like Japan, to keep the family's good name is the utmost concern of the head of the family regardless of his social standing. If his son, dissatisfied with the girl the father chose for him to marry, has an extramarital relationship with another woman, it is the father's responsibility to settle the matter quietly. In the following excerpt from *The Sound of the Mountain* by Yasunari Kawabata (1899–1972), the father of the young husband tries exactly that. Shingo, head of the family, visits his son's mistress, a war widow named Kinu. As this selection opens, the son's wife Kikuko has just had an abortion rather than give birth to the child of an unfaithful husband. The story was written in the late 1940s.

1

Shingo walked up the main Hongo street on the side that skirted the Tokyo University campus.

He had left the cab on the side lined by shops, and would of course turn from that side into Kinu's lane. He had purposely crossed the car tracks to the other side.

He was most reluctant to visit the house of his son's mistress. He would be meeting her for the first time, and she was already pregnant. Would he be able to ask her not to have the child?

Reprinted from Yasunari Kawabata, *The Sound of the Mountain,* translated by Edward Seidensticker (New York and London, 1970), pp. 226–235 (from the chapter entitled "The Cluster of Mosquitoes"), by permission of Alfred A. Knopf, Inc., and Martin Secker & Warburg, Ltd.

"So there is to be another murder," he said to himself. "Can't it be accomplished without adding to the crimes of an old man? But all solutions are cruel, I suppose."

The solution in this case should have been up to the son. It was not the father's place to interfere. Shingo was going off to see Kinu without telling Shuichi; and he was thus no doubt providing evidence that he had lost faith in his son.

When, he asked himself, startled, had this gap come between them? Might it be that this visit to Kinu was less out of a wish to find a solution for Shuichi than out of pity and anger at what had been done to Kikuko?

The strong evening sunlight touched only the tips of the branches. The sidewalk was in shade. On the university lawns, men students in shirt sleeves were talking to girl students. It was a scene that told of a break in the early summer rains.

Shingo touched a hand to his cheek. The effects of the *sake* had left him.

Knowing when Kinu would be finishing work, he had invited a friend from another company to a Western restaurant. He had not seen the friend in rather a long time and had forgotten what a drinker he was. They had had a short drink downstairs before going up to dinner, and after dinner they had again sat for a time in the bar.

"You're not going already?" the friend had asked in surprise. Thinking that, at this first meeting in such a long time, they would want to have a talk, said the friend, he had called for reservations in the Tsukiji *geisha* district.

Shingo had replied he would come after paying an unavoidable visit of perhaps an hour or so. The friend had written the Tsukiji address and telephone number on a calling card. Shingo had had no intention of going.

He walked along the wall of the University, looking across the street for the mouth of the lane. He was relying on vague memories, but they did not prove wrong.

Inside the dark doorway, which faced north, there was a shabby chest for footwear. On it was a potted occidental plant of some description from which hung a woman's umbrella.

A woman in an apron came from the kitchen.

Her face went tense as she started to take off the apron. She had on a navy-blue skirt, and her feet were bare.

"Mrs. Ikeda, I believe. You once honored us at the office with a visit."

"Yes. It was rude of me, but Eiko dragged me along."

Her apron wadded in one hand, she looked at him inquiringly. There were freckles even around her eyes, all the more conspicuous because she did not seem to be wearing powder. She had a delicate, well-shaped nose, and one saw a certain elegance in the narrow eyes and the fair skin.

No doubt the new blouse had been made by Kinu.

"I was hoping to see Miss Kinu."

He spoke as if requesting a favor.

"She should be home soon. Would you like to wait?"

A smell of grilling fish came from the kitchen.

Shingo thought it might be better to come later, when Kinu had had her dinner. On the urging of the Ikeda woman, however, he went inside.

Fashion magazines were piled in the alcove of the medium-sized parlor, among them considerable numbers of what seemed to be foreign magazines. Beside them were two French dolls, their frills quite out of harmony with the shabby old walls. From the sewing machine hung a length of silk. The bright, flowery pattern made the dirty floor matting look all the dirtier.

To the left of the machine was a little desk on which were numerous primary-school textbooks and a photograph of a small boy.

Between the machine and the desk was a dressing table, and in front of the closet to the rear a full-length mirror, the most conspicuous piece of furniture in the room. Perhaps Kinu used it to try on clothes she had made, perhaps she gave fittings to customers for whom she did extra work. There was a large ironing board beside it.

The Ikeda woman brought orange juice from the kitchen.

"It's my son," she said immediately. Shingo was looking at the picture.

"Is he in school?"

"I don't have him here. I left him with my husband's family. The books—I don't have regular work like Kinu, and so I do tutoring. There are six or seven houses I go to."

"I see. I thought there were too many for one child."

"They're all ages and grades. The schools these days are a great deal different from before the war, and I'm afraid I don't really do very well. But when I'm teaching I feel as if he were with me."

Shingo nodded. There was nothing he could say to the war widow.

The other, Kinu, was working.

"How did you find the place? Did Shuichi tell you?"

"No. I came once before, but I couldn't make myself come inside. It must have been last autumn."

"Really?" She looked up at him, and looked down again. "Shuichi hasn't been coming around lately," she said abruptly, after a time.

Shingo thought it might be better to tell her why he had come. "I understand that Kinu is going to have a child," he said.

The woman shrugged her shoulders very slightly and turned to the photograph of her son.

"Does she mean to go ahead and have it?"

She continued to look at the photograph. "I think you'd better ask her."

"I agree. But won't it be a great misfortune for both mother and child?"

"I think you can call Kinu unfortunate whether she has the child or not."

"But I'd imagine that you yourself might have been advising her to break with Shuichi."

"That's what I think she should do. But Kinu is much stronger than I, and it hasn't amounted to advice. We're two very different people, but somehow we get along well. She's been a great help to me since we started living together. We met at the war widows' club, you know. Both of us have left our husbands' fami-

lies and not gone back to our own—we're free agents, you might
say. We want our minds to be free too, and so we've put our husbands' pictures away. I do have the boy's out, of course. Kinu
reads all sorts of American magazines, and then she can get the gist
of French too with a dictionary, she says. After all, it's about sewing and there aren't many words. She wants to have a shop of her
own some day. We both say that when the chance comes we'll re-
marry. And so I don't understand why she had to be all tangled up
with Shuichi."

The front door opened. She got up somewhat hastily and
went out to the hall.

"Mr. Ogata's father is here," Shingo heard her say.

"Do I have to see him?" replied a husky voice.

2

Kinu went to the kitchen and seemed to be having a glass of
water.

"You come in too," she said, looking back toward Mrs. Ikeda
as she came into the room.

She had on a very bright suit. Perhaps because she was so
large, it was not apparent to Shingo that she was pregnant. He
found it hard to believe that the hoarse voice could have come
from the small, puckered mouth.

The mirrors were in the parlor, and it seemed that she had re-
touched her face from a compact.

Shingo's first impression was not unfavorable. The face,
round yet hollow, did not suggest the strength of will which the
Ikeda woman had described. There was a gentle roundness about
the hands too.

"My name is Ogata."

Kinu did not answer.

"You've kept us waiting," said Mrs. Ikeda, seating herself before the mirror stand. Still Kinu said nothing.

Perhaps because surprise and hostility did not show themselves well on the essentially cheerful face, she seemed about to

weep. Shingo remembered that in this house Shuichi had gotten drunk and had made her weep by insisting that the Ikeda woman sing for him.

Kinu had hurried home through muggy streets. Her face was flushed, and her rich breasts rose and fell.

"It must seem strange that I should be calling on you," said Shingo, unable to approach his subject with complete directness, "but I imagine that you will have guessed what brings me."

Kinu still did not answer.

"Shuichi, of course."

"If it's about Shuichi, then I have nothing to say." Suddenly she pounced. "Are you asking that I apologize?"

"No. I think the apologies should come from me."

"We've separated, and I will be no more trouble to you." She looked at Mrs. Ikeda. "Shouldn't that take care of things?"

Shingo had difficulty replying, but at length he found words: "There is still the question of the child, you know."

"I don't know what you're talking about." Kinu blanched, but all her strength seemed to go into the words. As her voice fell it was even huskier.

"You must forgive me for asking, but I believe you are to have a child?"

"Do I have to answer that sort of question? If a woman wants to have a child, are outsiders to step in and prevent it? Do you think a man would understand that sort of thing?" She spoke rapidly and there were tears in her voice.

"Outsiders, you say—but I *am* Shuichi's father. I imagine your child will have a father too?"

"It will not. A war widow has decided to have a bastard, that's all. I have nothing to ask of you except that you leave me alone to have it. Just ignore it, as an act of charity, if you will. The child is inside me, and it is mine."

"That is true. And when you get married you will have other children. I see no need at this point in having unnatural children."

"And what is unnatural about it?"

"I didn't mean that."

"There is no guarantee that I will marry again, or that I will have children. Are you willing to play God and give us an oracle? I had no children last time."

"Relations between the child and its father are the main point. The child will suffer and so will you."

"A great many children were left behind by men who died in the war, and a great many mothers were left to suffer. Think of it as if he had gone off into the islands and left behind a half-breed. Women bring up children that men have forgotten long ago."

"The matter has to do with Shuichi's child."

"I can't see that it makes any difference as long as I don't mean to bother you. I won't come crying to you, I swear I won't. And Shuichi and I have separated."

"The child will live for a long time. The bond with its father will last after you think you've cut it."

"The child is not Shuichi's."

"You must know that Shuichi's wife did not have *her* child."

"She can have as many as she wants, and if she has none the regrets are hers. Do you think a pampered wife can understand how I feel?"

"And you do not know how Kikuko feels."

In spite of himself, Shingo spoke the name.

"Did Shuichi send you around?" She set upon him like an inquisitor. "He told me I was not to have the child, and beat me and stamped on me and kicked me and dragged me downstairs to try to get me to a doctor. It was a fine show, and I think we have acquitted ourselves of our duty to his wife."

Shingo smiled bitterly.

"It really was quite a display, wasn't it?" she said to the Ikeda woman, who nodded.

"Kinu is already collecting scraps that she thinks might do as diapers."

"I went to the doctor afterwards because I thought the kicking might have injured the child. I told Shuichi it was not his. It most definitely is not yours, I said. And with that we separated. He hasn't been here since."

"Another man's, then?"

"Take it so, and that will be that."

Kinu looked up. She had been weeping for some time, and there were new tears on her face.

Even now, at the end of his resources, Shingo thought the woman beautiful. On close examination her features were not perfect; but the first impression was of beauty all the same.

Despite the apparent softness, she was not a woman to let Shingo come near.

3

His head bowed, Shingo left Kinu's house.

Kinu had accepted the check he had offered her.

"If you're leaving Shuichi it might be better to take it." Mrs. Ikeda had been very direct, and Kinu had nodded.

"So you're buying me off. That's the sort of thing I've come to. Shall I give you a receipt?"

As he got into a cab, Shingo wondered whether it might not be better to effect a reconciliation between Shuichi and the woman. An abortion might still be possible. Or should the separation be considered final?

Kinu had been antagonized by Shuichi and now by Shingo's visit. Her longing for a child seemed unshakable.

It would be dangerous to push Shuichi toward the woman again; and yet as matters stood the child would be born.

Kinu had said that it belonged to another man. Not even Shuichi could be sure. If Kinu made the assertion out of pride and Shuichi was prepared to believe her, then the world might be described as in order. There need be no further complications. Yet the child would be a fact. Shingo would die, and he would have a grandson on whom he had never laid eyes.

"And so?" he muttered.

In some haste, they had submitted the divorce notice after Aihara's attempt at suicide. In effect, Shingo had taken in his daughter and two grandchildren. If Shuichi and his woman were to part, another child would remain, out in the world somewhere. Were they not but a clouding-over of the moment, these two solutions that were no solutions?

He had contributed to no one's happiness.

On a different level, he did not like to think of the ineptness with which he had faced Kinu.

On Becoming
an Adoptee

In Japan, as in many societies, it is considered essential to the continua-
tion of a family to have a male heir. If no son is born, it is common for the
family, particularly if it has property to leave its descendants, to adopt a
grown man as heir. If the family has daughters, usually the adoptee mar-
ries the eldest daughter. The following excerpt is from an interview with
Morinosuke Kajima (1896–1975), a man who left his own family to marry
the first daughter of the Kajima family. A junior diplomat prior to his
marriage, he eventually succeeded to the presidency of the Kajima Construction Company. Here Kajima describes his thoughts on leaving his
own family and becoming an adopted son. The interview was conducted
in 1958 by Hikojirō Suzuki, a Japanese writer, for a radio broadcast. Kajima later added supplementary notes and included it in his memoirs.
The following dialogue begins with Dr. Kajima's recollection of the party
designed to set the stage for marriage arrangement.

Kajima: I attended the party to which Mr. Nagabuchi had invited me, thinking that the invitation was Mr. Nagabuchi's way of
repaying me for acting as his guide when we were both in Berlin.
To my surprise, however, Mr. Nagabuchi brought his wife along.*
He presented me with a proposal of marriage but I hardly considered it, since the marriage involved my entering the Kajima family

From Dr. Morinosuke Kajima, *Waga kaisōroku: shisō to kōdō* [Memories and
recollections of Dr. Morinosuke Kajima] (Tokyo: Kajima Institute Publishing Co.,
1965), pp. 73–80. Translated for this book by John Grossberg.
*Normally Japanese wives are not invited to such parties unless marriage ar-
rangements are under consideration.

as an adopted son. Mr. Nagabuchi was very persistent, though. All contractors are like that. Even if he is refused once or twice, a matter is not settled for Mr. Nagabuchi. After all, he is used to being refused. So he kept on discussing the matter with me.

Suzuki: Being in the construction business all his life, perhaps Mr. Nagabuchi had come to expect success in his bidding.

Kajima: He said as much himself. He also said the Kajimas had done a great many favors for him, and finding a husband for their daughter would be the best way to show his gratitude.

Suzuki: Miss Kajima had only one other sister, so the future of the Kajima family was at stake. Finding an heir was of great importance.

Kajima: I believed Mr. Kajima to be a truly great man—greater than any ambassador or minister I had served. His upright life inspired trust. The idea of becoming an adopted son was a little disturbing, but the marriage prospect was attractive.

Suzuki: I see. I'm sure the late Mr. Kajima had great confidence in you. What did Miss Kajima, your prospective bride, think about the marriage arrangement?

Kajima: She had set rather high standards for the man she wanted to marry and had turned down all of her father's earlier suggestions. It was Mr. Nagabuchi's opinion that this was the reason Mr. Kajima's hair had turned white. He was very concerned about Mr. Kajima. I think my wife-to-be already knew something about me from a book I had published in 1921 entitled *The Present Situation in Europe and America and Future Developments.* The book is a collection of the reports I submitted to the Foreign Office during my assignment in Berlin and my articles in *Foreign Affairs Review.* Another book, *The Pan-Asian Movement and the Pan-Europe Movement,* had come out three years after my first book, and I had sent copies of both to Mr. Kajima. It turned out that the father didn't read them. But his daughter did, and she apparently became interested in me as a result.

Suzuki: So even before the marriage negotiations your wife already had a good idea of your ideas and personality.

Kajima: Yes. When the marriage question was raised I knew less about her than she did of me. I wondered about the sort of person she was, and so I hired a detective agency to look into her background. I was told that the young lady was a philosophical person. This did not mean that she was a student of philosophy, but rather that she did not concern herself with petty matters. She focused on the essence of a problem whether it involved politics or business. People are seldom described as being philosophical but it is an extremely important quality to have.

Suzuki: I agree.

Kajima: Because of that quality I came to have a great respect for her.

Suzuki: Now that you have spent thirty years together, has your judgement of her changed? Do you regret your decision?

Kajima: Not at all. At first I had my doubts about being adopted. As I learned more about the Kajima family's circumstances it became apparent that they had to find someone who would marry their daughter and become heir. If such a marriage couldn't be arranged, it appeared the Kajima family's affairs would disintegrate. The business enterprise laboriously built by the two preceding generations would fall into disarray. Moreover, as the fourth son in my family there was no need to retain my family name—Nagatomi. It was also time to reconsider my career goals as a diplomat.

Suzuki: What do you mean?

Kajima: Well, while stationed in Berlin I enjoyed being under the tutelage of Ambassador Honda. Junior members of the diplomatic corps in general were responsible for telegraph communications. Political briefings were the responsibility of the secretaries.

Suzuki: Secretary being a more senior position. . . .

Kajima: Exactly. Ambassador Honda would put the third secretary and at times even the second secretary to work on the telegrams and allow me to work on the political briefings. I was so favored because I have good judgment in political matters. He even sent telegrams to the Home Office repeatedly urging that I be promoted to secretary status. Nevertheless, one has to wait fifteen years before being promoted to an Imperial Appointee status.

Suzuki: Is that a fact?

Kajima: That's why diplomatic success comes so slowly. In

fact, someone calculated that on the basis of that system one has to be one hundred and twenty-five years old before becoming ambassador.

Suzuki: That's assuming everyone was promoted in turn, right?

Kajima: A French philosopher once said that a civil servant is like a dray horse—a harnessed horse has his movement restrained. If one wants to move forward like a racehorse, one has to become a politician.

When Mr. Nagabuchi came, I told him I wanted to quit the civil service and become a politician. Nagabuchi thought that was fine and said that as a politician I could be of help to his business enterprises. So, under his auspices, I had the future option of becoming a politician. With this in mind I accepted the Kajima family marriage arrangement.

*   *   *

Kajima: I talked to my mother about it; she was not delighted. In our hometown there's a saying that if you have three handfuls of rice bran, don't allow yourself to take your wife's family name. My mother remarked that it wasn't as if my family hadn't been able to send me through school. I had in fact successfully graduated from the university and then became a diplomat. She couldn't understand what made me want to give up my own name at this point, since I didn't seem to crave money or anything. I told her that wasn't the reason.

As the fourth son I was looked upon as a relief pitcher. So as far as my natal family was concerned, I was expendable. For the Kajimas, however, the lack of a son was a serious matter that threatened the end of the family line. Accepting the Kajima's request would be the way to solve things amicably.

We diplomats who travel all over the world . . . we children of the world so to speak . . . for someone to take the likes of us into his family would require considerable confidence and trust. I met Mr. Kajima overseas; as a result of his confidence and trust he made a proposal to me. Shouldn't I respond to the trust placed in me? I also recalled my childhood: no one made much fuss over me.

I received the hand-me-downs of my oldest brother; and at meal-times, if the rest of us looked envious while my oldest brother ate his fill of meat and fish, we were told to make do with vegetables. I was never much more than second fiddle to my oldest brother.

One time I was reading a book which said that among the Greeks, who are a pessimistic people, a sage was asked to name the greatest good fortune. The sage replied that the greatest good fortune was not to have been born. I asked my mother if she knew the greatest good fortune. She didn't. "Shall I tell you?" I volunteered. When she remained silent, I quoted: "The greatest good fortune is not to be born." Without a moment's hesitation my mother replied: "It wasn't my intention to have you, but since you were born I brought you up." I was dumbfounded.

Suzuki: That was quite an exchange you had.

Kajima: Well, as long as I was a Nagatomi I was no more than a spare part. Taking care of my second and third oldest brothers was more important—I think I was regarded as a supernumerary.

Suzuki: What to do with other sons—that's always a problem.

Kajima: That's right. I remember happily my birthday not long after I was engaged. I had never celebrated my birthday before, but on that occasion I received splendid gifts from my future mother-in-law, my wife, and her younger sister. For the first time I, who had been so peripheral, felt that I counted for something and was appreciated. I cried when I received those gifts, and I resolved to dedicate myself to the happiness of my good mother-in-law, wife, and sister-in-law.

Suzuki: Then you were really determined to serve the Kajima family and their company?

Kajima: That's right. At first even my mother was quite against the idea. When we talked about the Kajima family's circumstances, however, she quickly changed her attitude and began to lecture me: "Not long ago there was a man of the Nagatomi clan who generously went as an adopted son to another family only to squander their fortune, though it was considerably larger than the Nagatomi's. To make sure you do nothing of the kind, pay attention to your father-in-law. It won't do to ruin somebody else's wealth." I always recall this lecture whenever I'm doing anything—

business, politics, or whatever. As a result, what I undertake I make sure to do well. I like to restrict my activities to those which are profitable financially and avoid anything that might cause problems for others. I also disapprove of gambling.

Suzuki: In the old days the construction business could not quite be called gambling, but it was certainly a speculative venture. Your dedication to your work is undoubtedly one of the major reasons for the current success of the Kajima Construction Company.

Memoirs of
A Successful Woman

Motoko Hani (1873–1957) was a journalist and educator. The following excerpts from her autobiography give a picture of her early family life in a household headed by her grandfather. She also tells of her unsuccessful first marriage and her close intellectual relationship with her second husband—with whom she founded the Jiyū Gakuen, originally a school for girls and later coeducational, and the magazine *The Woman's Friend*.

Memories of my family life are clearer than those of my school days. A large part of my character seems to be cast in the mold of my maternal grandfather. My family is not an old one, having been established by my great-grandfather, whose *samurai* rank had not been exalted enough to dictate a ceremonious way of life. Moreover, we were relatively free from the strict observance of convention. Our family was ruled by the straightforward, rational, and practical mind of my grandfather. My grandmother was very affable and competent in household management, though absolutely devoid of reasoning power or mathematical aptitude. She served her husband with faith and obedience, and my grandparents' marriage was a harmonious one, his dignity and inaccessibility well complemented by her warmth and openness. She was my mother's stepmother, without a child of her own, but she was truly a kind person.

From Motoko Hani, *Hani Motoko chosakushū*, vol. 14 (Tokyo: Fujin-no-Tomo Sha, 1955), pp. 33–46, 62–66, 78–81, 84–86. Translated for this book by Chieko Mulhern. Permission granted by the publisher.

When I was eleven, a tragedy struck our family. In a desperate effort to stem the tide of events, I had done everything within my limited power, but the situation proved to be past anyone's help. My father, who had married into my mother's family as the legal heir, was divorced and disowned due to complicated circumstances involving his extramarital affair. A few months prior to the final outcome, I overheard my mother and her friend discussing my father's conduct. The woman in question was one of the three Tokyo *geisha* who had come to work at a local restaurant. In connection with police investigations of the dubious management of that particular restaurant, my father was subpoenaed or was about to be. I only heard part of the story by chance, but it was enough to make me feel ashamed and wretched.

One evening only a few days later my father was reading a newspaper stretched out on the *tatami* floor in a room close to the outside wall. Anxious to have a talk with him, I was hovering about him when suddenly someone with an unfamiliar accent called out: "Hold it, Miss Hide!" Rushing outside, I caught sight of a woman peering into our house over the latticed top of the wall. It was not difficult to guess who it was. "Who's looking into our house?" I demanded sharply. The startled woman bowed to me and quickly joined another woman waiting some distance away. I immediately reported the little incident to my father and added that I could not bear the thought of him being involved with a woman like that. Taken by surprise, my father tried to dismiss the matter casually, but I insisted on having a serious discussion. He must have become angry and extremely overbearing in his attitude, for I fainted and later found myself in bed in another room.

While catching fireflies with some friends near the house of my grandmother's brother several days later, I met my great-uncle and learned that my father was not at his office. "Please take me to that restaurant," I pleaded with him. "Oh, well. I have some urgent business with him. Might as well take you along. Would you like to go home first to change?" "No, I will go as I am," I said, somehow wishing to preserve the spontaneity of my action. At the restaurant, my uncle and I stated that my father was needed at home. From upstairs, followed by a number of women, he came down into what appeared to be their living quarters. The eldest of the women offered me a pretty box, saying, "Poor little girl. You need not worry about your father. We are taking good care of him." "Thank you, but I don't want your gift," I said stiffly. Shortly after I arrived home, my father returned as promised.

My father's brother was manager of the largest bank in town. Having attained that impressive position and a great deal of wealth on his own, he had a large house built right behind ours. Just completed, it was the first three-storied house in the town of Hachinoe. A short plump man with pockmarks, my uncle was tactful enough to be sociable even toward women and children. Greed and overconfidence must have been untoward by-products of his ambitious nature. As a respected lawyer with a law office of his own, my father was often called upon to deal with his brother's avaricious and questionable ventures, and my family had been worried that my father might get himself into trouble.

My grandmother's brother-in-law by the name of Minamoto, an influential man who was later elected a member of the newly opened Diet, was entrusted with the task of persuading my father to straighten his personal as well as business affairs. But even he was unsuccessful. After Mr. Minamoto's second visit in one day, my grandfather sent for my grandmother, my mother, and myself. "I regret to say this, but I have decided to disinherit Tōtarō in order to protect our family name," he announced. My mother said, "Please forgive me for all this trouble. I have been ready for your decision." I was grief-stricken, feeling as if my father had just been deprived of his place in life.

In time, litigation was brought against a number of men including my father and his brothers in connection with some bank business, and they were placed under arrest. When the case against my father alone was dismissed at the preliminary trial, my grandfather rejoiced, saying "I knew he was incapable of committing a crime." I am of the opinion that being incapable of misconduct is not sufficient: a man's lack of fortitude to take positive action often leads to a catastrophe such as I witnessed.

My father remarried after the divorce, but he was never able to live in a house as large as ours or employ as many servants. Because of ill health suffered during his incarceration and trial, he continued to lose weight so that he looked like a different person every time I saw him. Whenever I was in his neighborhood or passing in front of his new house, I was torn between two conflicting emotions—I wanted to see him but felt restrained by the circumstances. On several occasions when I met his second wife on the street, she kindly invited me to drop in. Although I was burning with love and longing for my father, he did not show much affection or pleasure to see me. He might have been uncomfortable due to the abruptness of these encounters.

After finishing elementary school, I stayed home for a year seriously studying English and earnestly pleading with my grandfather to send me to a school in Tokyo. Study of English was very popular at the time, and a number of teachers taught reading and translation classes usually consisting of a handful of girls and a score of boys, among whom I was one of the youngest. While translating Parley's *History of the World* with the class, I memorized the meaning of every word in it. If my teachers had emphasized a broad comprehension approach rather than the verbatim translation method, my study might have proved more useful in my later years. My English study, as well as feverish pursuit of academic knowledge, ended with this period of my life.

In early February 1889, I went to Tokyo by sleigh, Santa Claus style, so to speak. My grandfather, an avid reader of newspapers, had found an announcement of the opening of the First Women's Higher School and decided to enroll me there. We set out early so that I would have enough time to get acclimated to the life in a metropolis before the start of the academic year in April. Besides, my grandfather must have been anxious to witness the promulgation ceremony of the constitution scheduled for 11 February.*

Railroad lines had yet to reach Hachinoe, and the sea route was the shortest way to Tokyo those days. For some reason, nevertheless, my grandfather chose the land route. We had a traveling

---

*A national holiday commemorating the enthronement of the legendary first emperor Jimmu.

companion, a Pure Land sect monk. Five days of straight riding in a horse-drawn carriage would take us to Sendai; from there Tokyo was only one day away by train. On the second day of our journey, however, it snowed heavily and we had to cross the Nakayama Pass by sleigh. February is the coldest month in Japan. The snow was already deep enough to conceal low-growing trees and bushes. Constantly calling to each other to keep in touch, our two sleighs proceeded in falling snow and arrived safely at an inn after dark. How bright was the lamplight of the inn! How warm and inviting the burning fireplace seemed to me that night! From Ishinomaki to Shiogama, we took a small steamship. The famous scenic island of Matsushima en route did not impress me much in the rain and snow. My aesthetic sensitivity had yet to mature before I could appreciate the beauty of nature.

At the Sendai Station early the next morning, how exciting it was to see a train for the first time in my life! It was a clear day under the brilliant sun. Suddenly brought into this bright land out of the gloomy northeast, I absorbed everything in sight with a sense of wonder and joy. Outside the train window, tree leaves were gleaming. The people in the crowded car were all strangers, each distinct from the other—so fascinating to a girl from a town where everyone knew everyone else. Curiously enough, while traveling to and from my hometown today, I can detect only uniform local characteristics in people's attitude, appearance, manners, and northeastern accent. On that first occasion, however, all the passengers seemed refreshingly individualistic to me.

When I stepped out onto the amazingly wide main street in Ueno, I actually felt the physical sensation of being in Tokyo. Our lodging was a pleasant inn overlooking the Sumida River. Until the school opening, my grandfather took me out every day on a sight-seeing trip, commenting upon the changes that had taken place since the days when he as a *samurai* had served in his lord's Edo residence.

I was eventually placed in a boarding house near the Eitai Bridge with other girl students from our area. The house was run by unpretentious, quick-witted, "lower town" Tokyoites, and I had an excellent opportunity to observe their language, manners, and daily routine, and to acquire a whole new set of practical ideas.

*   *   *

At any rate, the most powerful emotion driving me in this period was the love for a man. Our mutual attachment grew more intense despite the spatial distance between us, and finally he made an official proposal to my family by way of an intermediary with proper social standing. My grandfather, who knew nothing of his character or our relationship, gave an instant and clear-cut answer that he intended to keep me as his heir, eventually to marry a man who would take on our family name. It was as simple as that. My grandfather lacked wisdom and poignant insight to surmise how and why a man from a distant city came to make the sudden proposal. Since I had neither the courage nor sense enough to plead earnestly with him, we had no choice but to persevere for the time being.

At this point, I had yet another source of anxiety to face. Since the man I loved took a new job in a town near Kyoto, I began to detect gradual but radical shifts in his thinking and taste, from his former puritanical simplicity to an extreme vulgarity. I felt compelled to leave my teaching position and get married in order to save our relationship before it was too late. My grandfather gave me his blessing upon listening to my sincere plea. My grandmother told me later that my grandfather had somehow become aware of my feeling and had already been sympathetically disposed. The man I wanted to marry, on the other hand, rapidly lost his earlier zeal, and his reluctance and coolness appeared more and more pronounced in spite of his effort to conceal his true feelings.

In discussing my life years later, a newspaper article ventured to speculate that the reason for our divorce within a half year of the wedding was my incompatibility with my mother-in-law and concluded that the clash between the new and the old, which destroyed our love, actually contributed to remaking me into a resolute woman. The poor old lady is a victim of erroneous accusations, for she never even lived with us, much less did she cause any conflict of beliefs. The truth was that an educated woman from the northeast could not tolerate the vulgar taste of the Kansai (Kyoto–Osaka–Kobe area) small towns, a taste which her husband was assimilating readily. I was unable to put up a fight to protect our marriage—neither fortified with enough determination nor aided by foreknowledge of such a society diametrically opposed to the environment familiar to me. It was a painful half year heaped with unpleasant experiences; I was tortured by a sense of helplessness.

By nature, I am a small fish who wishes only to live in pure water. I am unable to contemplate a feat such as thriving in mud. My husband was basically a good man, but also an unfortunate man who was burdened with a wretched susceptibility to outside influences and temptations; this weakness became apparent only after he began drinking. At last, I made the drastic decision to relinquish my love as if giving up my own life. The profound implication behind the cliché "as if giving up one's own life" can never be fully appreciated by anyone who has not felt the desolation of despair. Bidding farewell to the cherished but cold corpse of love in my heart, I resolutely set out to find a way of life with more meaning.

Boarding the Tokyo-bound train at the Kyoto station, I thrilled at the anticipation of coming battles yet unknown. The man who had been my husband stood by my window, saying over and over again, "I have no doubt you will make something of yourself in the future." I could not help but feel respect for the man standing there humbly repentant. I have a persistent apprehension that this painful period of my life, of which I am ashamed to this day, might be seen as a stigma reducing the effectiveness of my public service. Not for a moment, nevertheless, do I regret my decision to liberate myself from the enslaving hold of emotion and from a life rendered meaningless by the willful profanation of conjugal love by the other party. I am grateful to the greater power that granted me the fortitude when I bitterly needed it.

*   *   *

For some thirty years since then, my public life has evoked various reactions from various quarters. As one might expect, the Japanese society of the day was not exactly ready to welcome with open arms its first newspaperwoman. Looking back over my experiences, I find, nevertheless, that the insults, hostility, and harassment against me were basically the result of undefined fear, jealousy, dissatisfaction with life, or a lack of ideals, while the encouragement, empathy, and anonymous help stemmed from personal integrity, sincerity, and insight. In fact, there have been far more occasions on which I was overcome with gratitude for kindness and support than times when I encountered sheer malice and complete lack of understanding.

It was always gratifying to know that an article elicited a response among readers. Even the editors were pleased when my coverage of a child-care association inspired some women to join the worthy organization. While another article of mine on an orphanage was being serialized, I had an occasion to interview Prince Konoe, then the president of the House of Lords. "You are the author of the orphanage report, aren't you? It's wonderful to see an article written by a woman, so rare in newspapers. You should be proud of yourself and continue the good work," the prince said with sincerity.

By that time, the Reverend Nishiari was installed in a new temple bearing his name in Yokohama. One summer, while he was teaching at a Sōtō sect Zen temple school in Azabu, Tokyo, I attended his morning lectures every day, alone among the host of monks. I was vaguely toying with the idea of becoming a nun at the time. It might have been motivated by my thirst for social recognition, or possibly by the deep-seated loneliness of which I was unaware in the excitement of the job. The reverend told me that, unlike today, some nuns of former times were so highly honored as to be allowed imperial audience, and consequently they exerted far-reaching spiritual influence on society. He even introduced me to a certain monk who was able to tell me about nunneries. The Nishiari Temple was the home for my soul during this period. When the reverend returned to our hometown after a long absence, he found time in his tight schedule to send for my grandfather and informed him of my latest desire. (I learned of their meeting later.) "I have tried not to interfere with her wishes in the past," my grandfather said to him, "but I want her to reconsider her plans this time." "I don't blame you," the reverend commiserated. Despite his advanced age, past eighty, and his exalted position as the head of a Buddhist order, he extended great compassion and help to me, a mere young lay person.

Yoshikazu Hani (1880–1955), who was to become my husband for life, joined the newspaper *Hōchi Shimbun* some time after I had and also received praises and commendations from the owner of the paper. The year 1901 was when my love and ambition found a single, perfect means of fulfillment in our marriage. Ever since, our home has been the center of our work, and our work has been an extension of our home life: the two are completely merged without demarcations of any kind. I am truly grateful for this ideal unity that is the very essence of both our work and marriage. Together, we have found our place in life.

It has been already twenty-five years this April since we began to speak to the world and our friends through our magazine, which one of us managed and the other edited. In 1903, I was an editor-clerk-manager of the journal of the Women's Education Association, the most influential women's organization at the time. In spite of my pregnancy and a heavy workload with the journal, I was healthy and eager to continue working until two days before the birth of our first daughter on April the second. The very next day, our first magazine, *Friend of the Home*, published its inaugural issue. It was only thirty-two pages long, but written entirely by one person—myself. I do not even recall how arduous it must have been for me to launch a new magazine just before giving my first birth or how concerned I must have been about the next issue.

Stimulated by firsthand observations of social scenes during several years of newspaper reporting, our concern extended beyond the narrow scope of housekeeping hints to include social mores and psychological aspects of family life. Our fourth issue carried a story relating how the loyal and loving wife of a gifted man succeeded in breaking his stubborn drinking habit to restore his professional productivity. In answer to a continuous wave of readers' requests, that issue went into the third and even fourth printing. This single item earned us numerous new readers who discovered our little magazine and wanted to read its back issues as well. Thus, we es-

tablished a bond with society and began to make our contributions.

One day, on the street in the foreign quarter in Tsukiji, my attention was caught by the sight of foreign children at play comfortably dressed in Western clothes. I could not help but feel sorry for
our own young who were encumbered by ponderous *kimono*. I immediately went to a nearby kindergarten and learned all I could
about Western clothes from its superintendent, Mrs. Tapping. Our
magazine did not stop at simply introducing a new idea or merely
advising the readers to adopt it. We instructed them how to cut
material, how to make Western clothes, how to wear them, how to
launder them. To follow up the subject over the years, we reported
the experiences of those who actually tried Western clothes, discussed the costs involved, and held study classes. This is just one
example of our editorial policies.

Grandfather
Sōhachi

Finding one's roots is for many people, Japanese and non-Japanese alike, a crucial aspect of their search for identity. In the following excerpt from the collection of essays *Rekishi to shōsetsu* (1969), Ryōtarō Shiba (real name Teiichi Fukuda, b. 1923) tells of his attachment to a grandfather he never knew. Although he had never even seen a photograph of his grandfather, his curiosity was aroused when he was told of his resemblance to him. Shiba visited his grandfather's hometown and found his grandfather's name on the stone post of a small shrine.

I do not know what grandfather looked like. He was an old man when my father was born, and he died when father was a boy. So I, his grandson, never knew him. I have never even seen a picture of him because all his pictures were burned in a number of fires. My father says that I look like my grandfather and that my voice sounds exactly like his. I am told that grandfather was shorter and more roundfaced than I, and that he was lame because of a stroke in his later years. The fact that he looked so much like me makes me especially interested in him.

Grandfather Sōhachi was from Harima. He came from the village of Hiro, which is close to the seashore in the suburbs of Himeji City in Hyōgo prefecture. He was born to a family that had engaged in farming throughout the Edo period (1600–1867). I am told during the sixteenth century one of the family ancestors was under siege in Miki castle in Harima, but nobody knows what his

From Ryōtarō Shiba, *Rekishi to shōsetsu* (Tokyo: Kawade Shobō Shinsha, 1969), pp. 207–218. Translated for this book by Takeo Hagihara.

rank was. After the castle fell he went to the nearby village of Hiro with other soldiers who had been in the castle and became a rice farmer. He was a devout follower of the Pure Land sect of Buddhism and a member of the West Honganji temple. When Ieyasu won the battle of Sekigahara, he divided the West Honganji temple into two temples, the East Honganji and the West Honganji. Sōhachi's ancestor apparently was extremely stubborn. Although his name was on the roster of the Saifukuji temple, a temple under the authority of the East Honganji, he decided to continue to chant the sutras in the style of the West Honganji. His children and grandchildren all followed his example. Grandfather Sōhachi, like his ancestor before him, tenaciously chanted the sutras in the style of the West temple all of his life. When I think of my ancestors, who were otherwise undistinguished, I am proudest of the fact that they continued to chant the sutras in the style of the West temple for over three hundred years even though they belonged to the East temple.

Grandfather was probably eighteen or nineteen at the time of the Meiji Restoration (1868). Until then most commoners were not permitted to take surnames. All of Sōhachi's relatives in the village met to decide what name to take. They agreed on the name Miki, I'm told, because of their ancestor who had been under siege in Miki castle. At the time Sōhachi was not on good terms with his relatives and they told him to take a different name. He was living with his widowed mother and was probably in straitened circumstances financially. I doubt that he took his work very seriously. He apparently did not find the plodding nature of farmwork very appealing and preferred to speculate on rice instead. When he lost, he sold his fields. When he won, he got them back. The other farmers disapproved of Sōhachi's way of life. They respected steadiness.

Sōhachi went to register his name at the village office. Although the office was formally under the new Meiji government, the people working there had all been functionaries under the shogunate. A former *samurai* helped Sōhachi. When Sōhachi told the *samurai* that he wanted to register his name as "Sōzaemon," a name he had been using, the *samurai* said it was too presumptuous. Grandfather was registered as Sōhachi instead. In later years grandfather recalled the episode with great indignation, claiming that the *samurai* had made an ass of him. In retrospect grandfather's anger was unjustified. It was a policy of the new government to abolish names with "zaemon," "emon," and "bē" in them because these endings had signified imperial government posts in former times. During the Muromachi period (1338–1573) the general public began to use names of that sort. Since the new government considered this practice disrespectful to the emperor, its supporters voluntarily abandoned the use of such names. The Harima official was not, as Sōhachi thought, making a fool of him because of his penchant for speculating on rice.

After 1868 Sōhachi speculated more heavily than he could afford and lost all his money. Unable to stay in the village, he stole away in the moonlight and at the port of Shikama boarded a boat bound for Osaka. His pockets were nearly empty. The only one who went to see him off at the pier was a village child Sōhachi had liked very much.

In Osaka Sōhachi opened a rice-cake store at Namba, where he made rice cakes and crackers. The business could not have been very big since that was all he sold. He apparently sold the kind of crackers ordinary farmers made and ate in the country. His business was successful enough to enable him to collect the inexpensive clocks he loved. His neighbors and other cracker merchants considered him an eccentric.

Sōhachi was a firm proponent of the antiforeigner policy of the former government. That is not to say that he was a man of profound thought. At the time, most ordinary people favored the exclusion of foreigners. The people of Osaka and Sakai were especially strong supporters of the antiforeigner policy and it was they who, naively, were the most exhilarated when, in the first year of Meiji, warriors of the Tosa domain embarrassed the new government by wounding some Frenchmen and killing others in Sakai. Because of his xenophobia, Grandfather Sōhachi never ate beef. And since he had never liked fish, all he ate, other than rice, was vegetables. Fried bean curd was his only source of protein.

He was very much opposed to public education because he

thought it was a part of Western culture. He allowed his daughter to attend a public primary school and high school, but he did not let my father go to public school because father was to carry on the family name. Instead, father attended various private schools, a school specializing in mathematics, an English school, a school of Chinese classics. As a result, father could not get a primary school diploma, and without it he could not be accepted by any high school. He would also have had some difficulty in taking an examination for the military conscription, so grandfather made great efforts to buy a diploma for father illegally. Finally he succeeded in getting one at a high price from the principal of a primary school.

Sōhachi's business was fairly successful until after the Sino-Japanese War (1894–1895), when it began to decline. Cheap rice flooded the Japanese markets as a result of the colonization of Taiwan. Sōhachi called the rice "foreign" and would not buy it. "The only foreign things I own are my watch and umbrella," he always bragged. Sōhachi's competitors used the cheap rice from Taiwan to make less expensive rice crackers. Sōhachi never did use the despised "foreign stuff." Naturally his prices were higher than those of his competitors and it was hard for him to compete. His principles got in the way of his business.

He continued to gamble on rice as before, but he does not seem to have been very adept at speculation. He came out ahead only a few times in his life. Just before he died, though, he had a streak of unaccustomed good luck. He went to the Dojima stock market every day and earned more than he had ever gained before. In fact, he got so excited that he had a stroke there. He was already dead when he was put on the door they used as a stretcher.

My family has suffered from several fires since Sōhachi's time, and nothing of his is left. The only traces of him are on my face.

I had been thinking of visiting Sōhachi's hometown near Himeji for some time, but had not had a chance to do so when on New Year's Day of this year I received an unexpected call from Himeji castle. I was asked to give a lecture in commemoration of the completion of the repair work on the castle. Ordinarily I refuse such offers because I think lectures of that sort are utterly meaningless. This time I decided to accept because I thought I could visit grandfather's village at the same time.

Odd as it may seem, the next day I received a call, completely unrelated to the first call, asking me to give another lecture at Himeji. I was astonished by the coincidence. The second caller was a friend of mine who is a little older than I. His name is Koh Shimizu, and he is a resident priest of a branch of the East Honganji temple near the town of Shitennōji. Koh's younger brother, Shū Shimizu, is a composer, and Koh himself, who is well known for his study of Japanese ceremonial court music, is a member of the Shitennōji court music society.

Since Koh and I had been friends for nearly twenty years I felt that I ought to do as he asked, but I did not want to make two trips to Himeji. This reason would have sounded a bit blunt, though, so I explained my sentimental reasons for going to Himeji. I told him of my ancestors' family temple—the Saifukuji in Hiro village where my ancestors' names had been on the temple roster until Grandfather Sōhachi sold his land. Koh was dumbfounded. After an awed silence he said, "Why, that temple is run by the Takahama family. That's my wife's family, and what's more my older sister's daughter is married to the present resident priest of the temple. So we are twice related to the temple family."

It was my turn to be surprised. The East Honganji temple had some nine thousand branch temples. One of these was the Saifukuji temple in the suburbs of Himeji, and it was only in that temple that any trace of my grandfather might be found. Since his house had been destroyed a long time ago, I decided to visit just the temple. What a surprise to discover Koh's connection with the temple! Koh was as excited as I. He offered to go with me to the temple.

Later I told my father the whole story. He too was surprised. He told me that memorials for my grandfather could be found not only in the Saifukuji temple but also on a stone post of the fence surrounding the village shrine. In fact, he said that grandfather's name, Sōhachi Fukuda, was probably engraved on the post. He explained that after Sōhachi had sold his land and left the village, the guardian of the shrine decided to rebuild it and asked for contributions. Sōhachi, who was in Osaka at the time, was asked to contribute also. He probably wanted to show his hometown what a success he had become in Osaka, and so he made an extravagant contribution for his means. His name was therefore probably among the contributors cited on the stone posts. According to father, the posts were still there.

I went to Himeji. The sun was just setting when I finished the lecture and the streets were growing dark. I thought it would be pitch black by the time I got to Hiro village. Reverend Takahama, the resident priest of the Saifukuji temple, had come all the way from Hiro to meet us. He told us it would take about half an hour to get to the temple. The priest and I got into Koh's car.

We arrived in Hiro village. The Fuji Steel Company had taken over most of the former rice fields. The village had changed completely; it was cluttered with modern housing units. There was almost nothing to remind one of the village as it had been in Sōhachi's days. In fact, the Saifukuji temple itself had just been rebuilt, in reinforced concrete, a short distance from its original location.

It was very dark. Just as I muttered to myself, "Where is the village shrine?" the priest said "Here it is," and asked Koh to stop the car. We parked in front of the *torii,* the gateway to the shrine. The site of the shrine seemed spacious. Since it did not have any of the trees that typically surround village shrines, though, it gave the impression of being very dusty. At least that was my reaction to it. The night was so dark that I could not really see anything.

We went through the gateway. It was difficult to walk in the darkness, and I had little hope of being able to check the names on the stone posts. There were far more of them than I had expected.

Suddenly Koh, a practical man in spite of being a priest and court musician, remembered that he always carried a flashlight in his car for emergencies. He went back to the car, picked up the flashlight, and hurried back.

Stepping through the bushes, Koh led the way with such agility that it was hard to remember he was a priest. He held up the flashlight to light the nearby posts. Suddenly, there in the light, was a stone post bearing the name Sōhachi Fukuda. "That's it," said Koh, turning back to me. I was so overwhelmed that I almost cried out. Only the fear of being embarrassed kept me from doing so. I pretended to be nonchalant. Trying to control my voice, I said, "Oh, we found it." Still, I could tell that my voice was trembling.

"Life is full of mysteries . . ." Koh said while continuing to shine the flashlight on the name. He probably meant that such inexplicable events as finding the right post the first thing and in the dark do in fact happen. As a follower of the Shinran sect of Buddhism, which rejects superstition, he must have been reluctant to see this as a mysterious event. I could understand that. What complex feelings he must have built into the simple statement: "Life is full of mysteries. . . ."

At last I felt I had met Grandfather Sōhachi. I had had enough excitement and asked Koh to turn off the flashlight at once. He switched it off. Darkness returned. Grandfather Sōhachi, once again, disappeared into the night.

Advice to
Young Mothers

Michio Matsuda (b. 1908) is a pediatrician who is rapidly gaining the fame in Japan that Dr. Spock has in the United States. He urges Japanese women to return to traditional methods of childrearing—methods which he claims recognize the needs and idiosyncrasies of each child. The following excerpts from Dr. Matsuda's books on child care, *Nihonshiki iku-jihō* [Childrearing Japanese style] and *Ikuji no hyakka* [An encyclopedia of child care], illustrate the Japanese encouragement of children's dependence on their parents from early infancy. In neither of these books does Dr. Matsuda discuss the way to discipline children—probably because, as a rule, Japanese mothers rely on the child's dependence rather than on discipline for control.

BABIES WHO SLEEP WELL WILL THRIVE

The zoologist Edward Morse, who lived in Japan during the late 1870s and early 1880s, noted in his book *Japan Day by Day* that he had seldom heard Japanese babies cry or seen Japanese mothers lose their tempers. In no country in the world, he wrote, are babies more closely attended or better behaved than in Japan.

Why is it that Japanese babies do not cry? This question goes to the heart of traditional Japanese care. In writing this book I read many of the major works on child care, and I came to the conclusion that Japanese mothers used to have a rich supply of milk. At

From Michio Matsuda, *Ikuji no hyakka* (Tokyo: Iwanami Shoten Co., 1967), pp. 208, 445, 469–470, 552–553, and *Nihonshiki ikujihō* (Tokyo: Kōdansha Co., 1973), pp. 62–63, 65, 99–100. Translated for this book by Keiko Sellner.

the time Morse came to Japan, Western women probably were not able to produce as much milk as Japanese women. A baby usually cries because he wants milk. Japanese babies were quiet, to Morse's surprise, because their mothers nursed them with abundant milk whenever the babies were unhappy. It did not matter where they were or what time it was. Morse was also surprised that Japanese mothers nursed their babies in public. In his book about Japan, Alcock, the first British ambassador to Japan, drew a sketch of a fisherman's wife who, bare breasted, was nursing her baby as she carried fish home on her head from the sea. What seems natural to us profoundly shocked the Westerners.

In traditional Japan a mother nursed her baby whenever he cried, and the baby, satisfied, fell asleep. The proverb "Babies who sleep well will thrive" is pertinent here. If a mother did not have enough milk, the baby would have cried a great deal because he could not get sufficient nourishment. Generally speaking, the amount of milk a baby drinks becomes fairly regulated at two or three months after birth. So do the intervals between feedings. Nature has seen to it that a baby "can follow what he wants without transgressing what is right." *

The idea of feeding a baby on a fixed schedule every three to four hours came from German medical practice. It was the result of the penetration of Prussian militarism into childrearing.

SLEEPING WITH THE BABY

I approve of the practice of mothers sleeping with their babies. I have visited many women over sixty years old who have raised five or more children. All the women told me they slept with their children. Because it is convenient for mothers to sleep with their children, it became a common practice in Japan for thousands of years.

Westerners think it is bad to sleep with their babies. They believe in putting children to bed in a room separate from their parents. At first the children cry hard, but soon they give up and en-

---

*Quotation from the *Analects* of Confucius.

dure the loneliness because their mothers do not come. In Japan, when mothers sleep in the same room with their babies it is impossible for them to ignore the baby when it cries. The parents cannot sleep. It would take great determination not to pay attention to the baby. The baby knows his parents are in the same room and so, naturally, he cries all the more rather than learning to endure solitude.

The construction of Japanese houses lends itself to the practice of families sleeping together. The Japanese house is of a simple design with sliding doors instead of walls inside the house. . . . Even if a baby is in the next room his cries can be heard through the sliding door. In a farmer's house, the bedrooms are very small and the children are numerous; mothers have no choice but to sleep with their children.

THE PROS AND CONS OF PUTTING THE BABY ON HIS STOMACH

In America it is common practice to put a baby on his stomach and turn his head to one side when he sleeps. It is believed to be safer than putting the baby on his back in case the baby spits up.

This concern might be warranted in a hospital where babies are separated from their mothers, but it is not necessary in Japanese homes where mothers sleep in the same room with their babies and can watch them. The belief that babies will become flatheaded if they sleep on their backs has not been proved. The infant's skull grows in its own way in the third or fourth month no matter what position he sleeps in. Human beings are most comfortable when they can turn freely in their sleep. I was pleased to see a baby turn himself and sleep on his back as soon as he was able to roll over—even though he had been put on his stomach for the first six months of his life in America.

PUTTING THE BABY TO BED

It is a mistake to expect a baby to fall asleep more easily at age two than at age one just because he is bigger. A baby becomes increasingly dependent on his mother as he grows older. No baby will fall asleep as soon as he is in his pajamas and under the covers. When he is sleepy, a child becomes infantile. Even children who have become quite independent during the day are apt to cling to their mothers at night. Most babies need to have their mothers stay with them for ten or fifteen minutes until they fall asleep. After much trial and error, mothers have found that it is best to let the child fall asleep naturally.

Even if a child is toilet trained and able to hold his own spoon he will still feel a strong attachment to his mother. Because of this bond he will want his mother to stay with him as he falls asleep. I wonder if we can in fact make a child self-reliant by refusing to stay with him. Surely the child's resentment toward a mother who refuses to fulfill his wishes will be injurious to his development. If a child cannot put on his own shoes, help him. He will be able to put his shoes on by himself eventually, but the sense of rejection he feels when his mother refuses to help him will stay with him and harm his development. It may cause him to punish his mother by refusing to be independent in the daytime as well as at night. I recommend that the mother stay with the child as he falls asleep if the child wants her to do so. It is wise to give the child a sense of security so that he falls asleep contentedly. It is only natural to do that in Japan. After all, parents and children sleep in the same room anyway. If your child falls asleep more easily after taking a bath, give him a bath.

Many babies suck their thumbs. In many cases, the baby starts sucking his thumb after his mother has forced him to sleep alone. The mother could have avoided the thumbsucking if she had lain beside her baby and held his hand when he first started to suck his thumb. Even if thumbsucking has become a habit, you need not worry about it too much. If the mother stays with the baby as he falls asleep, he will go to sleep easily and eventually forget his thumbsucking.

When a baby takes a nap in the daytime, he tends to stay awake late at night. Consequently, it is better not to put the baby to bed too early. A baby cannot lie awake for long without doing something; he will suck his thumb or chew on his blanket. It is better to let him stay up until he is tired enough to fall asleep right away.

With a child who has been breast fed it is a good idea to let him nurse as he falls asleep. Breast feeding is harmful only when the baby nurses so much that he will not eat other food. In deciding when to wean a baby, we have to consider his personality and the environment. It all depends on the readiness of the child.

CARRYING A BABY ON YOUR BACK

Is it all right to carry a baby on your back? If a baby is more than three or four months old and can hold his head up, you can certainly carry him on your back. A baby of four months cannot yet hold onto his mother's shoulders by himself; you must carry him in a baby carrier. Child care books since the late Meiji era (1868–1912) have been against carrying a baby on one's back because it puts pressure on the baby's chest. This advice is mainly the result of the influence of Western methods (and particularly those of Germany). One reason Western women do not carry their babies on their backs is that they wear dresses. The *kimono* is better suited to carrying a baby on one's back than a Western dress is. Even Japanese women do not carry babies on their backs when they wear Western clothing. It is only to be expected that a woman values her good dresses. But when you wear everyday clothes you should carry your baby on your back.

Suppose that your baby is crying in his bed and you have housework to do. To solve this problem do not hesitate to carry him on your back.

STAYING UP AT NIGHT

Most people do not believe that a baby should be put to bed at eight o'clock. It is the general practice of most city dwellers to relax in the evening, and a child who is part of the family naturally shares in the family evening. It is best to put a child down for a nap so that he can stay awake at night until nine-thirty. That way he can play with his father at night—a pleasure both for the child and the father. If you keep him from napping in anticipation of an early bedtime, he will be sleepy and cranky even at dinner. Then if you put him to bed at eight o'clock he will wake up early in the morning, and neither the parents nor the child will be happy.

SIBLINGS

It is better to have more than one child. Pediatricians recommend having more than one child because they see a considerable difference in attitude between mothers with one child and mothers with more than one. When a mother raises her first child, she is always unsure of herself. She worries about when to wean the child and whether he is ready for nursery school. Whatever she does is a new experience for her. With the second child, however, a mother is more confident. She has had experience with different approaches to childrearing. She can relax and follow the one that is best for her. When mothers are confident, children are less tense.

It is not only convenient for the parents to have more than one child; it is better for the children to grow up together in a family. It is one of the joys of life to live with siblings. A child without brothers and sisters is like a book without pages. The love of one's parents is too precious for one child to keep to himself. A child wants to share the boundless love of his parents with his brothers and sisters so that he can better appreciate it. An only child never has the experience of fighting with brothers and sisters or asking them questions or working out the problems of being in a large family.

Housewife
and Woman

Housewife and Woman is a collection of papers from a seminar entitled "What Women's Problems Mean to Me." The purpose of the seminar, held at the Kunitachi-Shi Community Center in Tokyo from December 1971 to March 1972, was stated as follows:

> One of the things on the minds of many women today is the disquieting feeling that being a woman is not the same as being a person. What is the cause of this feeling? Instead of trying to answer this question in terms of general theories and knowledge, let us examine the status of women from the perspective of everyday life: the realities of marriage, childbearing, and child care; daily life as a housewife; self-realization as a woman; the significance of having a job for women; and so forth. From this viewpoint we can gain insight into the historical position of women and their present status in society.

Twenty-five housewives were admitted to the seminar from among numerous applicants. The topics were selected by the participants themselves, and at the beginning of each discussion one member of the group gave a report. The following two reports were written by two housewives who participated in the seminar.

From *Shufu to onna: Kunitachi-shi kōminkan shimin daigaku seminā no kiroku* (Tokyo: Niraisha, 1973), pp. 54–56, 68–72. Translated for this book by Hiroko Kataoka.

LOOKING AFTER MY FATHER-IN-LAW: IN RETROSPECT
By Hideko (Eiko) Yamanaka

Whenever my friends and acquaintances tell me how admirable I was to take care of my father-in-law, I feel pangs of guilt. These last eight years I have been at odds with myself, torn between my real feelings and my desire to be a good daughter-in-law in the eyes of the world. Today I would like to talk about these feelings.

When my father-in-law was well, he was very active as head of the family. He was a farmer, and he also ran a small business manufacturing Japanese paper. He also worked in the village government. When he was fifty, his wife died. He decided to stay in the village alone even though his five children had all left after finishing school. At the age of sixty-four, however, he had a stroke and was in the hospital for a year. My husband, who is the eldest son, decided that we should take care of his father after he left the hospital because his father was paralyzed slightly on his right side and could not live alone. My father-in-law did not like the idea at all. It was not because he disliked us; rather, he was sorry to leave his home for an unfamiliar place where he felt lonely and uncomfortable. And, of course, he was upset about his poor health.

At the time my father-in-law came to live with us, my husband and I had been married for six years and had two children, aged five and two. Most of the time my father-in-law talked about the good old days. His mind was too crowded with memories for him to be able to play with his grandchildren. Since he had no income of his own, he never disagreed with us. On the whole, he was not at all like his former self. When he first came to live with us, many things bothered me which now sound petty—he needed a special diet; he asked me to cut his toenails (that was quite a shock); I had to clean his false teeth every morning. Of course I did not express my annoyance to anyone because of my zealous desire to be a good daughter-in-law. That soon became a source of tension. I tended to scold my children, and I quarreled with my husband repeatedly over small things. My husband was callous in his attitude toward his father. When the children and his father fought with each other, he would take the children's side. When his father wet the bed, my husband chided him. Sometimes I could not help wondering if they were really father and son. When I saw my husband reacting in that way, I started to reconsider the value of having a son, and finally my feelings turned into sympathy for my father-in-law. As I think back on it now, my husband may have acted that way on purpose to arouse in me sympathy for his father. When my father-in-law first came to live with us there were many problems, but by the second year things became more stable.

The feeling that my family needed me gave me a sense of mission and confidence in my own worth. My husband called himself the breadwinner and left all family matters to me. When my father-in-law started to use a chamber pot all the time, we wanted him to have a room of his own. After two years we bought a small house. My husband left it to me to decide which house to buy and how to arrange the financing. I found the strength to make these decisions in the knowledge that the family could not do without me.

My father-in-law's condition continued to grow worse. At first he only dragged his right foot; then his right side became completely paralyzed. Slurred speech was the next stage. By the time he had to be hospitalized, he was wetting the bed frequently. My husband told me to use diapers, but I could not do it. I simply could not humiliate my father-in-law. His mind was still clear.

During his last stay in the hospital my father-in-law was very conscious of his Kyūshū dialect. Because of it he could not call for the nurse when he wanted to use the bedpan and so he frequently wet the bed. I stayed with him all day to take care of him. At night I asked the nurse to look after him when I went home. That was the most difficult time of those eight years. It was not my physical exhaustion but the mental anguish I felt that made it so hard. Sometimes I found myself thinking that only his death would end this hardship, and that made me feel even more guilty.

The year before last, in the fall, my father-in-law died at the age of seventy-three. I still remember how difficult it was for me to leave the hospital the day before he died—he looked so lonely. If I had been his own daughter, he might have asked me to spend the night with him. I imagine that he thought of my position as his daughter-in-law and repressed the desire. Why didn't I stay there instead of going home to my husband and children? If it had been my husband or one of my children in the hospital, I would have stayed. My father-in-law and I got along very well even though we were not real father and daughter. But there was always something lacking between us that only a true father and daughter could have. I think that is why I could not be with him when he died. I tried to take the place of a real daughter, but I could not. Often I was made to feel that I was only his daughter-in-law. When my sister-in-law emptied his bedpan, for example, she always complained, but I think she sympathized with her father in her heart. As his daughter-in-law, however, I would tell him that I didn't mind while I was thinking quite the opposite. After all, I was only a daughter-in-law.

After the death of my father-in-law, my life became serene again. At first I was filled with a sudden feeling of emptiness. I started to gain weight because I no longer had to work so hard. That made me feel guilty and ashamed. It was a surprise to find after eight years how much free time a housewife has if she does not have to care for an elderly person. It was almost as if I were in a different world.

I have the following suggestions as a result of having nursed my father-in-law:

1. When parents reach old age, they should avoid living with their children. The feeling of estrangement from one's own children that comes from living with them may be much harder to bear than the loneliness one feels when living alone. We need well-equipped homes for the elderly.
2. Everyone should have a hobby. As long as our society remains as it is, there is no place for the aged except in the homes of their children. To make this situation less difficult, everyone should have something to do that interests them throughout life.

3. We should not spend all our money on our children. It would be better to save some money for our old age, even if the children have to work to earn their school tuition. I feel strongly that we must improve society so that we can grow old without worry.

I WANT TO WORK, BUT. . .
By Tomoko Tamura

When I graduated from college and was looking for a job, my sole purpose was to earn enough to support myself until I married. I did not seek a lifetime career or a job in which I could develop my abilities. I had a high school teaching license, but even though I knew that teaching was a suitable job for a woman, I did not want to be a teacher. Surely there was more to being a teacher than simply spreading knowledge. I knew that it involved shaping the moral character of the students and thought I was too immature to handle such a demanding job. Since I was already engaged to be married at the time, my first concern was that my job be compatible with housework. It had to leave me enough time to do other things than work. So I took a job as a translator in an office.

After I had worked at the job for two years, I became pregnant. Our financial situation did not allow me to quit working and settle down at home, although that is what everyone at work thought an expectant mother should do. I must admit I had no strong desire to continue working while trying to reconcile the demands of work with the responsibilities of child care. My parents lived far away and there were no relatives living nearby with whom I could leave my baby. Nursery schools do not normally take very young babies. I could have found one to take the baby when it reached one year of age, but that would not have been practical in my case because we lived too far from any of the nursery schools. I would have had to spend a great deal of time taking the baby to and from school. Nursemaids were scarce and we would have had to wait a long time to get one. Worse yet, the salary of a nursemaid was much more than I could afford. I felt that I had no choice but to leave my job. More than child care problems, what discouraged me most from keeping my job were the comments of those around me. People said things like "Children in nursery schools are skinny" and "The poor children who have to go to nursery school." After all, I wanted to be a good mother. I decided to quit working and stay at home.

When the baby was born, I was surprised at how much trouble child care could be. Before the baby was born, I had thought my life would be richer and more rewarding. When I actually began to care for my child I was awestruck—he was so painfully cute and fragile, and yet so demanding. He clung to me both physically and emotionally; it felt as if I were at the mercy of my child. Spending most of the time in our small house with the baby and not being able to read books or newspapers easily, not to mention the impossibility of going out, made me feel as if I had been segregated from the rest of society. Our difficult financial situation may have been one reason why I felt that way. I was frustrated because I had no time to myself and, at the same time, I worried about my child's development. I tended to direct my resentment toward my child, but I was concerned that my attitude might be a bad influence on him. As for my husband, I often took my feelings out on him, and that put a strain on our relationship. At that stage, my desire to go back to work was still faint. Certainly it was not as strong as my desire to find a babysitter. Instead of doing anything, I just kept wishing for some time to myself.

About three years passed and I had my second child. From then on, my anxiety was much less than it had been. For one thing I was now used to child care and knew that children could be left alone to a certain extent. For another, I became less nervous as I grew older. The main reason, however, was that I gave up the idea of ever having time to myself once I had two children. Since I thought I could not help spending all my time with them, I used this as an excuse for neglecting everything else.

When my younger child was almost two, he started asking to play outside with other children. That meant I could not take my eyes off him. Often I spent all day chasing after him. Soon it became routine. Each day was a repetition of the one before. I became incapable of detaching myself from my child. I got involved in his quarrels with other children and was angry whenever he lost. I had no sense of my own identity at all and was unable to concentrate on anything when I was alone. Although I wanted some time to myself, I felt lost when my child was away and I could accomplish nothing at all. Child care became a convenient excuse for laziness.

Being a housewife means spending every day in the endless repetition of routine affairs. You get up in the morning, take the children to nursery school, do the laundry, and clean the house. Later you must keep the children company, fix meals, and do the dishes. Only late at night can you relax and even then it is not always possible. Housework is like an obsession. If you leave one task undone, you feel uneasy. When I was employed, I was detached from my housework. Whenever I had time I would clean or do the laundry. Now that I don't have anything else but housework as a job, I tend to let it tie me down and I'm never done with it.

Because I was frustrated, I began to think that mothers and children should have separate lives. I felt my life would be wasted if I let my house rule me. I also felt that my real worth could only be proved outside the home, and that feeling may explain why housework and child care did not satisfy me.

My husband opposed my ideas. He argued that I was too optimistic in thinking I could find a job and fulfill myself. Even if I found such a job, he said, I would never stick with it. It was irresponsible of me to want a job just because I didn't want to stay home. In his opinion, only economic reasons such as buying a house or paying for the children's education would justify a woman's desire to work. As long as there were babysitting expenses, he said, a woman could not contribute to her family financially. In the long run it might be more expensive to work than stay home. "Let me remind you, too, that you chose to be a housewife when you were expecting the first child so that you could devote yourself to child care and housework. If you become so self-centered that you think only of your own sense of accomplishment, it will be impossible to have a home. Think of it this way—we divide the work between us and you take the housework."

Despite my husband's admonitions, I was not convinced. I

couldn't help admitting, however, that we could not afford to lose money. After looking at the want ads in the newspapers, it was obvious that the job market for married women over age thirty was very limited. Moreover, I didn't know what kind of work I wanted to do. Without my husband's cooperation I would have been exhausted both physically and mentally had I taken a job. When I thought about the fact that my children would suffer most from the situation, I was stymied. Rationally I thought it best for the children to spend most of their time with their peers; emotionally I was afraid to leave the children at the day-care center all day.

As I struggled with my thoughts, I started to think I should value my home life with my husband and children above all else. I began to think it was selfish to want a job, as my husband had said, and that it would be impossible to make a home if each member of the family thought only of himself. When I think back on the past, I don't think I treated my children in the way I believed to be right. Nor did I devote myself to my housework. I still want to get a job, but I will wait until my youngest child enters grade school. I am thinking about doing something at home for the next few years.

Part 3

THE COMMUNITY

These selections on the community illustrate the relationship between people who, though not members of the same family, depend on each other socially and economically and share a common set of norms and a common view of the world. Since this interdependence often takes place between people of different social levels, the community is characterized by vertical or pseudo-familial human relationships. Interdependence is most evident in rural Japan, where for centuries the majority of the population lived. The "Laws of the Hamlet" and *The Earth* are both set in rural Japan and exemplify the functioning of the rural community.

The most important aspect of rural life throughout Japanese history has been cooperation. The growing of rice, the staple crop of Japanese agriculture, requires irrigation, and the sharing of water and maintenance of irrigation systems necessitates cooperation and community solidarity. The organizational unit through which cooperative efforts were carried out is commonly referred to in English today as the hamlet. While the hamlet in Japan no longer has the formal legal status it had in the premodern period, it remains an important extralegal, political, social, and economic unit in the countryside. The number of households that make up a hamlet may vary, but the size always ensures close physical proximity and allows for face to face relations among its members. In addition to maintaining irrigation systems the households of the hamlet join together to repair roads, paths, and ditches. Members help each other with the construction of buildings, the roofing of houses, and the preparation for ceremonies and festivals. All the households assist at weddings and funerals and send a representative to attend.

In the selection from the novel *The Earth,* the story of a husband and wife takes place against a background of community concern and activity. When the wife becomes sick, a neighbor leaves his fields to bring her husband back from a construction site where he had been working to supplement the family income. Another neighbor goes to get the doctor while others sit with the dying wife. Members of the community also take an important part in the funeral arrangements; the women dress the body and prepare food for the funeral. Neighbors make offerings of money to the family and accompany the funeral procession. In fact, the funeral is more the concern of the community in which she lived than of her distant relations. In "The Laws of the Hamlet," too, members of the community take part in a funeral and the writer of the essay is obliged to give up his own plans to help make the coffin and march in the funeral procession.

The hamlet assembly acts as a governing body, and any resident who does not uphold the interests of the hamlet or join in the assembly's decisions is disciplined. Great emphasis is placed on harmony and standards of conduct. Any misbehavior or disloyalty that would disturb the peace of the hamlet is subject to immediate and unanimous sanctions. Gossip is a powerful sanction in the hamlet as in many small communities; and if all else fails, the offending household may be ostracized. Among the offenses that might bring community censure are theft, failure to carry out obligations to other hamlet households, or failure to acquiesce in decisions of the hamlet association. One of the most serious crimes a member can commit is to report to the police a community activity or decision with which he or she does not agree. Loyalty to the hamlet is supposed to take precedence over obedience to national law. The writer in "The Laws of the Hamlet" is not recognized as a member of the hamlet until he joins his neighbors in gambling. By gambling, illegal under national law, he takes part in an offense committed by community residents and so becomes one of them.

In the same essay one member is punished for complaining to the police about an action by the hamlet. This resident believed that the hamlet association had cut one of the trees on his property, and so he reported the matter to the police. Hamlet residents, angry because their honor had been questioned publicly, decided to punish the offender. Now the ultimate form of punishment in a hamlet is ostracism—all members of the community cut ties with the offending household and offer no help with planting and harvesting. The ostracized household cannot attend hamlet association meetings, and marriage arrangements for its children may be difficult. But there is some reluctance to apply ostracism since it is a public admission of the hamlet's inability to control its members. In this instance, rather than voting the offending household out of the assembly, the members all resigned, leaving the household the only member. In another case, the theft of potatoes was stopped when the hamlet voted to ostracize anyone caught stealing the potatoes. The threat alone was sufficient to establish discipline.

With the introduction of national transportation and technological advances in agriculture, fewer people are needed for farming and community solidarity is less essential than it once was. Moreover, there has been a marked reduction in the size of farm households and their number. Nevertheless, the hamlet remains a source of continuity and solidarity in modern Japan. Rural communities still remain a cohesive force, particularly in remote areas, although they no longer have the autonomy they had in the premodern period and members of the community have greater personal independence from the local system than ever before.

Urban centers developed in Japan long before the modern period, and when, in the Meiji period, restrictions upon changing residence and occupation were removed, the growth of the urban population accelerated rapidly. Younger sons of rural families moved to the cities to find work, and since the 1960s entire families have left their farms and moved to the urban areas. These emigrants exchange the cohesive rural community for an urban neighborhood that has far less autonomy and functional significance. In contrast to the hamlet, the boundaries of the urban neighborhood, for adults in particular, are vague; mobility in and out of the neighborhood is common; and the neighborhood associations have little authority in comparison with the hamlet assembly. Since World War II many urban Japanese have moved into huge and impersonal apartment complexes. "The Talisman" is the story of a man who feels alienated from the urban environment around him. There is nothing to replace the sense of identity and status that hamlet life provided.

"Relations with Neighbors" is a selection of excerpts from a contemporary book of etiquette written for urban dwellers. The very fact that a book on how to get along with one's neighbors is published at all says something about community life in a city. In the rural hamlet neighbors were expected to help each other in an emergency; indeed, collaboration was essential for survival. The etiquette book exhorts neighbors to go to each other's aid, but the need to *urge* urban dwellers to do so indicates that mutual assistance is far less a part of city life than of rural life. Moreover, the advice on how to move into a new neighborhood shows the contrast between the rural and urban community. Even today, relatively few people move into the rural hamlet. The major exception is the new bride who has married a hamlet member; on the occasion of her marriage the rural bride pays a visit to the village shrine and is then accepted as a member of the hamlet. There is much more mobility in and out of the urban neighborhood. In middle-class neighborhoods the wife and husband may move in after their marriage. The wife gradually becomes part of the neighborhood after she visits her immediate neighbors and brings them small presents. A foreigner who moves into a Japanese neighborhood is often expected to do the same before being accepted.

The urban husband, if he is employed by a large company as a blue-collar or white-collar worker, may find his sense of community in his work group. While the men in rural farming communities, like the women, work and live in the same area, the urban husband, particularly the white-collar worker, commutes to another part of the city to work. If he lives in Tokyo, he will probably spend at least an hour commuting to work and another coming home. His emotional commitment and sense of group solidarity will often be with his fellow workers. This commitment is often solidified by social activities involving others in his work group but not his wife and children. The story by Keita Genji, "The Thirty-Fifth Anniversary," illustrates in a comic vein the way in which a company president promotes loyalty among his employees by arranging for a

celebration to commemorate the firm's anniversary. The vertical relationship between senior and junior members of a Japanese firm is
evident in the story. The relationship between the former president
and the current one is almost familial—that of father and son. The
president is beneficially disposed toward junior members and be-
friends them; they in turn accept his assistance and even look to
him to act as honorary matchmaker. The prosperity of the corporation is a goal shared by every employee under the lively encouragement of the company's president and directors.

Minority peoples in Japan live in communities of their own
that are often separate from the rest of society. Two such groups are
Korean residents and the outcasts (often called *burakumin* or the
pejorative *eta*—literally, "filled with filth." The outcasts make up
approximately two percent of the Japanese population and the Koreans less than one percent. In two of the selections presented here,
"One Woman's Outcry" and "Korean Residents at Inoshino,"
members of these two minorities express their feelings about their
position in Japan. "Korean Residents at Inoshino" is an interview
with a Korean who grew up in a Korean community in Osaka.
Many Koreans in Japan today still live in their own enclaves, preserve their ethnic identity, and send their children to Korean
schools. In this interview the Korean, a writer and businessman,
tells of the social discrimination he felt as a child when he ventured
outside his community. As an adult he has taken a Japanese name,
but resents the fact that he has had to in order to succeed outside
the Korean community.

Like the Korean communities the outcast communities tend
to be held together as much by exclusion from the rest of society as
by inner cohesion. "One Woman's Outcry" is a letter written by an
outcast to an Osaka newspaper in 1958. Outcast status derived
originally from involvement in occupations that other Japanese regarded as polluted—butchery, the execution of criminals, the handling of dead bodies, leather work. According to Shinto belief,
death is a source of defilement. And the introduction of Buddhism
with its injunctions against the taking of life added stigma to the
tasks the outcasts performed. Other Japanese tended to avoid the
outcasts from a belief in defilement by association. The woman

writing the letter is protesting the misconceptions and prejudice directed against her community. She herself tried to leave her community by marrying a man who was not an outcast, but public recognition of her origins led to the breakup of her marriage. The *"All Romance* incident" to which she refers took place in Kyoto in 1951 when a city official wrote a short story attributing bestial sexual practices and squalor to those who lived in the Kyoto *burakumin* community. The incident triggered vehement protest from leaders of the militant outcast organization and won from Kyoto officials the promise of extensive improvement in housing and sanitation for the outcasts.

The modern media have made it possible for people all over Japan to observe events and react to them as if they were happening in their own community. The Asama Villa incident was such an event. In early 1972 the police surrounded a mountain villa where they had learned that five members of the Red Army were hiding. The Red Army is an extremist group of Japanese in their twenties who are committed to a philosophy of violent world revolution. Many of its members have been sought by police for crimes they committed to support their cause. In this case Yasuko Muta, the wife of the villa manager, was taken hostage, and, in the siege that followed, three policemen were killed and twelve people injured. After the extremists surrendered it was learned that the Red Army had murdered several of its own members for being too "soft." The senseless violence turned the usual tolerance of the Japanese for youthful idealism to public revulsion. The newspaper accounts presented here demonstrate the public pressure that was exerted against the families of the extremists. One account tells of the harassing calls received by people who happened to have the former telephone number of an extremist's family. In other instances the families received threatening letters and cards. One father resigned from his job; another committed suicide. As in the rural hamlet, pressure is brought to bear on the entire family of an offending member—a striking example of the continuity and change that have characterized the community in Japan throughout its history.

The Earth

THE EARTH is a novel written by the poet, Takashi Nagatsuka (1879–1915). Though born to a wealthy landowning family in Ibaraki prefecture, Nagatsuka felt deep sympathy toward the poor peasant families who tilled his father's lands. On the recommendation of the novelist Sōseki Natsume (1867–1916), Nagatsuka was commissioned by the newspaper *Asahi Shimbun* to write a novel about peasants. The novel was first serialized in *Asahi Shimbun* and in 1912 it was published in book form. *The Earth* is considered to be a faithful representation of the life of the peasants whom Nagatsuka had known as a boy. The excerpt offered here, which involves an abortion that eventually causes the death of a peasant woman, shows the suffering of the family and the community's response to it.

Kanji went to work on a construction project on the Tone River. A laborer had come around during the fall to recruit workers, offering very good wages, and several men from the nearby villages had agreed to go. Kanji had no idea what construction work was like, but he was attracted by the high wages of more than fifty *sen* a day. The construction site was in bottomland near the Kasumigaura Lake, where a dike divided river from lake. In times of flooding, the lake would overflow its grassy banks and merge with the river. Kanji was amazed at how desolate the place was in comparison with his home, and the foreman worked the men like animals.

Before he left for the job, Kanji had to take care of the fields.

From Takashi Nagatsuka, *Tsuchi* (Tokyo: Shun'yōdō, 1927), pp. 21–31, 47–71. Translated for this book by Margaret B. Dardess.

He worked frantically to harvest the potatoes and white radishes and especially the rice before the onset of winter. He worked from dawn until dusk. His wife, Oshina, got up and lit the kitchen stove while Kanji spread straw mats in the yard to dry. He hulled the rice, turning the hand mill himself. He spread some of the white radishes out to dry in the sun and stored others in the earth. He had not quite finished everything he wanted to do before his departure, but Oshina promised to take care of the rest.

The construction site was about fifty miles away. Since he would start earning money as soon as he got there, Kanji put only one *yen* in his pocket. He took enough food with him so that he would have to spend money only for the ferry ride. He reached the construction site in the evening and, though exhausted from the trip, started work the next morning. He did not want to use up his food supply when he was not working. But the work was very hard, and the next day the muscles in his hands ached so badly that he was not able to work for a few days. Some time later a cold wind began to blow from the west. Kanji wrapped himself in a thin quilt at night. His feet had been thoroughly chilled during the day and he could not get them warm. Unable to sleep, he tossed and turned all night until daybreak.

That morning he gripped the cold shovel with his stiffened hands and went back to work in the mud. He was covered with it when a neighbor from his village arrived unexpectedly looking for him. There was such a crowd of men that the neighbor had great difficulty finding Kanji. When he finally did, he told Kanji repeatedly how happy he was to see him. Kanji was surprised and puzzled. The neighbor made trivial comments about his trip. He did not explain why he had come until Kanji, unable to stand the suspense, demanded to know what the neighbor was doing there. Finally the neighbor told Kanji that Oshina had sent him. When he learned that Oshina was sick, Kanji feared the worst. Again and again he asked the neighbor how she was, and despite the neighbor's assurance that Oshina was not very sick, Kanji was uneasy. It was as if something were stuck in his throat.

They left for home that night. Since Kanji was in a great hurry and the neighbor was too tired to go on foot, they took a steamboat down Kasumigaura Lake to the town of Tsuchiura. In Tsuchiura Kanji bought a packet of sardines. He left the neighbor there and walked on as fast as he could. When he finally reached the village, it was dusk. He could hardly see the people he passed on the road. When he reached his door, he saw that the lantern was not on the outside pillar. One hand lantern was all he had. Through a crack in the door he could see that Oshina lay wrapped in a quilt. Otsugi, their daughter, was rubbing Oshina's legs.

Kanji opened the door all the way, saying only "How are you doing?" Oshina, hearing Kanji's voice, stirred on her pillow. "Kanjisan? You didn't miss Minami, did you?"

"I saw him. How do you feel?"

"I didn't think it was going to be so bad, but I've been in bed for three or four days. I'm a bit better today. I think I'll be all right soon."

"That's good. If I'd been alone I could've walked all the way, but I didn't think I should make Minami go any further on foot. We took a boat to Tsuchiura and I left Minami there. He was tired and would've had a hard time walking again today. The boat was late."

Kanji removed his straw sandals. He took the packet of sardines he had tied in the corner of his handkerchief and put it down next to Oshina. Lifting off the bundle from around his neck, he went outside to wash his feet, and then came and sat down beside Oshina.

"I'm glad that you don't feel too bad. I was really worried. Are you eating well?"

"Otsu boiled some rice for me a while ago. I've managed to eat some of it."

"Here, try some of these. I bought them on my way home." Kanji carried the lantern to Oshina's side and opened the packet of fish. The fish glistened in the lantern light.

"Oh my!" Oshina exclaimed, still lying on her stomach.

"Otsu, make a fire there," Kanji directed.

"Kanjisan, they must've been expensive. I didn't need so many." "They'll keep a long time in this weather. Eat them and get your strength back."

"Didn't the boat cost a lot?"

"Yes, it was about sixty *sen* for the two of us. I paid for it. I couldn't ask Minami to pay his own way."

"You must've used up all the money you earned."

"No, I still have some more in my purse. I worked for about seven days and probably saved about two *ryo*. I'm planning to go back. I got a little in advance because the men from around here vouched for me," Kanji told her proudly.

"I wanted to see you so much when I was feeling bad." Oshina pushed her face against the pillow.

"I left without putting everything in order so I had to come back once anyway," Kanji said looking at Oshina. "But I see that you've already put the rice in straw bags." Oshina was still lying face down.

"I don't need any money when I'm there. I don't smoke even a puff. We get paid every two weeks. The cost of the rice and firewood we need is taken out of our pay so our purses aren't so fat on payday. Still there is a lot left." Kanji told Oshina more about his job.

"We need to eat quite a lot of rice every day, the work is so hard. But if I work hard I can save a good deal of money. I will have a fair amount before I come home, and then we can even buy some salted salmon."

"That's good. I've been worried because I heard that most construction workers are pretty rough." Oshina lifted her head.

"I don't have much to do with them. I keep to myself, and they don't bother me."

As Kanji talked, Otsugi broke twigs and made a fire in the *hibachi*. Kanji laid skewers across the fire and put three fish on the skewers. Drops of grease fell into the fire and the flames blazed up. The smell of fish and smoke that filled the room made Oshina hungry. Still on her stomach, Oshina ate a fish.

"It's not too salty, is it?"

"It's so good."

"The peddlers around here don't carry fish like this," Kanji said as he looked affectionately at Oshina.

Oshina started to eat a second fish. As she picked up her

chopsticks she looked at her son, Yokichi, asleep beside her. If he were awake he would be very excited.

"Have some more," Kanji urged.

"I've had enough. Give some to Otsu." "I'll eat now, too," Kanji said, and he took some leftover rice balls from his bundle and nibbled at the cold rice.

"Otsu, is the tea still warm?" Oshina asked.

"I don't want any tea. I never drink tea when I'm at work." Kanji licked a pickled plum slowly. When he finished his rice, he gave some fish to Otsugi and ate a little himself.

"It's good, but it's not salty enough for me." Kanji drank a few cups of lukewarm water. Then he took a bag from his bundle and put it by Oshina.

"This rice was left over and so I brought it along. It's safe enough when I'm there, but the others would eat it while I'm away. I'll give it to Otsu."

Kanji handed the small bag of rice to Otsugi.

"I was wondering what it was," said Oshina gaily.

"I had some firewood, but I couldn't manage that." He smiled as if laughing to himself. Let me rub your legs, Oshina."

"That's all right, Kanjisan. I'm feeling pretty good today and you're tired, aren't you," said Oshina, her spirits rising.

Later that night Oshina suddenly took a turn for the worse. Kanji had just fallen asleep when Oshina cried out in misery, "I can't open my mouth!" It seemed to her as if her jaws had been nailed shut and her throat was tight. She couldn't swallow. She felt so helpless!

Kanji started up in alarm. "What's the matter? Do you feel very bad? Hold on until morning." Kanji tried to cheer her up, but he did not know what to do. He tossed restlessly all night. In the morning he sent a neighbor for a doctor while he stayed at Oshina's side. Someone like Kanji would not send for a doctor except in an extreme emergency, but he was too frightened to worry about the cost. The doctor lived to the east across the Kinu River.

Kanji rubbed Oshina's legs, and asked if she were getting tired. He was deeply disturbed by Oshina's obvious exhaustion. Unable to wait until afternoon for the doctor to come, he ran after the doctor himself as soon as a neighbor came to see Oshina. On the ferryboat crossing the river, Kanji saw the neighbor he had sent to get the doctor, and they shouted to each other as their ferries passed. Kanji asked the neighbor to tell Oshina that he would soon be back with the doctor.

When he reached the doctor's door Kanji found that the man, in no hurry, was just leaving. Even though the doctor told Kanji that he was going in the direction of Kanji's house and would stop by, Kanji could not feel confident of the visit. He followed the doctor from patient to patient carrying his bag for him respectfully and waiting outside each door. With an old hat on his head and a small bag in his hand the doctor always made his rounds on foot because his patients were poor farmers who could not pay his carfare. As they walked along Kanji described Oshina's condition to the doctor and wanted to know his opinion. The doctor said he would not be able to tell anything until he saw the patient. As soon as the doctor examined Oshina, however, he knew that she had tetanus, and he was afraid for her life. He excused himself from the case by saying that he did not have the right hypodermic needle.

Kanji rushed off to find another doctor. The second doctor wrote down the name of some medicine on a pad and told Kanji to buy it at the pharmacy at once. He gave Kanji another piece of paper and told him to take it to the doctor's house, where he said Kanji would be given something else. Kanji again rushed off across the river. The pharmacist gave him two containers of medicine, and Kanji felt his purse become considerably lighter when he paid the seventy-five *sen* for the medicine. He then hurried off to the doctor's house where he was given a hypodermic needle. The doctor returned to Kanji's house toward evening after seeing his other patients. He asked Kanji to hold the lantern for him and in its clear light he wiped Oshina's thigh with wet gauze, pinched her flesh, and gave her an injection. He withdrew the needle, pressed the mark with his finger, and then put a piece of adhesive on it.

The next morning the doctor came again and gave Oshina another shot. He left saying that she would be all right now. But Oshina showed no sign of recovery; in fact, she seemed to be getting worse. Toward evening, she suddenly went into convulsions. Her whole body shook violently and her arms and legs jerked as if pulled by some powerful force. With each convulsion her face distorted in pain and her mouth twitched uncontrollably. Kanji, with only Otsugi beside him, did not know what to do. When the sky began to lighten he again ran to the doctor. The doctor sent him back to the pharmacy, but the serum the doctor needed was out of stock. The pharmacist said that he did not keep it on hand because it lost its effectiveness after a certain time and was very expensive besides. Out of curiosity Kanji asked how much it cost and was amazed to discover that he could not have paid for it even if it had been available.

The doctor again sent Kanji to the pharmacy. Only when he was rushing around was Kanji's mind at all at ease because then he felt he was doing something to save Oshina's life. The doctor gave Oshina more of the first serum, but it was no use. The convulsions became more frequent. Her breathing was labored. Three or four neighbors sat by Oshina's bedside in great sorrow.

The doctor gave Oshina a shot of morphine to ease her pain. After a while she regained consciousness; her body quivered and then went limp.

"Doctor, what's going to happen to me?" she asked suddenly.

"What do you think, doctor?" Kanji, too, wanted to know.

The doctor whispered to Kanji, "It might be a good idea to tell her that she will be all right."

"Oshina, the doctor says you'll be fine. Just be patient and don't give up," Kanji shouted in Oshina's ear.

"But I don't think I can last until tomorrow. I'm so scared," Oshina said. Her voice was very faint, but she was clearly conscious. Finally the doctor gave her the heaviest dose of morphine he could and left.

That night she convulsed continuously. Her hair was wet with sweat; the quilt smelled of it.

"Kanji, don't leave me," Oshina pleaded as she fought for breath.

"I'm right here. I won't go anywhere."

"Kanjisan."

"Yes, Oshina."

Oshina may not have heard him. After a pause she said, "Kanji, I'm really . . ." and grasped Kanji's hand.

"Otsu, you are . . . Yokichi, you, too. . . ." She had another convulsion.

"Kanji, if I die, put me in a coffin. . . ."

Kanji tried hard to understand her disconnected words.

"In the back rice paddy, under the oleaster tree by the path. . . ."

Kanji understood.

The night was hushed and still. The shutters moved a little; the fallen leaves rustled in the wind. Oshina's body grew cold. As soon as they realized that she was dead, Kanji and Otsugi began to sob uncontrollably, all of their suppressed emotions welling forth. The neighbors cried with them. Only Yokichi, asleep beside Oshina's body, was unaware that Oshina had died. One of the neighbors put Oshina's hands together on her chest. He put her weaving shuttle on the quilt. It was commonly believed that a cat that walked across a dead person would turn into a ghost; cats were said to stay away from a body if a shuttle were put on the quilt next to it.

As the night wore on it grew colder. There was not a single lump of coal in the house. The neighbors could not move away from the bedside until Kanji and Otsugi stopped crying. They tucked their hands inside their clothing to keep them warm. After a long time Otsugi stood up, made a fire in the stove with dried leaves, and boiled water for tea. They all drank the tea in silence.

After drinking tea by Oshina's bedside one of the neighbors left to tell Oshina's relatives of her death. Then they all discussed the funeral arrangements. They decided to hold the funeral the next day, inviting only close relations and neighbors. At daybreak some of the neighbors went to the temple to borrow things for the funeral and others went to tell the sad news to relatives in neighboring villages. Back at the house neighbor women came to give their sympathy to Kanji. Since Oshina had no close relative to help with the preparation of the body, Kanji, with Otsugi's assistance, rolled up the straw mat, put a basin on the dirt floor, and cleaned

Oshina's body himself. The severe pain of Oshina's illness had left her body very thin. Kanji put the body back onto the quilt and threw the dirty water onto the dirt. Then he put back the straw mat. He aired out the house and swept it thoroughly and on the floor he spread several sheets of straw borrowed from his neighbors. In keeping with local custom Kanji left the dressing of the cleansed body to the neighbors.

Several neighbor women cut a large square of white cotton cloth in two pieces and made a short shroud and a hood to cover the face. They shaped triangular pieces of cloth to cover the feet in place of socks. Then they fastened a piece of cloth around the legs with a cord. Some coins, said to be the cost of the ferry across the river to the underworld, were put in a bag of the same cloth and tied around Oshina's neck. Her body was bent with knees drawn up and placed in the coffin.

Before it was fully light that morning Kanji had left the house and walked between the oak trees behind the house to the rice field. He looked carefully around the oleaster tree. When he found a place where the ground had been disturbed, he carefully poked around the soft earth with a sickle until he found a parcel wrapped in a rag. Inside he found the tiny thing. He put it carefully inside his clothing and looked around as if in fear that someone would see. Then he wrapped it in a piece of oil paper. When Oshina's body was placed in the coffin, Kanji slipped the parcel in with her, arranging her thin arms so that they embraced it tightly and her face pressed against it.

Even though Kanji offered a meal only to immediate neighbors and close relatives, all the villagers came to express their condolences and offer two *sen*. They stayed only briefly. The chief priest and his young acolyte came on foot from a distant temple bringing with them a servant dressed in a faded yellow-green coat and carrying a lacquered box. The assistant removed the lid of the coffin right away. He lifted the white cotton cloth and touched the gaunt cheek lightly with a razor. After this ceremonial shaving, the lid was nailed in place.

A few people took part in the burial. Two white lanterns and a couple of bamboo flower baskets with green bamboo handles were held over the coffin. The baskets contained red, yellow, and blue paper flowers and some colored paper hung from the edge. A sheet of paper at the bottom of the basket contained the same number of coins as the number of years Oshina had lived. The person holding the baskets waved them from time to time and the coins fell through the bottom. The village children vied with each other to pick them up. With the lanterns and baskets leading the way, a group of villagers carrying red drums around their necks followed, chanting slowly and beating the drums. They carried the coffin through the main street. All of the villagers got a quick look at it from their doors. Probably because it was poorly secured the coffin kept jostling around. Kanji, dressed in formal clothes, held a mortuary tablet. Since he had borrowed the clothes, Kanji tied them with a twisted paper cord.

Although it was a very small funeral, when the funeral party left, the house looked as if a whirlwind had swept it clean. The women who had come to help had nothing left to do. They had had little to do from the start since not many people were served a meal. Almost all the food had been prepared by the farmers themselves. There was a little chopped white radish and carrot left over. Although the women nibbled a little on these and on the cold soup with bean curd, the white rice appealed to them most and they ate as much as they could hold.* They clustered together in the shadows by the back door and gossiped.

"Wasn't the coffin shaky? I wonder why."

"Of course. Don't you know that a departed soul moves around if it's worried about what's left behind?"

"Maybe she wants Kanji and it's hard for her to leave him."

"I hear that if a departed soul really wants you it'll take you along with it."

"How awful!"

"No one is going to come and get you even if you wanted them to."

They talked in this vein continuously. After a pause, one

---

*White rice was a luxury. Most peasants ate barley and coarse grains.

woman said, as if she had just thought of it, "But how sad for Oshina!"

"Really she just did what everyone does."

"She told me she had the flu. She said it was a very bad case and she couldn't get up to work. She played innocent."

"It's always the poor who die."

"But I hear that Oshina didn't do it just to herself."

"Yes, I've heard that too. Just between us I understand she did the same for others too and charged anywhere from fifty to eighty *sen*."

"Eighty *sen!* It's really something for a woman to earn that much money. But dying herself like this. . . . We really shouldn't do it."

"It could be punishment for committing a sin."

Their talk went on without interruption.

"Don't talk about a person who has just died. You'll be haunted." With that the conversation stopped. Everyone was quiet for a while. One woman picked up some white radish from a plate and put it in her mouth.

When someone warned her against doing that the woman laughed and answered, "That's all right. I don't expect anyone to marry me at my age."

They all burst out laughing. The gossiping did not stop until the people who had gone to bury the coffin began to come back one after another. Women like that ordinarily have very little to console them so that when two or more of them get together they wag their tongues without considering the consequences. On rare occasions they take clean clothes from the drawer and comb their hair, and while they are offering their condolences, they are very diffident. That is because they are concentrating on the formalities. But once they step down into an earth-floored room, tuck up their sleeves, and start washing and drying the dishes, their minds return to gossip. Even if it is a sad occasion for others it is one of the few times they can get together with friends. Ordinarily they eat only enough to keep up their energy. In a day of mourning, however, they can eat their fill at someone else's expense. No matter how grief-stricken others are, it is no concern of theirs. Consequently, whenever they get together the laughter never stops.

Once Oshina was one of them and today she returned to the cold earth leaving laughter behind her.

In a sense Oshina took her own life. A year after giving birth to Otsugi at the age of nineteen, Oshina became pregnant again. She and Kanji were at the low point of their poverty then, and so Oshina's mother, who has since died, performed an abortion when the fetus was seven months old. It was fall and still warm. Oshina, then full of health, started cutting grass in the forest a few days later. Although she did not become seriously ill she strained herself and took some time to recover completely. Yokichi was born when Otsugi was thirteen. This time both Kanji and Oshina were happy with the baby. Otsugi at thirteen could help with Yokichi so that both parents could work in the fields. When Yokichi was three, they decided that Otsugi should enter domestic service somewhere. At that time a girl of fifteen could earn only about ten *yen* a year. But it would mean one less mouth to feed, and even that small sum would make a big difference to a poor household. But just as the rice began to mature, Oshina started to worry. She knew that she felt strange. For ten years before Yokichi was conceived, she had not become pregnant; but since Yokichi's birth her womb seemed to be in the habit of getting pregnant, and she had conceived again. Kanji and Oshina did not know what to do. If they sent Otsugi into service, Oshina with two small children would not be able to work. Loss of income, however small, would be a great blow to them. Meanwhile harvest time came and the couple was busy reaping the rice and drying it. Aware that taking the life of a fetus was a sin, they passed each day not knowing what to do. At night they lay down exhausted and for a few minutes before falling asleep they exchanged their troubled thoughts. Kanji lacked the determination to make the decision himself so it was difficult to decide which of them should take the lead.

"Do whatever you like. It's your body," Kanji would say. This response did not mean that Kanji did not care, but rather that he shrank from ordering Oshina to do anything.

"But I don't know what to do either," Oshina would reply.

Kanji would not oppose whatever Oshina wanted to do. But the matter was too important for her to make the decision alone. Pressed with farming chores, they did not resolve the problem. Meanwhile cold winds began to blow. The zelkova trees dropped their red leaves on the ground. The small light fallen leaves rolled along the ground as if searching for a place to hide. They were everywhere—in the dried hay and on the straw mats used for unhulled rice. Soon Kanji had to leave for the construction site.

"It's time for us to make up our minds," Oshina again urged Kanji.

"I don't know what to say. Do whatever you like," Kanji replied simply.

After Kanji had gone Oshina felt confused, alone, and helpless. Finally she carried out the sin. She was four months pregnant. It is said that four months is the most dangerous time of pregnancy. That is the reason for Oshina's death. Since the fetus was four months old it was easy to tell its sex. Between the tiny legs Oshina saw a bump as small as a grain of rice. As might be expected she felt sad and empty. She was afraid that someone would find out what she had done. Although at first she buried the fetus under the floor as women often do, she dug it up again, wrapped it in a rag, and buried it again by the oleaster tree in the field.

She might have lived if only she had stayed quietly in bed until she had recovered. The first time her mother had taken care of everything for her, but this time Oshina had to do everything herself since Kanji had gone. She also forced herself to work because she wanted to act as if nothing had happened so that no one would be suspicious. How did the germ that killed her get into her body? . . . It is impossible to tell now.

The Laws
of the Hamlet

In the traditional social pattern that is still characteristic of much of rural
Japan, the customs of the village often take precedence over national
written law in determining behavior. People who do not follow village
customs are outsiders even though, as in the following essay, they may
live in the village. In this selection, Minoru Kida (1895–1975), a novelist
and popular anthropologist, describes his experiences in a rural hamlet.
Kida is considered to be an outsider until he gambles with the villagers—
thereby joining them in an activity which is illegal under the national law
but very much a part of village life. Once he has shown his allegiance to
the village by breaking the law of the outside world, he is an insider.

Fifteen or sixteen years ago I went to live in a rural hamlet. Soon after I arrived, the worthy Shin-san, boss of the hamlet and chief parishioner of the local temple, led me out to the house that was to
become my home. I well remember that day. I followed Shin-san
up a path that climbed through a green forest. Alongside flowed a
fresh clear mountain stream. After a time we passed through a
grove of cedars and came out on a plateau about halfway up the
mountain. There stood a dilapidated temple and a small, equally
dilapidated, house for the priest. We were surrounded by an un-
earthly quiet, and the atmosphere was sharp and sweet. The buildings seemed suddenly to have emerged from among the quivering
bamboo trees behind them. I liked the place.

Reprinted from Minoru Kida, "The Laws of the *Buraku*," *Japan Quarterly* 4,
no. 1 (January–March 1957), pp. 77–87. The Japanese term *"buraku"* used
throughout in the original article has been translated here as "hamlet."

"How long has the house been vacant?" I asked Shin-san, at the same time opening the rain shutter of the little shack.

"Well, it must've been around ten years now—ever since the last priest died. Go on and take a look at the rooms!"

I glanced in. The living room, which had a matted floor, was about nine by twelve feet. Next to it was a somewhat larger kitchen with a wooden floor. It contained a hearth for cooking and a sink. The building had been vacant for so long that the paper-covered windows and doors were all in tatters. I had never seen such a desolate house, but somehow the very desolation appealed to me. I decided to rent the place.

"How much is the rent?" I inquired.

"Oh, anything'll be all right. We were looking for somebody to take care of it, and that would've cost us money. When there ain't anybody in it, the house gets run down, and people cut down the trees. If you'll stay in it, you don't need to pay more than five or ten *yen*—just as a token, sort of. But there's one thing I do want you to do. Thirty families belong to the temple, and I want you to go pay your respects to every one of them."

I heaved a sigh. "I don't mind paying a call on them," I told him, "but it's going to be a mess having thirty landlords."

"Oh, I'll take care of all that. Don't you worry about it." He displayed a self-confidence befitting his status as boss and chief parishioner.

"Where's the well?"

"There ain't any well. You can draw water from the little river in the marsh. It's real good water."

Shin-san guided me to the stream. The water was clean and beautiful. A few water-bugs were skating over the surface, and I saw some small crabs crawling about at the bottom. I scooped up some water in my hands, and it tasted good.

"But don't forget," he admonished, "you can't do your washing here. The water from this stream is piped to fifteen houses, and they use it to drink."

The place was beginning to seem like a campground rather than a house. Suddenly it occurred to me to wonder what the neighborhood did for funerals with no priest. I asked Shin-san.

"Oh, yes," he replied, "I was going to tell you about that. Come look at the temple. This may be the country all right, but we're pretty modern up here in some ways. It ain't a rich neighborhood, and there ain't many parishioners, so we decided there wasn't any use in keeping a priest. Come on and look."

I was puzzled. He led me to the temple and opened the glass door. Then I found out what he meant. Before the altar there was a cabinet for scriptures, and in front of that a large satin-covered cushion for the priest. But on the cushion, instead of a priest, there sat a phonograph.

"Whatever you say," argued Shin-san, "it's the scriptures that get people to heaven and not the priest. And this here priest don't drink, and he don't chant a long time for the ones who pay him a lot and a short time for the ones who can't pay him much. Everybody in the neighborhood who dies gets the same treatment. That way, they all go to the same neighborhood in heaven, and they can all sit around and drink tea and talk just like they did here."

Well, well, I thought to myself, a great religious reform has taken place here, with neither war nor bloodshed, and all through the courtesy of Mr. Edison and Shin-san, it having been the latter's idea to use the phonograph.

Just then some birds darted up from the forest before us and flew off across the mountainside. Then a dog barked, and a hare scampered up from the side of the stream, past the temple, and into the bamboo grove behind it. The dog had caught the scent and was hot on the hare's heels.

"Somebody's hunting out of season," commented Shin-san.

*   *   *

I rented the house.

When I first moved in, my five-year-old boy was with me. One day he looked rather listless, and when I asked him what he would like me to fix for lunch, he said he didn't want anything. I felt his pulse, and it was a little fast. He looked as though he had a fever. I suggested eggs, and he said he thought he could eat eggs. I recalled that Sanzō-san, the combination tobacco, *sake,* kitchenware dealer, raised chickens, and I walked down the hill to the village to see whether he would sell me some eggs. As it happened, Sanzō-san was out, and the store was being presided over by his wife O-kon, who had the reputation of being an awful skinflint. I thought, oh well, and asked, "Say, do you happen to have any eggs?"

"What d'ya want 'em for?" she asked noncommittally.

"Well, my boy has a fever, and he's lost his appetite, but he says he'd like some eggs, so I thought maybe you would let me have some of yours."

As soon as I said that, O-kon's expression softened. With a touch of worry in her voice, she said "Oh, that's too bad! So the little rascal has a fever. Now that's a shame—I know you must be worried. I'm sure we've got a few eggs around here somewhere, so you take 'em along and give him some. Did you bring a thermometer up here with you? If you didn't I'll lend you one."

She went inside to a shelf and came back with a basket and the thermometer. In the basket were ten eggs.

"Just take the whole basketful, and give the boy all he wants." She sounded extremely solicitous.

"How much will that be?"

"Oh, I don't want any money. When we're in trouble we have to help each other out. Indeed we do."

I took the basket and started back home. On the way I envisioned the boy's happy face and thought what wonderful people these country folks were, how honest and generous and kind. I was almost moved to tears.

My son happily gobbled up his eggs.

Later I sent the boy back to Tokyo, but remained behind myself to do some work. One day I decided I wanted an omelette, so I went down to the village again to ask the gracious O-kon for some eggs.

She was watching the store as before, and I again asked if she had any eggs.

"Yeah, I think we've got some."

"How about letting me have a few?"

"What d'ya want 'em for?"

"I'm going to eat them."

I got her to let me have five, but this time she demanded a higher price than the highest I had ever heard of—even on the black market. I was startled by the naked greed in her eyes.

I started back up the hill, and on the way I tried to figure out what had happened. Why had the same O-kon who had once moved me so with her honesty and generosity and kindness now displayed such avarice? What had caused the sudden change? It was as though I had been dealing with two completely different people.

Time and again while I lived in that neighborhood I received the same impression, and it was only after watching these people in action for quite some time that I came to know the answer, which was, in effect, that they were generally nasty to each other. To be sure, if someone suffered a misfortune, they all managed to look sympathetic when they were with him, but secretly they were delighted. Conversely, when one person made some money, the others were hysterical with envy. When it was rumored, for example, that Masao-san had saved up some money and wanted to buy some land for gardening, everybody attempted to squelch the rumor by insisting that Masao-san couldn't possibly have acquired that much money. This was their way of comforting themselves over Masao's good fortune. I have no doubt but that the reason for the popularity of gambling in that neighborhood was a general desire to take money from someone else and watch him suffer. Nor was the attitude limited to gambling. When members of the community traded with each other, all money arrangements were purely on a person-to-person basis, with no regard whatever to going prices elsewhere. Everyone simply tried to do everyone else out of as much as possible.

One day O-kon, whose store was the only one in the hamlet, let fall a precious pearl of commercial wisdom.

"If you're going to use something yourself," she allowed, "it doesn't make any difference what the price is. You can't lose."

When I first heard this curious bit of philosophy, I did not really comprehend it, but later I began to see what she meant. If you want something to eat or use yourself, you should be willing to pay for your wants. And once you have paid, it's better to be satisfied with what you have got. A person can lose only when he buys something high and sells it cheap, that is to say when he resells. To put it bluntly, the people in the hamlet are utterly unconcerned with the market anywhere else. Their commercial philosophy is centered entirely about their own little group.

Their urge to gyp other people, their joy over other people's misfortune, and their envy of each other's good fortune may have a social basis. Within this little neighborhood, after all, when someone else's house prospers, one's own grows relatively less influential, and vice versa. The situation is in some ways similar to the dog-eat-dog practices of international politics: as among the rival nations of the world, there is no specialization in labor—every family is in the same business, farming.

Eventually, however, I found that in the midst of the constant battle to squeeze each other, the hamlet maintained a number of oddly different conventions.

One day when I came down the mountain with the intention of going to Tokyo, I saw a crowd gathered in the garden of Yoshi-san's house. I went up and asked what had happened.

"Well," replied Boss Shin-san, "last night Yoshi-san's old man died, and the neighborhood is here helping with the funeral. I was just going to send word to you."

"Is that so? I certainly am sorry to hear it. I have business in Tokyo today, but as soon as I get back I'll call on the family."

"Oh, no," he said firmly. "I don't care what kind of business you've got in Tokyo, you can't go today. It would've been all right if you hadn't known about it, but now you know. You live in the same neighborhood and belong to the same group, and you've got to help with the funeral."

I didn't go to Tokyo. Instead I helped make the coffin. It was the first time I had ever done anything like that, but I joined right in with the rest of them, planing boards and driving nails. All the people there, men and women alike, were busy. Some of them had gone to tell other people. Some, like myself, were making funeral equipment. Some were making a funeral banner, and some were

making baskets or umbrellas. The women were charged with preparing noodles for the men to eat, and some of them were knead-
ing flour, while others boiled water in a great caldron.

When the funeral procession formed the next day, Shin-san
looked around until he spotted me and said, "Now let's see—what
can I have you do?"

Shū-san, who was at his side, spoke up: "He's tall, and if you
let him carry the casket with us, the weight will all fall on us. Get
him to carry the banner! The parade will look real good with a big
fellow out in front."

So I marched with the banner at the head of the procession.

*   *   *

One year there was a serious food shortage, and by spring almost everyone in the hamlet had exhausted his store of grain.
Around noon one day in April a certain Shō-san passed through his
garden and noticed that the stems and leaves of his potato plants
were wilting. Examination proved that someone had dug up the
potatoes. Now no one but a farmer could steal potatoes without
disturbing the plants, and Shō-san was sure that the thief was another farmer in the hamlet. But who? There was no particular person on whom he could vent his wrath, and this made him all the
angrier. He soon thought of a way, however, to calm himself. That
night he went out and stole someone else's potatoes, and this completely satisfied his sense of justice.

Shō-san's solution to the problem was not especially unusual.
There was another man who went to work in the mountain and left
his bicycle at the foot only to return and find that a passing urchin
had slit his tire with a scythe. He was so disgusted that when on the
way home he spotted another person's bicycle he went after it with
his hatchet. The owner may not have been the person who had
wronged him, but it calmed his spirit to get even with someone.

The attitude reflected here is something like the one behind
the old law of talion, but by the law of talion, the actual sinner is
punished. In Shō-san's case, it was obvious that someone had
stolen the potatoes, and Shō-san felt it only proper that he should
pay this person called "Someone" back in kind. He was, in a word,

taking his revenge against society. The person whom Shō-san robbed was Kaku-san, and Kaku-san chose to avenge himself against society in the same way. Potato stealing suddenly became rampant.

The hamlet was called together in emergency session to consider means of dealing with the problem. At the first meeting it was decided that anyone caught stealing potatoes would be turned over to the police, but though the stealing continued, no one was actually caught. A second meeting was held, and a night watchman appointed to watch over the gardens. That evening, however, the watchman was Kume-san, and as luck would have it, Kume-san, having just been the victim of a potato thief the night before, welcomed the opportunity to take his revenge and did so. A third meeting was convened. This time no watchman was appointed, but it was decided that anyone who stole potatoes would be asked to leave the hamlet. This was a grave decision, and everyone in the hamlet had to sign and seal it.

After that night there was no potato stealing.

To be asked to leave the hamlet is to be ostracized completely and irrevocably. The village, which is merely an administrative division, composed of a collection of hamlets, does not have enough strength to enforce sanctions of this sort, but the hamlet is able by tradition to do so, and in the interest of local peace and harmony it does so in the case of certain violations.

When I first moved to the hamlet I had a chat with Sanzō-san, the second in command to Shin-san, and as we sat by his hearth drinking tea, he told me the basic laws of the hamlet.

"If your house burns down," he said, "you can't stay in the hamlet."

"Even if it's only your own house?" I asked.

"Yes," he replied. Then he added, "Naturally you can't set fire to somebody else's property, or kill anybody, or wound anybody, or steal, or do anything that would make the hamlet lose face."

Children are taught by their parents that if they break one of these prohibitions they cannot remain in the hamlet. Of course, a family in need of food or fuel is not inclined to chastise one of its members for swiping them from other people's gardens or from untended mountain property, but the potato stealing had gone so far that the life of the community was threatened, and this was enough to make the hamlet as a whole band together and make a forceful decision, to which everyone signed his name and affixed his seal. The interesting fact is that where the threat of calling in the police—that is to say, the threat of national law—had no effect, action by the hamlet itself put an immediate end to the whole affair. This testimony to the power of the hamlet raises a point to which I shall revert below.

*   *   *

The hamlet is, to be sure, in Japanese territory, and theoretically anybody can live in it. That is not to say, however, that a new resident is immediately taken in as a member of the group. To be so recognized sometimes takes a long, long time. When the hamlet as a unit holds a good deal of forest land, as is sometimes the case, a new resident is often not granted the privilege of exploiting a portion of this land for as long as twenty years. At the same time, to be sure, he is not required to serve in community labor forces, such as those which build or repair local roads.

There was no fixed rule on this point in my hamlet, but when I first went there to live, I was treated distinctly as an outsider or a guest. One day, however, all this came to an end. It happened in the following way.

The hamlet observed two important festivals, one on the first day of the year, and the other on July 15. On New Year's Day a religious official came especially to perform services to the gods. He would stretch a sacred rope with paper festoons hung from it across the entrance to the local shrine, a small building about six square yards in area, and inside he would say prayers designed to ensure the happiness and prosperity of the hamlet during the coming year. Then he would lightly brush the heads of the representatives from each family with a branch from a sacred tree, to which strips of white paper were attached. The religious ceremony was essentially the same on July 15.

When the ritual ended the members of the community gath-

ered beneath a great cedar, which was considered holy, and spread
straw mats around on the ground in the shrine enclosure, an area
of about twenty square yards. Everyone sat down on the mats to eat
and drink, singing songs and amusing themselves otherwise as they
feasted. It was a very primitive sight.

The first time I attended a festival was on July 15. That morning Shū-san, who was one of the persons in charge of the affair,
came to invite me. He looked completely different from usual. Instead of the patched field clothes that he always wore, he had on a
silk *kimono,* and his unruly hair was combed and anchored in
place with pomade.

"Come on down," he said. "There's a celebration today.
Starts at the shrine at ten o'clock."

"Sure, I'll be there," I replied, and I laid down my work for
the day.

When I arrived at the shrine it was just ten o'clock, and only a
few people had gathered. More came as time went on, and eventually there was quite a crowd, but still no religious official.

"In the country, nobody's ever on time," complained
Shin-san.

His deputy, Sanzō-san, wearily seconded him: "Yeah, that's
the way it always is in the country!"

At eleven the religious official finally arrived, wearing an ordinary suit and riding a bicycle. First he went into the shrine and
changed into a ceremonial outfit that must have been about thirty
years old. Then he emerged and performed a ceremony of purifica-
tion followed by prayers and blessings. The whole thing took only
about thirty minutes. When it was over, everybody spread mats
under the big cedar tree and began to eat, drink, and be merry. After a time the feast ended, but they all continued to loll around on
the mats talking to each other. Somehow, despite the festive atmosphere, they seemed uncomfortable.

Finally Sanzō-san announced, "Well, the ceremony's all over
now. It's time to go home."

But there was something wrong. Nobody paid any attention
to him. They all continued to lie where they were and talk.

Then Shin-san addressed me: "The party's ended now. You

better not stay away from home too long, or a thief might break into your house. You've got to be careful, you know."

"I'll go home when everybody else does," I replied. I was wondering why nobody made a move to leave.

After a time Shū-san spoke up.

"Well, everybody, let's go on and do it!"

"Yeah, let's do!" shouted someone.

"Sure, it's all right!" shouted another, and there were more cries of approval from the rest. Then the people who had been lying down got up, and the ones who had been talking grew silent.

Shū-san wrote numbers on twenty or thirty strips of paper and rolled each of them up tightly.

"What's all this?" I asked Masao-san, who was standing by me.

"It's a lottery," he replied. "One of the tickets is left out, and the number above the number on that one gets first prize. The number below gets second prize. One chance costs a *yen*."

"There are thirty chances in all," announced Shū-san. "The big prize is twenty *yen*, and the little one is ten."

The crowd made sounds of approval and gathered in a semicircle around him. I wormed my way in and shouted, "I want to buy one!"

I have never said anything to anyone that broke the ice as quickly as those magic words did. Every face looked at me with a mixture of surprise and relief.

The trusty Shū-san was too startled at first to do more than drawl "Oh?" But he quickly regained himself and said, "So the professor's going to buy a chance too, eh! Well, if that's the case, there wasn't any reason to fool around. There we were lying down and getting up and getting up and lying down like a bunch of fools waiting for him to go home." And then to me: "Are you really going to buy one, sir?"

"I sure am. I'm going to buy three."

So that was why they had all been lying around doing nothing for so long. I could hardly keep from laughing.

I bought my chances, and we all laughed and talked while we waited for the number to be read. For the shrine congregation, this

lottery was in a way a divination ritual designed to reveal whom the
gods smiled on. It was repeated several times, but as time went on,
the players wearied of the low stakes and raised the price of chances
to two *yen* and then to five. Still the game was a little too monoto-
nous to keep them amused long. Or perhaps I should say they were
still looking forward to a couple of more interesting ways of determining whom the gods favored.

At length Shū-san said, "This is no fun! Let's go to that house
over yonder and play cards." Then he added, "I wonder if the professor plays cards too."

"Sure," I answered.

"Do you really know how?"

"Of course I do."

But the card game was not destined to be the real battle-
ground. After we had played for a while, someone said, "This
game's too slow— let's get some dice. Hey Shū! Go look for some
dice!"

"If it's dice you want," answered Shū-san, "I've got 'em right
here. You don't suppose the professor would like to play 'single,'
do you?"

"Single," as the name implies, is played with one die, and instead of getting double his money, as is usual, the winner takes five
times what he put in. I had never played "single," but I had
played roulette in France, and I wasn't afraid of this.

"I'd like to play, all right," I answered, "but what if the police come?"

"What do you mean, the police! The police wouldn't come
nosing around here. This is a religious festival, and we're just finding out who the gods like. Why, there's nothing wrong with this—
our grandfathers, and our great-grandfathers, and our great-great-
grandfathers all did it. We don't have much of a chance to have
fun around here, you know, and even the village mayor himself
wouldn't stop us."

As the game turned out, I was lucky. After watching me win
for a time, Shū-san exclaimed "Say, what's going on here? This
professor must be a professor of dice throwing. Why he's better
than I am, and I thought he was only a stuffy old egg, like a school-

teacher. We sure were dumb to worry about him—he's just like one of us, aren't you, Professor?"

Participating in the dice game, which was of course forbidden by law, had the effect of making me a full-fledged member of the hamlet.

*   *   *

One family in the hamlet has been ostracized. That means that no one else in the neighborhood will speak either to the master of that house, whose name is Tetsu-san, or to his wife, Aki-chan. Their children are allowed to play with the others, and when candy or cookies are passed around, they are given some. But no one will have anything to do with the parents, let alone call on them.

Why did this situation arise? Well, Tetsu-san's land borders on that of the shrine, and near the boundary there was once a large oak tree. Some time ago, when a new middle school was to be built in the village, the hamlet was called upon to make a contribution, but it happened that times were bad, and when the deadline came, the money had still not been raised. The other hamlets in the village had already put up their shares, and if our hamlet did not do its part, its honor and reputation would be badly stained. In the face of this crisis, an emergency meeting of the hamlet was called, and after the boss and everyone else had wracked their brains for a time, they hit upon the idea of cutting down the trees in the shrine enclosure and selling them. It was generally agreed that when times got better new trees could be bought for the shrine.

The trouble arose when in cutting the trees, the workmen chopped down the oak on the border of Tetsu-san's land. Tetsu-san, incensed, ran to the police and accused the hamlet of stealing his tree. He figured that it was a case of him against all the rest, and that it would do no good to appeal to the boss of the hamlet, who was as much involved as anyone else. By tradition, however, he should have gone to the boss and tried to settle the affair within the hamlet. By going to the police instead, he had not only created discord within the hamlet, but had exposed the discord for all outsiders to see. As a result, even though the money for the contribution was raised, the honor and reputation of the hamlet were seriously damaged, and it was considered that Tetsu-san had violated one of the basic rules of the community.

When the police examined the disputed land, they found that the oak had belonged to the shrine after all. This was reported to a meeting of the hamlet, and everybody agreed that it wouldn't do to associate any more with anyone who had "treated us all like thieves." Tetsu-san was ostracized. But the formal action of the hamlet took a curious turn. This was now, after all, the age of Democracy, and this business of ostracizing people had been widely criticized in the press. Consequently, when it came to dealing with Tetsu-san, the hamlet had to resort to other means. At the meeting, the boss and his two aides got up and said, in substance, "We're not going to have anything more to do with this fellow, and he's in this hamlet, so we guess we'll have to leave the hamlet. Anybody else who didn't like being called a robber by Tetsu-san ought to do like we're doing."

Everybody in the hamlet except Tetsu-san resigned from the association, so that instead of being cast out, he was the only one left in. The effect was of course exactly the same.

Tetsu-san afterward said ruefully to me, "I thought the laws of the nation were stronger than the laws of the hamlet, but now that I've gone to the police, I've found out better."

On the other hand, Sanzō-san, the assistant boss, said, "The country can have all the laws it wants, but the hamlet has its laws, too, and it's had them since our ancestors were around. If you live in the hamlet, you've got to obey the laws of the hamlet or get kicked out."

In other words, a person may be a human being, and he may be a Japanese, but above all he is a member of the hamlet.

*　　*　　*

After living in the hamlet for a time, I realized that it thinks and feels differently from the State about crime. The actions that are punished by ostracism are invariably actions that damage the hamlet itself. As a rule, of course, most crimes against national law are also held to be criminal by the law of the hamlet, and the hamlet assists the police in prosecuting them. But if a violation of the national law does not happen to cause any harm to the hamlet, the hamlet is little concerned with it. For instance, blackmarketing, gambling, hunting out of season, and tampering with the election process are all illegal, but the hamlet makes no attempt to stop them. These are all things that either have existed for centuries or are recognized as means of bringing money into the hamlet, and the hamlet will not cooperate with the police in their efforts to stop them. Indeed, when a person guilty of one of these crimes is caught by the police, everybody from the mayor of the village on down attempts to secure his release as soon as possible, and when he returns to the hamlet, he is still regarded just as highly as before. The society of the hamlet simply does not classify such actions as criminal.

Relations
with Neighbors

In a society that places heavy emphasis on group solidarity, relations with
one's neighbors are crucial to one's comfort. Up until the twentieth century Japanese society was relatively stable and most people lived as their
parents had lived in the same location their families had occupied for
generations. The rules of social etiquette were well understood by everyone. With an increasingly urban and more mobile society, however, the
Japanese, like people in modern industrialized societies throughout the
world, have become more transient. Many live far from their families, often in apartment houses next to neighbors who have no connection to
them other than the proximity of their dwellings. To assist the Japanese in
working out new relations, countless etiquette books are being written
and sold to people who want to live in harmony with their neighbors. The
following excerpts are taken from an etiquette book entitled *Zoku zoku
kankon sōsai nyūmon* [Twice revised and enlarged version of Introduction
to Various Social Occasions] by Yaeko Shiotsuki.

**When you plan to be away from home for a long time,
leave a neighbor an address where you can be reached.**

Let us discuss relations with neighbors. These days we never
even hear phrases such as "my immediate neighbors"; yet harmonious relations with our neighbors are vital. There is a saying, "It's
better to rely on unrelated neighbors than on far-off relatives," for
in a pinch it is the neighbors who come promptly to your aid. As
long as the bounds of privacy are not overstepped, we should meet

From Yaeko Shiotsuki, *Zoku zoku kankon sōsai nyūmon* (Tokyo: Kōbunsha,
1971), pp. 67–68, 70, 76–80, 144–148, 150–151, 153. Translated for this book by
Hiroko Kataoka and John Grossberg.

our obligations to our neighbors, cooperate with them, and maintain friendly ties with them.

When asking a neighbor to look after your house while you're out, be sure to tell him the hour you will return. For instance, you might say, "I'm going to the P.T.A. meeting; I'll be back by four." When you're going on a trip for a number of days, leave an address where you can be reached. On your return, in addition to thanking the neighbor, leave a gift.

When leaving your children with a neighbor, leave snacks for their children, too.

We occasionally hear the tragic news of a small child being burned to death because the mother went out and left the child locked in the house. It is certainly helpful to have neighbors with whom we can leave our children and whose children, in turn, we would look after as needed. When leaving children with a neighbor, tell the neighbor when you will return. And if the neighbor has children, leave snacks for both your children and the neighbor's.

People who look after the children of others should make sure that the children don't injure themselves. And when serving meals and snacks don't differentiate between your own children and the neighbor's children—treat them all equally. But if the neighbor's children should do something wrong, don't hesitate to scold them. It is an adult's responsibility to scold children when they do wrong regardless of whose children they are. Mothers whose children have been reprimanded should be prepared to thank their neighbor.

Working couples should contribute their financial share to neighborhood functions.

Our community life is based on the premise that the wife is in the home. Therefore, families in which both husband and wife leave the house to work tend to inconvenience their neighbors in such matters as cleaning, disposing of garbage, and taking care of visitors, bill collectors, store deliveries, or children (as previously discussed). Couples who habitually inconvenience their neighbors in these matters should show their gratitude and compensate them adequately for their services. Arranging to pay bills through your bank and offering to pick up small packages and registered mail at the post office are positive ways of avoiding inconvenience to neighbors. Be sure to excuse yourself from neighborhood duties by giving monetary compensation or sending sweets to those who do the work.

When a death occurs, offer your help to the person in charge.

When there is a death in the neighborhood, you should rush to offer your condolences provided you are on intimate terms with the bereaved. If the bereaved family is short-handed, offer assistance.

One woman on hearing of a death in the neighborhood offered her assistance to a member of the bereaved family but was refused. Some time later she heard that the family had said of her, "Although we've assisted her so often in the past, she didn't even come to help!" This shows that in offering assistance you must be sure to speak with the chief mourner or the person in charge. Otherwise, your good intentions and sincerity are likely to go unappreciated.

When the bereaved live in an apartment you can be of great help by lending extra cushions, tea utensils, and ashtrays or by offering to look after the young children.

The cost of donations should be borne by the neighborhood association and paid for from membership fees.

When requested to sign something or make a donation, read the statement carefully and ask questions on points which are not clear. If you are not satisfied, refuse the request. "I would like to discuss this with my husband before I make a decision" is a good way of avoiding a request without giving offense.

A certain woman had to care for a sick person and was thus unable to help shovel snow from the neighborhood roads. From then on, I understand that others in the neighborhood treated her coldly. It is unreasonable to compel every family to perform neighborhood duties. Cooperative functions and shared events should be treated as concerns of the neighborhood association, not as whispered transactions among individuals.

When you're bothered by neighbors' noise, first bring it to their attention. Then, if they continue to disturb you, bring it to the attention of the police.

Playing the piano, the violin, or the electric guitar early in the morning or late at night will disturb your neighbors. Even during the day, shut all windows while practicing any musical instrument. When practicing intensively before an audition or concert, have the courtesy to rent a practice room outside the neighborhood. One should also be careful not to play radios, televisions, or stereos loudly.

When bothered by noisy neighbors, call it to their attention politely. Say such things as "We have a baby sleeping" or "We've someone convalescing." If they still ignore you, call it to the attention of the police department's office of household consultation.

When bothered by factory noise, check to see if the industry involved is legally permitted to operate in your district. If it is in violation, appeal to the authorities.

When you find it hard to respond to a neighbor, shift the responsibility to your husband.

Troublesome matters often arise in dealings with neighbors. You may be asked to lend money or belongings, or be pestered for contributions or a signature. If you are prepared to do so, you may lend small amounts of money or such things as personal possessions, sugar, and soy sauce. If you are satisfied with the request and genuinely desire to offer support, you may lend your signature or agree to make a contribution. If you wish to turn down a request or find yourself in a difficult position, however, you can get out of a pinch by saying "I'll have to talk this over with my husband." By shifting responsibility to your husband you avoid giving offense. Even when trouble arises you may use your husband as an excuse: "You are absolutely right, but my husband is so insistent that he would never allow me to comply."

Give your neighbors notice if you plan to move.

We tend to forget to inform neighbors of an intended move. A few days prior to moving you should visit your neighbors and inform them of the moving date and apologize for any disturbance the moving might cause.

After clearing out your belongings give the inside and outside of your former house a good cleaning. There is an expression: "It is a foul bird that defiles its own nest." I have rented houses all my life and changed my residence a number of times. Whenever I move out of a rented house, I return it to the owner in perfect shape.

When about to leave, visit the neighbors and express your thanks to them, wish them well, and invite them to drop by should they ever be in your new neighborhood.

Give notice of your intentions to move into a neighborhood.

It is customary to offer noodles to the three neighbors opposite and the two on either side of one's new home. These days people often give their neighbors envelopes with three noodle coupons enclosed. This can be easily arranged with the neighborhood noodle dealer. Instead of noodles, some people give their neighbors postcards or matches; tea makes a good gift too. Whatever you choose, be sure to keep the gift small so that you do not embarrass the recipient.

You should introduce yourself to the neighbors on the day you move in or, at the latest, by noon of the following day. Rather than waiting, it is much better to introduce yourself and greet your neighbors before moving into the neighborhood.

It is good for the entire family to go greet the neighbors.

Formerly one greeted the three new neighbors opposite and those on either side. In apartment dwellings, however, one visits all the occupants sharing the same stairwell, and depending on the construction one may also want to visit the neighbors on the other side of the building. Those with young children might find it wise to introduce themselves to more families, as children tend to have a wide sphere of activity.

A good time to call neighbors is around seven or eight in the evening during the family relaxation period following dinner. If there are children in your family, it is ideal for the entire family—husband, wife, and children—to call on the neighbors. If the neighboring families also have children, ask to be introduced to them. Once the members of a family introduced themselves to me and left the husband's calling card on which were included the names of his wife and children. I was deeply touched.

If you have mischievous pets, apologize to your neighbors beforehand.

One often hears of mischievous cats and dogs which snatch a shoe from a neighbor's yard or steal fish from a neighbor's kitchen. People judge such pets according to their likes and dislikes. Some are oblivious even to mischievous dogs and cats; others grow frightened at just the sight of them. Since some people throw stones at troublesome dogs or cats, owners of pets which roam freely about the neighborhood should apologize for them ahead of time.

If you own a dog which habitually causes trouble in the neighborhood, visit the neighbors at regular intervals with a small gift. Strictly speaking, it is forbidden to allow dogs to roam at large.

In apartments and crowded housing complexes, flush the toilet sparingly late at night.

An acquaintance of mine who moved into an apartment in the center of Tokyo suffered a neurosis and subsequent insomnia because of the noise caused by toilet flushing; it was so bad she had to move back to the countryside. The violent sound of toilet flushing is especially bothersome to women. It may not bother us once we get used to it, but the case of my acquaintance was extreme. Her neighbor, a bar hostess, would inevitably flush the toilet two or three times late at night. That flushing sound, reverberating at my acquaintance's bedside, made it impossible for her to sleep. One can't place a late-night ban on bodily functioning, of course, but think of the neighbors late at night and have the courtesy to leave the toilet unflushed after use.

When loud construction noises continue late into the night, make apologies to the neighbors ahead of time.

When remodeling or adding onto your house, let your neighbors know ahead of time as a matter of course. You should tell the neighbors not only that there will be construction but also its purpose, extent, and duration. When adding an extra story onto a one-story house, the neighbor's right to sunshine may be compromised and that can cause trouble. It is absolutely necessary in such cases to let the neighbors know ahead of time.

Even when only minor remodeling is involved, loud noises from the construction may last well into the night. If you apologize and request the neighbor's patience ahead of time and leave a box of sweets, strained feelings may be averted. Once trouble and unpleasantness have been created, offering a box of sweets will hardly compensate.

To repair a strained relationship with neighbors, take advantage of a joyous event in your neighbor's household.

Neighbors who may have been closer than relatives often become upset over some trivial matter and break off their relationship. As time passes and things calm down, one may regret having quarreled but find no good opportunity to seek a reconciliation. A good time to restore a strained relationship would be any joyous event in your neighbor's household—as when their child is admitted into a school, or passes an entrance examination, or is married.

If, while you are still on bad terms, there is a death in the neighbor's family, do no more than make an appearance and offer incense at the funeral. Trying to make use of such an occasion to gain a reconciliation will only lead to misunderstandings: your neighbors may think you are rejoicing in their sorrow. Restoring such a relationship takes time and should be postponed till later.

When pressed to vote for a certain candidate, say that you are undecided.

At election time one is beseeched to vote for a particular candidate by those to whom one is indebted. For the sake of friendship one says to Mr. A, "Fine, I'll vote for him," and to Mr. B, "Fine, I'll vote for him." In so doing one's integrity is compromised, and one may lose the trust of others. When pressed to vote a certain way, gently push the request aside by saying that you'll give it full consideration but are still undecided. In the event that you meet the person after the election, tell him you voted as he requested. But don't let this behavior lead to the point where you really are undecided and consequently don't vote.

If you have a daughter of marriageable age, pay a courtesy visit to your neighbors.

These days on the occasion of employment and marriage people often hire private investigators or detective agencies to look into the personal history of the prospect. Personally, I do not like this practice. I want nothing to do with those who can't trust a person without sneaking around the neighborhood to ask questions. Since it involves not only one's self, however, but also the future happiness of one's son or daughter, one must on occasion put up with it.

To prevent false critical reports by investigatory agencies, those who have daughters of marriageable age should pay a courtesy visit to the neighbors. One may even find that this countermeasure to private investigations will be good public relations for your daughter and lead to a fine marriage proposal.

When no one is at home, hang up a sign: "Please go to our neighbors the So-and-so's."

It is not very pleasant to hear a visitor standing in front of your neighbor's house calling out the neighbor's name in a loud voice over and over. A neighbor, unless given prior notification, has no way of knowing whether or not you really are absent from home and thus can't take effective action.

When the entire family goes out, ask your next door neighbor to look after the house. So that visitors don't yell out loud in the streets, place a sign at the entrance to the house. Since a sign might attract the attention of a robber, write "I'm at my next door neighbor's; please inquire there." When planning to be away from home for a long period of time, ask for your neighbor's cooperation.

Don't give a present to neighbors each time they do a favor.

When we need someone to look after the house in our absence, or supply us with extra cushions, or watch after our children in an emergency, we often turn to our neighbors.

These days there are young people who, wishing to avoid any feeling of obligation, pay back their neighbors each time they are rendered a service. I do not admire relations among neighbors based on such calculated acts as returning a favor right away to avoid feeling indebted. I think it far better to show one's respect and heartfelt gratitude by offering truly significant gifts—seasonal, home-made delicacies such as rice cake dumplings covered with bean paste for example—or by sharing some unusual item one has received.

The Talisman

"The Talisman" is a short story written by Masao Yamakawa (1930–1965) in 1963. It depicts a typical middle-class man who lives in a large modern complex in which each apartment is identical to the others. The story illustrates his feeling of lost identity: his life, like his apartment, is indistinguishable from that of his neighbors. He attempts to assert his individuality in a very unusual way, but even then he finds that he is not unique.

"I don't suppose you need any dynamite?"

This was the question my friend Sekiguchi asked me. I had not seen him in four or five years. We had run into each other on the Ginza, and were drinking in an upstairs room of a small restaurant.

I had been with Sekiguchi through high school. He was now working for a construction company. It was not strange that he should have access to dynamite; but the question, however peculiar an old friend he might be, was a little sudden.

"I don't know what I'd use it for."

"I have it right here if you want it."

It would be a joke, of course. I smiled and poured a new drink for him. "It would blow up right in my hands. And what is the point in carrying dynamite around with you?"

This was the story Sekiguchi told me.

Masao Yamakawa, "The Talisman," reprinted from *Life,* 11 September 1964, pp. 94–97.

*   *   *

My wife and I live alone in an apartment house. I put my name on the list two years ago, and got married last spring, before I had a decent place to live. And then last fall I got one of the apartments. I couldn't have been happier.

Everything seemed new and fresh—the grass that hadn't taken to the ground, the beanpoles of cherry trees. Before that we had been with my family, a big family at that. We had had only one room, and we wanted a place where we could lock other people out. Well, now we had a room with a lock. You can imagine what it meant to us.

We had it, a place of our own. But I had not been there six months before I began feeling uncertain and irritated. I felt somehow that I was disappearing. No one's fault—call it some sort of neurosis. I can't say it was his fault either, I suppose. But I can say that Kurose made things start going this way for me.

It was late one night. I had been to a party. There were no more buses, and I took a taxi and got off at the main gate. I hoped that by the time I got to my wing of the building the night wind might sober me up.

There was a man in front of me. I had the feeling that I was looking at myself from behind. He had on the same felt hat, and he had the same package in his left hand. You could tell by his walk that he had been drinking too. It was a foggy night, and I wondered if I might be seeing my own shadow.

But it was no shadow. He walked on, the image of me, I thought—and he went into Wing E, where I lived. He went up the stairs I always go up.

It was a big complex, I grant that; but I knew at least the people who went up and down the stairs I used. And I did not know him. He went up as if they were the stairs he knew best in the world. He came to the third floor and knocked on the door to the right.

It was my apartment. And then I was even more startled. The door opened and he was taken in, like any tired husband home from work.

I thought my wife must have a lover. That was it. I climbed the stairs quietly. I would catch them in the act. I put my ear to the door.

The way I felt—how can I describe it to you? I was wrong. He was not her lover. He was I myself.

No, wait. I'm not crazy. But I thought I was. I could hear her saying "Jirō, Jirō," and laughing and telling me what my sister had said when she had come calling that day. And I could hear my own tired voice in between. She was off in the kitchen getting something to eat, and "I" seemed to be reading the newspaper. I did not know what to think. There was another "I," that was clear. And who, then, was this I, standing foolishly in the hall? Which was "I" and which was I? Where should I go?

I had thought that I was sober, but I'm afraid I was still drunk. The confidence that I was I had left me. It did not occur to me that the man in the room was a false "I," a mistake. I opened the door only because I could think of nothing else to do with the I that was myself.

"Who's there?" she said.

"I," I finally answered.

It was quite a scene. My wife came screaming out. She looked at the other "I," and screamed again, and threw herself on me. Her lips were moving and she began to cry. The other "I" came out. His face was white.

His name was Kurose Jirō.

*   *   *

Sekiguchi fell silent, a thoughtful expression on his face. He poured himself a cup of *sake*.

"Another you," I laughed. "A fine *Doppelgänger*."

He glanced up at me, but seemed to pay no attention to my words. Unsmiling, he went on with his story.

*   *   *

Kurose was all apologies. When he handed me his name card I saw what the mistake had been. I lived in E-305, he in D-305. He had come into the wrong wing and gone up to my apartment.

My sister is named Kuniko. He was a civil engineer, and he had a cousin named Kuniko. His name was Jirō, so is mine. He lived alone with his wife. The coincidence was complete.

"I did think she seemed a little young. I've been married four years, after all," he said as he left. He said it as if he meant to flatter, but I was not up to being pleased. It weighed on my mind, the fact that until I opened the door neither of them had noticed the mistake.

"But I went off to the kitchen, and he sprawled out with the newspaper the way you always do. It didn't even occur to me that it wouldn't be you."

I reprimanded her, and she looked timidly around the room.

"Not just the room. They must be exactly like us themselves. You saw how he thought I was his wife. It scares me."

I was about to speak, but I did not. To mistake a person or a room—that made no difference. It happened all the time. What bothered me was that Kurose had mistaken our life for his own.

Kurose had been mistaken for me by my own wife. And were they as alike as all that? These apartment-house homecomings?

I knew of course that all the apartments were the same. But I asked myself: had our very ways of life become standardized?

You know what apartment-house life is like. It does have a terrible uniformity about it. The qualifications for getting in, and the need to get in—they mean that the standard of living is all on the same general level. All of us are even about the same age. But it seemed to me that the uniformity had gone beyond externals. It had gone to the very heart of things.

Take for instance when I have a quarrel with my wife. The wind always brings the same kind of quarrel in through the window from another apartment. It all seems so foolish that we stop fighting. So far so good; but then you come to realize that the people in the other apartments have their quarrels on this and this day of the month at this and this time of the day, and you are no exception yourself; and—this may seem a strange way to put it—the sacredness of quarreling disappears. A quarrel comes to be no more than a periodic outburst of hysteria. Think about it. It's not very exciting.

You go to the toilet, and over your head you hear someone pulling the chain and the toilet upstairs flushes. The same thing day after day. I hadn't paid too much attention, but it began to weigh on me.

I began to wonder whether identical surroundings and identical routines were bringing us to identical emotions and identical outlets for them. And if so we were like all those toy soldiers lined up on a department-store counter. Like standardized puppets.

Where was there something that was mine? No one else's but mine? In this mass of people who so resembled one another, I was no more than one bean spread out to dry with the rest. I could not even identify myself among them all.

My wife said something that did not help matters. We were in bed.

"It's very strange. I go off to the toilet, and I hear water running up above and down below. We all do exactly the same thing."

I pulled away from her. We men of the apartment house proceeded every night, as if upon a signal, to go through the same motions.

And so I began to lose interest in them too. Each time my wife would whisper something to me, it would seem to me as if all through the building wives were whispering. I would hear a gale of whispers in the darkness and I would find myself frowning.

We may think we have something of our own. But we only have standardized days with standardized reactions.

It seemed intolerable. I was not a puppet!

Could I put much importance on my life when I could no longer be sure that I was myself and no one else? Could I love my wife? Believe I was loved by her?

*   *   *

I started to laugh, but did not. Sekiguchi was gazing earnestly at me.

Presently a faint smile came over his face.

He had always been a man, I remembered, who placed a high value on a smile.

"It's a very serious story," he said.

*   *   *

Kurose became for me the representative of all those number-less white-collar workers, all the apartment-house husbands, the toy soldiers, exactly like myself. The representative of all those numberless people who were "I."

You will have guessed that after that foggy night I did not want to speak to the man. We were too much alike, and it would seem that, as he clutched his briefcase to his chest, he was avoiding me too. He always seemed to be scurrying off.

He had become a scapegoat for all those standardized toy sol-diers—I hated them through him. I rejected all those standardized articles that were "I."

I resented him. He was not I. I was not one of them, those of-fice workers so much like myself. I was *I*, I was most definitely not he. But where was the difference? Where was there positive evi-dence to establish the difference?

I was not a random spot. I was I, a particular person with the name Sekiguchi Jirō, someone not to be substituted for another, whoever he might be. So I said over and over to myself.

And yet where were the grounds for distinguishing me from them? Was there more than my name? A name is only a tag. Aside from my name, where was the evidence that I was not a random apartment-house dweller?

I had to build it—my independence, my individuality. I had to find something to distinguish me from those numberless ones who were Kurose Jirō.

A couple of weeks ago I found it. A charm. I've kept it secret from my wife. The problem is my own private one.

This is my charm.

*   *   *

Sekiguchi opened the heavy leather briefcase behind him and took out a bundle just small enough to hold in one hand. It was elaborately tied up in oil paper.

"Dynamite. The real thing."

With great dexterity he undid the knots, and for the first time in my life I saw dynamite, the real thing. There were four iron tubes perhaps eight inches long, bound tightly in wire, heavy for their size.

"This is my charm—my talisman," said Sekiguchi. "We talk and talk, but we can't get away from the uniformity. But when I am of a mind to I can blow all of them up and myself too. This is what I came on. The secret that keeps me going. My uniqueness."

I handed the tubes back, and Sekiguchi turned a caressing gaze on their dark luster.

"I don't think I need any dynamite, thank you."

"Oh? That's too bad. I don't need it any more myself. I'm going to have to hunt up another charm."

"I don't know whether you're being funny or not, but it's dangerous. . . ."

Sekiguchi raised a hand to silence me. "Make no mistake," he laughed. "You're a very lucky person. I don't need it any more, because it's not my uniqueness any more." He paused. "Did you hear the news on the radio this evening?"

"No."

He smiled a wry smile. "There was a dynamite explosion on a bus. Three people were killed on the spot. The others got by with cuts and burns. It was near my apartment house."

"How did it happen?" I felt the effects of the *sake* leave me.

Sekiguchi did not look at me. Slowly and deliberately he put the bundle away.

"He always did carry his briefcase around like the most important thing in his life. And he avoided me. He must have resented me as much as I resented him. He needed a charm too."

"Oh?"

Sekiguchi stretched out on the matting. His voice rose in a sort of lament. "They said it over the radio. The police think the dynamite was in a briefcase of one of the three people killed. An engineer named Kurose Jirō."

The Thirty-Fifth
Anniversary

"The Thirty-Fifth Anniversary" is from a collection of humorous short stories by Keita Genji which were serialized in the weekly magazine *Sandē Mainichi* from 1951 to 1952. Keita Genji is the pen name of Tomio Tanaka (b. 1912), a former employee of the Sumitomo Company who won his first prize in popular literature in 1930. His stories and novels depict the life of the middle class company man in Japan. The story translated here illustrates the way in which a company director promotes company morale and employee loyalty. He not only heads the company but also performs the honorary function of matchmaker for many of those who work for him. The vertical structure of human relationships within the company, typical of this level of society, is evident here. The writer is intentionally satirical.

The Nankai Corporation is a prestigious company with a first-rate reputation in a provincial city. In theory, therefore, the president of the company should be a prominent man of some renown. In fact, Mr. Kuwabara, the present head of the company, is a different sort of person from what one might expect. He used to be a director of the third rank, so to speak, before he was promoted to the presidency upon the forced resignation of Mr. Nara, the former president, during the purge of big corporations carried on under the Allied Occupation. In short, Mr. Kuwabara was a lucky man who unexpectedly became president under unusual circumstances. For

From Keita Genji, *Santō jūyaku* [Third-class executive] (Tokyo: Shinchōsha, 1961), pp. 620–639. Translated for this book by Michiko Y. Aoki.

a while after his appointment to the presidency Mr. Kuwabara felt uneasy whenever he sat in the president's chair too long. At such times, he had to remind himself that he was a president.

But that was a long time ago. Mr. Kuwabara has worked hard to carry out his responsibilities as company president and has convinced himself that he is now as capable a man as any of his predecessors. He could now sit in the president's chair for the rest of his life without feeling uncomfortable.

One day Mr. Kuwabara was sitting comfortably in the president's chair deep in thought. He was mulling over what Mr. Urashima, the chief of the personnel section, had said to him a while before. Mr. Urashima had said, "Mr. President, this coming April thirteenth is the thirty-fifth anniversary of this company. Everybody is expecting a bonus envelope in honor of the occasion. I beg you, Mr. President, to take a hint from what I have just said and act accordingly."

The president's office was quiet. If he were to take one step out of the room, however, he would see his two hundred or so subordinates all working earnestly for the good of the company. Mr. Kuwabara was stirred by this thought. He looked up at the portraits of the former presidents on the wall in front of him. Only one of them, Mr. Nara, was still living.

"Thirty-five years—Hmm—"

Those years had not been uneventful. It had been a stormy period and the company had suffered through a series of crises before it had reached its present prosperity. It was Mr. Kuwabara's ambition to make his company leap one more step forward, and for that he had to do something to enhance the esprit de corps of his employees.

"Ah, I have it!" he cried. Soon afterward Mr. Kuwabara summoned the five company directors who were all expected to fly to his bidding. They, too, were called directors of the third rank because, like the president, they had been promoted to directorship after capable directors had been purged for one reason or another. All the directors, looking anxious, appeared before the president. Mr. Kuwabara took the chair and opened the meeting by saying

that the company would soon have its thirty-fifth anniversary and
that the chief of personnel suggested that a bonus be given in
honor of the occasion.

"I would like to know what you think about it."

The five directors looked at each other for a while. One of
them, Mr. Hayakawa, took the lead.

"What do you think, Mr. President?"

"I, of course, think it is a good idea," said Mr. Kuwabara.

"Then we agree with you. It's a great idea, sir!" That means
we too will receive big bonuses, the five directors told themselves
happily. Mr Kuwabara looked at them ruefully. My goodness, they
haven't changed a bit. They still think like ordinary employees.

"Furthermore," Mr. Kuwabara continued, "I'm thinking
about something to commemorate the company's thirty-five years
of prosperity. What do you think about that, gentlemen?"

"Well, Mr. President, what do you think?" asked Director
Matsuda.

"I want *your* reaction to my idea. What do *you* think?"

The five directors whispered to one another. This time Mr.
Yamano spoke for the directors.

"We are generally in agreement that we will support you in
whatever you decide. So please do whatever you think best."

"Well, then," Mr. Kuwabara cleared his throat, "I will tell
you my idea. Please listen carefully. First of all, the current prosperity of the Nankai Corporation is the result of the accumulated efforts of former presidents, directors, and regular employees. Therefore, I would like to conduct a memorial service for all the deceased
members of this company."

"That's a good idea, sir."

"Secondly, we shouldn't forget our debt of gratitude to our
customers. I would like to give each of them a token gift. As for the
retired directors, I would like to send gifts to them if their whereabouts are known to us."

"Hear, hear! We are all in agreement with you, Mr. President."

"Well, yes, you should be."

Mr. Kuwabara was satisfied and continued. "Third, the day of the anniversary fortunately falls on a holiday. Therefore, I would like to have a recreation day, a sort of picnic for employees and their families. I'm afraid it's going to be expensive, but fortunately we have made a substantial profit this year—more than we anticipated. Our financial situation is sound. So we can do it. I'll tell you why I am considering doing something for the employees. Upon careful consideration of their conduct, I reached the conclusion that they are exemplary by any standard. Our employees are capable, gentle, and sincere. Although they are unionized, they never go on strike. We should congratulate ourselves on that. That is why I am inspired to do something nice for them. I am convinced that we must reward the sincerity and earnestness of our employees. What do you gentlemen think of my idea?"

"Mr. President, it's a great idea! To tell the truth, we have been thinking the same thing that you have," said the five directors each in turn.

"Hmm, is that so?" said Mr. Kuwabara.

"Yes, indeed, sir. It certainly is," said the directors.

"Well, that's almost hard to believe, but it doesn't matter. Now I am going to instruct the personnel chief to take charge of the commemorative gathering."

"Mr. President, please do so," said the directors.

"Well, I will entrust the whole matter to Mr. Urashima, the personnel chief. Ah, yes, there is one more thing. It is not directly related to the thirty-fifth anniversary, but I have been thinking about promoting Urashima to the position of department chief. He is quite a capable man as you know. You might say that he is my right hand and I need him—a very trustworthy fellow."

"Mr. President, we agree with you one hundred percent."

The matter of promoting Mr. Urashima, too, passed unanimously.

Beginning on the next day Mr. Urashima, the personnel section chief, was remarkably busy. All the employees welcomed the good news about the bonus and the commemorative picnic. Each section selected two delegates for a committee to prepare for the coming events. The committee met nearly every day to exchange the various messages and wishes of its members.

"Don't skimp on the budget, Mr. Urashima. Make it a lavish, relaxed, and carefree occasion."

"We want a concert half an hour long. An hour-long concert, of course, would be even better."

"As for the bonus, we male employees want to receive it without our wives' knowledge. We want to stash it away as petty cash. You understand that, don't you, chief? If that's not possible, please arrange it with the treasurer so we can receive our bonuses in two different envelopes—one for an overt bonus and the other for a covert bonus. That is an absolute *must*, Mr. Urashima."

"We would like to put on a play, a very romantic and passionate one. Would that be all right, Mr. Urashima?"

Mr. Urashima was busy handling such requests while at the same time making the arrangements for the anniversary. He just kept smiling and saying, "Leave it to me. Leave it to me."

As the atmosphere of the company became increasingly lively, the efficiency of the personnel increased, and so did productivity. No one complained even when asked to work overtime.

The wives of the company employees, too, were getting excited as Commemoration Day approached. The Magnolia Beauty Parlor was filled with the wives of Nankai Corporation employees. (The Magnolia was run by the daughter of Mr. Nara, former president of Nankai. When Mr. Nara had a stroke and needed money, Mr. Kuwabara had been instrumental in setting up the beauty parlor, and since then it had been company policy to encourage the wives of employees to patronize the Magnolia.)

Cigarette cases and shopping bags with the Nankai emblem were made ready to give to customers as token gifts. The gifts had been chosen with both the customers and their wives in mind.

Three days before Commemoration Day, Mr. Kuwabara summoned Mr. Urashima for an interim report.

"Mr. President, I can assure you that the plan will be a success. All the employees are saying they are so touched by your intentions that they will work harder for the company."

"Good, Urashima. That's exactly what I had in mind. It's very satisfying to learn that they understand how much I care about them."

"It all comes from your good guidance and leadership, sir," said Mr. Urashima.

"Well, I'm flattered, Urashima." Mr. Kuwabara's tone changed. "By the way, I'm thinking about paying a visit to Mr. Nara, my predecessor. Do you think you can go with me to-morrow?"

"Yes, Mr. President, I can go with you."

"Well, then, be sure to bring along some gifts for Mr. Nara."

"By all means, sir."

The following day the two men drove to the Naras'. Mr. Nara had been bedridden since his stroke, but he had been recovering rapidly. He was now able to walk a little and his speech was almost normal.

Mr. Kuwabara recalled his younger days when Mr. Nara was a vigorous and capable company president of the Nankai Corporation. The young employees had nicknamed him "Thunderstorm" and were very much afraid of him. Mr. Kuwabara, too, had been in awe of him. When Mr. Nara picked him as his successor, Mr. Kuwabara made every effort to follow Mr. Nara's example. He could not change his character, of course, but at least in outward appearance he could be like him. . . .

The limousine ground to a stop on the gravel in front of the Naras'. Mr. Nara was delighted to see Mr. Kuwabara and Mr. Urashima.

"Oh, hello, hello, welcome! I'm glad you came."

A thousand things crossed Mr. Nara's mind. Then he remembered the purpose of Mr. Kuwabara's visit.

"The thirty-fifth anniversary. I didn't realize that it's been so long."

Mr. Kuwabara told Mr. Nara about the accomplishments of the Nankai Corporation, adding that his company was planning to celebrate its anniversary.

"That's a splendid idea, Mr. Kuwabara. Very good, very good."

Mr. Nara nodded in response to everything Mr. Kuwabara said to show his approval. Then he thought for a while.

"Mr. Kuwabara," he said, "it may seem irrelevant, but I have something to tell you just for your information."

"Yes, sir." Mr. Kuwabara's expression became intense as Mr. Nara continued.

"You've led the company well during difficult times. I've been very impressed by your performance. However, your task from now on may be more challenging than ever. You must be prepared for that. When one is successful, he feels as if he were walking on air. But that's dangerous. The time will come sooner or later when the task of management will be more difficult. The financial situation is already becoming unstable. Recession is under way. We must always keep an eye on the business world. Mr. Kuwabara, I urge you to be cautious."

Mr. Nara's tone was dignified, yet gentle. It was as though a father were giving advice to his son.

"Yes sir," said Mr. Kuwabara and he suddenly bowed to Mr. Nara. "I will keep in mind what you have said."

Mr. Urashima, too, bowed deeply to Mr. Nara.

"Well, you don't have to thank me so profusely. I'm only glad that you understand what I mean. By the way, I have something to ask you, Mr. Kuwabara. I wonder if you would do me a favor?"

"By all means, sir, if there is anything I can do."

"It's about my daughter. You have been so kind as to help her open the beauty parlor. It is doing well, and I cannot thank you enough for that. But there is one more thing that I am concerned about, and that is her marriage. Mr. Kuwabara, do you think you could find a good husband for her?"

"That's right! Miss Yukiko *has* reached marriageable age." Mr. Kuwabara was elated and came close to saying that matchmaking was his specialty and his achievement as a matchmaker was even greater than his success in directing the company, but he managed to restrain himself. He said, "Yes, sir, I will look for a good candidate among my acquaintances. By the way, do you have any specific conditions for the prospective husband?"

"None in particular. I don't care much about the man's social status or wealth. I just want a nice man who will make my only daughter happy. A man of sincerity."

"Well then sir, he must be from the Nankai Corporation."

"That's fine, Mr. Kuwabara. I could not agree with you more."

"Then I assure you I'll find a nice man for Miss Yukiko. She is invited to celebrate Commemoration Day with us. She can look over the young men of our company on her own without attracting attention."

April 13, 1952, was a fine day. The thirty-fifth anniversary of the Nankai Corporation was celebrated first by a memorial service in honor of the deceased members of the company. After the service, everyone was left to enjoy themselves.

The entrance of the company building was decorated with the national flag and the flag of the company. Inside, the building was decked out in multicolored crepe paper. A stage had been set up in the dining hall for the occasion. Small bottles of *sake* and bags of candies were passed around to all those present. All the offices were opened to employees' families and on the roof of the building were booths of sweets. The company facilities were available for everyone to use as they liked.

At eleven o'clock it was announced that Mr. Kuwabara was going to give a speech, and everyone gathered in the dining hall to hear him. Mr. Kuwabara showed up on stage with a large flower in his buttonhole. He was beaming as if this were the best day of his life.

"Ladies and gentlemen, I would like to congratulate all of you and myself as well because today we are gathered here to celebrate the thirty-fifth anniversary of the company. . . ." Mr. Kuwabara went on about his reasons for holding the commemorative celebration, and he added Mr. Nara's warnings about preparing for difficult times ahead. By the end of his speech a few employees were already inebriated and the gathering turned to merriment. The women's chorale group started the entertainment.

A little while after the end of the speech Miss Yukiko, Mr. Nara's daughter, appeared. Miss Seiko, the president's secretary, was to retire on that day to prepare for her coming marriage to Mr.

Wakahara, a colleague of hers in the company. She had been following her fiancé around since morning, not leaving him alone for even a minute, and she would glare at any female employee who tried to tease him about his prospective marriage as it was customary to do.

Mr. Urashima was quite busy running around here and there. He, too, wore a large flower in his buttonhole. From time to time he paused to smile broadly.

His wife, seeing him, said, "My goodness, dear, why on earth are you grinning like that? What's the matter with you? People will think you've taken leave of your senses. Can't you keep a straight face? It's very embarrassing."

"Oh, am I grinning?" Mr. Urashima couldn't keep back another grin.

"There you go again. Good heavens!"

"Well, my dear, I'll tell you why. . . ." Mr. Urashima whispered to his wife.

"How splendid!" Mrs. Urashima exclaimed. "Then you are going to be a department head!"

"Hush, it's not official yet, but the president told me so a while ago."

"Congratulations, my dear."

"Look at you. Now you are grinning!"

"I can't help it. How can I?"

"Well, I don't blame you, dear."

Just then a young man and woman passed the Urashimas. The woman was Miss Yukiko. She was with Mr. Nanno of the department of general affairs.

"Well, I didn't know they were dating," said Mr. Urashima.

"You didn't know!" Mrs. Urashima exclaimed. "I saw them together about a month ago. I thought they were. . . ."

"Hmm. . . ." Mr. Urashima pondered: Mr. Nanno is quiet, a man of deeds not of words. He joined the company three years ago. He is the slow maturing type, but definitely a promising young man.

"Well, if that's the case, it wouldn't be a bad match," murmured Mr. Urashima softly.

* * *

The Commemoration Day program went along with much frivolity. Onstage proud amateurs sang. The refreshment booths were busy. Children ran around in the hallways. Everyone was happy. In the afternoon a Mrs. Murao went to look for Mr. Urashima. She had worked for the company until, after dating him for some time, she married Mr. Murao. Mr. Kuwabara had arranged the match. The Muraos' marriage was Mr. Kuwabara's first achievement as a matchmaker.

"Chief, I'd like to make an urgent request for you to take to the president," Mrs. Murao said.

"What is it?"

"I just realized that all nine couples who married as a result of the president's matchmaking are here today. This is a rare occasion, and so one woman suggested that we all go to see Mr. Kuwabara to thank him for his matchmaking. Everyone agreed."

"Oh, that's a commendable idea, Mrs. Murao."

"Yes, we thought so. We very much want to do it because we owe Mr. Kuwabara a great deal. Without his matchmaking, we would not have become such happily married couples. Incidentally, we also want to thank you, Mr. Urashima."

"Are you just thanking me incidentally?"

"I'm sorry, Mr. Urashima. But you have to be satisfied with that today."

"Oh, well, I guess that's life. I'll accept that and give your message to the president. He will be very much in favor of it, I'm sure."

"Yes, we all thought so. That's why. . . . Well, then, we shall be waiting for him in the conference room."

Mr. Urashima walked into the office of the president's secretaries looking for Mr. Kuwabara. There he found Mr. Nanno and Miss Yukiko sitting together. Mr. Wakahara and Miss Seiko were there too.

"Where is the president? Do you know, Wakahara?" asked Mr. Urashima after greeting Miss Yukiko.

"He is in his office with Mrs. Kuwabara."

Mr. Urashima was just about to knock on the door when he paused to explain to the young people what was to take place in the conference room in the presence of the president.

"I think you'd better join them. Yes, do attend the thank you meeting for the matchmaking. This is a good opportunity for you."

"But we aren't married yet. We aren't qualified to attend, are we?" asked Mr. Wakahara hesitantly.

"That's all right, Wakahara. It is important to let everyone in this company know that you and Seiko are going to be married as a result of the president's matchmaking. It will also save much unnecessary speculation."

"Do you think so?" asked Mr. Wakahara.

"Then we want to be introduced in that way, too, Mr. Urashima," said Yukiko. "Will you let us attend the meeting?"

"Well . . . I see, Miss Yukiko. You have already gone that far, . . ." said Mr. Urashima.

"Yes indeed, already, . . ." said Yukiko, blushing and turning to Mr. Nanno. "Don't you agree with me?" asked Yukiko. "I want to take this opportunity to announce our engagement. Otherwise, I will have to worry about the other girls who might snatch Mr. Nanno away."

"I don't mind at all," said Mr. Nanno looking fondly at Yukiko.

Mr. Urashima delivered all the messages to the president of the Nankai Corporation. Mr. Kuwabara was immensely pleased.

"Well, it's a praiseworthy thing to hear these days. Hmm . . . is Miss Yukiko coming with Nanno? But that's good news. I am satisfied. Mr. Nara will be very happy to hear the news."

When the Kuwabaras walked into the conference room, they were greeted by applause from the nine couples whose marriages Mr. Kuwabara had arranged and from the two prospective couples and others who had learned of the grand "Thank You for the Matchmaking" meeting in time to attend.

Mrs. Murao, the first bride to have been married by Mr. Kuwabara, stepped forward and said, "Mr. President and Mrs. Kuwabara and Mr. Urashima, all of us here who are married because of you want to express our gratitude. We are deeply indebted to you for our marriages or prospective marriages. Those of us who are already married have family fights from time to time, naturally, but that's not so bad because they only make our relationships better afterward and we are happier. The happier we become, the more grateful we are to you, Mr. President, Mrs. Kuwabara, and Mr. Urashima. We thank you very much."

The men in the gathering gave sporadic applause to Mrs. Murao's speech. In contrast to the men, the women were enthusiastic. Mrs. Kuwabara was very happy; she, too, fights with her husband from time to time, only to have her relationship stronger afterward. Mr. Kuwabara looked embarrassed but happy. He seemed pleased by Mrs. Murao's speech. He got up and said, "Thank you, Mrs. Murao, ladies and gentlemen. I'm really happy to know that my matchmaking has been so successful. I feel highly honored. I hope you'll be happily married throughout your lives. I, of course, will continue my good marriage along with you young folks. May our marriages be as successful as the Nankai Corporation's future."

The Commemoration Day program drew to a close. It had indeed been a memorable day. At the end Mr. Kuwabara climbed up on the stage in the dining hall to conclude the occasion. He started by saying, "Ladies and gentlemen, let us return to work tomorrow with this spirit and devote all our efforts to our company's success. Let us now end this unforgettable day with three cheers—Nankai Corporation, *banzai, banzai, banzai!*

The cheers echoed in the dining hall. When the final *banzai* died down, someone in the back of the room cried out, "Third-class executive, *banzai!*"

Incident
at Asama Villa

One snowy day in February 1972 a group of young extremists known as
the Japanese Red Army stormed the Asama *sansō*, a villa in the mountain
resort area of Karuizawa in Nagano prefecture. The group had been hiding out in the region and robbing banks to finance their political activities. When the police discovered their presence, the group shut themselves up in the villa and took the housekeeper as hostage. The skirmish
that followed was broadcast throughout Japan continuously on every television station until the group surrendered. The medium of television
brought a sense of community to the entire nation and individuals responded to the crisis as they often do in smaller community units in Japan: by putting pressure on the families of the extremists. The following
excerpts are taken from daily newspaper accounts of the incident.

28 February 1972
THROW AWAY YOUR ARMS THE PARENTS CRY
"It takes courage to come out."
"Show us you're not heinous criminals."

Police have confirmed that they have completed preparations
to rush the Red Army members under siege in Asama villa and res-
cue the hostage. From the outset of the incident the police have
tried to persuade the radicals to come out of the building voluntarily. On 2 February the parents whose sons are among the criminals
joined the attempt to talk them into surrendering, but the youths
did not answer. The parents persisted, however, and on 27 Febru-

Excerpts from the newspaper *Asahi Shimbun* (Tokyo), 21, 22, 24, 26, 27, 28,
29 February and 3, 5, 14 March 1972. Translated for this book by Hiroko Kataoka.

ary, the day before the planned confrontation, they again admonished and even begged their children to come out. The parents' appeals brought no response from the mountain villa. The villa remained silent as a tomb.

21 and 22 February

The mother of Hiroshi Sakaguchi:
"Think of your life. You've created such a sensation—please, throw away your guns and free Yasuko. . . . If you want a substitute, I will come in. You're surrounded by the police. I only hope you survive.

"It would take real courage to put down your guns and come out. Your family is worried—so worried we haven't slept for nights. Have you ever thought of that? Please, don't lock yourself up in there. Make a fresh start!"

The mother of Masakuni Yoshino:
"Mā-chan, please listen if you're in there. If you'd only connect the telephone, I could say this to you privately. The reason you're doing this . . . I really don't know if you're in there or not, but I think you are. I guess you didn't expect things to turn out this way. I know you haven't lived a decent life. . . . Surely Yasuko is suffering in there. If you don't do something, you're no better than a common criminal. I'm your mother—I want you to live. I think circumstances have made things turn out this way. I know it's hard, but throw away your arms and. . . .

"Listen, we didn't come here because the police told us to come. As a parent I just can't bear to see what you're doing. Things have turned out for the worst and . . . you've had your own way for a long time, haven't you? But you shouldn't break the law. I want you to show us you're not a detestable criminal. As long as you come out, the police won't shoot you. Come out with Yasuko!

"If you keep on this way, you'll be ruined for life. I realize you have your self-respect. I know it's terrible; I know it's hard; but I want you to come out. Please, I beg you, Mā-chan!

"I want to hear how you honestly feel. You've never listened to me, but it's heartbreaking that your honest intentions have been misunderstood. As things stand now, you're far from a martyr. You wanted to sacrifice yourself for the sake of society, right? If you really want to sacrifice yourself, please come out in front of everyone even though they have guns and bullets.

"Please, I beg you to act with decency. . . . I'm almost close enough to see you."

24 February

The mother of Kunio Bandō:

"Trust your mother and come out with Mrs. Muta, please! Let's go home together, all right?

"If you hurt someone, you'll be hurt too. I'll wait here for you all day—even for two days, so please come out! I've never lied to you, have I?

"You've been such a good boy. I've lost all hope for you now that you've done this.

"I came here because I was so worried. I've had a hard time. . . . (sob) . . . Come out, and let's eat a meal together. I'll fix a dinner and be waiting for you. Come out please, please I beg you."

26 February

The father of Koichi Teraoka:

"It is a distinctive trait of Japanese to resist to the last. From now on your character depends on your behavior.

"Language is a good weapon. Be brave; come out and talk with us. The year before last you came to the funeral of your grandmother unexpectedly and cried for her. I was so glad. Your picture is in the room with the Buddhist altar, and I look at it every day."

26 February

The father of Masakuni Yoshino:

"Listen. It's your father. What you're doing now will only hurt your cause. Come out immediately. You have already achieved your purpose. Please, for my sake, come out."

27 February 7:00 A.M.

The mother of Masakuni Yoshino:
"I'm really sorry to shout so loudly this early in the morning. I guess you take turns sleeping. But listen to me.

"Yasuko, are our children treating you kindly? I certainly hope so.

"I talked with the parents of one member of your group last night, and I understand that you are self-sacrificing people who consider others before yourselves. I can't imagine how this has happened. . . . (sob) . . .

"When you let Yasuko out, please put a piece of cloth on her eyes. There's a great deal of snow outside, and the glare is very bright.

"Your friend is waiting for you. Please give yourself up today. Masakuni, my shouting may hurt your pride—forgive me. But I feel as if I'm going mad.

"You're only a few steps away from me, and yet I can't see your face or hear your voice. . . . When I'm watching the building, the whole thing looks like your face and your body. Please don't shoot any more, just sit there. I've put up with so much. . . ."

29 February 1972
FATHER OF KUNIO BANDŌ TAKES LIFE

Moments before the arrest of the Red Army members on 28 February at Asama villa in Karuizawa, Yoshiko Bandō, the mother of 25-year-old Red Army leader Kunio Bandō, found that her husband Motonobu had hanged himself in the family home in Awazu-chō, Otsu City. Mrs. Bandō immediately reported her husband's suicide to the police.

According to the police and the Bandōs' friends, Motonobu had locked up his inn and drawn all the curtains on that day, and had stayed in the house with his wife and daughter to watch the telecast of the "conquest" of Asama villa by riot police. Just before 6:00 P.M. the television announced that "The riot police are about to enter the attic," and at this point Motonobu quietly stood up and disappeared. His wife and daughter found him at 6:10 P.M. in the earth-floored room in front of the washroom, where he had hanged himself with a laundry rope hooked around a pole.

According to Mrs. Bandō, the family had received four threatening telephone calls from Osaka and Kyoto demanding that Motonobu substitute himself for Yasuko (the hostage of the Red Army at Asama villa), and Motonobu had repeatedly apologized to the callers. On a small piece of drawing paper in the change pocket of Motonobu's coat, the police found a note written in pencil. The note said, "I deeply apologize to the person who was taken hostage. Even my death is not enough, but I do not know how to make my apology other than by my death. Please do not blame the rest of my family any longer. Thank you, my Yoshiko, and allow me to leave our daughter in your hands. I thank all of you who have given me consolation. I regret that I must leave my daughter alone, but. . . ."

According to the police, Motonobu was a quiet and timid person, and Yoshiko herself was managing the inn. The inn had been closed since 23 February, when Yoshiko went to Asama villa to persuade her son to surrender.

Yoshiko, looking exhausted, met the crowding reporters and repeatedly said "I'm sorry" while bowing again and again. She finally added, in a choked and faint voice, "I feel very sorry for the people who were killed. Watching the television, I was praying to a spirit of mercy every minute . . . but. . . ."

5 March 1972 (Sunday)
DON'T MAKE THREATENING CALLS—THINK OF THE FAMILY'S PAIN

Noriko Konishi (a housewife):
"A little after 11:00 P.M., just as we are about to go to bed, the telephone rings. Even after one or two o'clock in the morning, the phone still rings. We never know the people on the other end of the line. Helplessly, my husband sets the telephone by the bed and covers it with a quilt before he goes to sleep. We receive these

phone calls because of the people who used to live here. Until a year ago, when we moved here from Osaka, the place belonged to the family of one of the criminals of the Asama villa incident, and we are mistaken for them.

"The people on the other end of the line never believe what we tell them. And they never change their rude attitude, no matter how we insist we are not the family. They always hang up with some horrible parting words. Even if they understand that we are not the family, they never apologize for their rudeness. Of course they never give their names, and they have absolutely no consideration for our feelings.

"Since we have no connection with the incident, we answer the telephone even though we get angry. If we were the family of the criminal, though, their words would cut like a knife.

"We should not allow another crime to be committed in retribution for the first crime. We sincerely hope the police will be more careful about such cases."

3 March 1972
FATHER SUBMITS LETTER OF RESIGNATION

Threatening letters and phone calls have been directed to the family of two brothers who were among the Red Army members arrested at Karuizawa. The police in the city of Kariya have decided to investigate the matter. In the meantime, the father of the brothers, an elementary schoolteacher, submitted his letter of resignation to the school on 1 March.

On the evening of 28 February when the brothers were arrested, the family began to receive threatening phone calls. Although the family knew that the brothers belonged to an extremist group, it did not have the slightest knowledge of the siege at Asama villa. The family was both surprised and pained by the news. As if repeatedly attacking a defeated enemy, the phone calls went on all day. The father said, "Because one of the members of my family was ill, we left the receiver off the hook for a while."

Since the beginning of March, the family has been annoyed by a rush of postcards. Post office cancellations identify the cards as coming not only from Kariya, the home of the family, but also from such places as Tokyo, Hyōgo, and Osaka. All the postcards are seven-*yen* cards, the cards used before the price hike, probably because the senders suspected that the family would never receive them. The family has gotten almost twenty postcards in the last two days.

The father has been a schoolteacher for thirty-two years. Since he has a reputation as a teacher of serious and upright moral character, the municipal education board has not taken action on his resignation at this time.

"I WAS WRONG"——FATHER OF KATŌ BROTHERS

Masuo Katō came home to Ogawa-chō, Kariya City, Aichi, from the area of Mt. Haruna the afternoon of 13 March after identifying the body of his son Yoshitaka. Yoshitaka, a member of the Keihin Joint Front Army Against the US–Japan Security Treaty and a student at Wakō College, had been killed at a lynching by the Red Army. In addition, Katō's second and third sons were among the criminals arrested at Asama villa. All the relatives crowded into the house, but Mr. Katō only stared at them—there was no conversation. Everyone silently decorated the Buddhist altar for the funeral. Mr. Katō's hair had turned gray and his face twitched. He was at a loss. . . . How could he express his sorrow and anger? "I am questioning myself . . . as an educator and as a father," he said. He went on speaking in a weak voice:

"I have been an elementary schoolteacher for thirty-two years and have taught thousands of pupils. Despite my confidence in myself as an experienced teacher, I now realize that I made some mistakes in educating my sons.

"When I was young, my parents could not afford to buy the books I wanted to read. For my own sons, therefore, I provided as many novels and philosophical books as they wanted, and encouraged them to study hard. My sons read avidly, including every page of a juvenile encyclopedia. I was always pleased when my wife told me, 'The children were reading today.' They were such obedient and gentle sons.

"About twice a year the whole family, all five of us, would take a trip. To Nara, to Kyoto. . . . We harvested rice in our rice field and had a lot of fun. . . . But when I think of it now, maybe I was the only one who was happy. Perhaps I was only satisfying myself. The whole family never laughed together; there was always some sort of tension in our home.

"My program of education for my sons was too demanding. I always spoke of 'effort' and 'guts': I thought these were the best words for inspiring educational purpose. Rather than such words, I should have taught my sons 'the joy of life' and 'the brightness of life.'

"I grumbled a lot, too. I devoted myself entirely to education, but when I went home I often grumbled about my dissatisfaction. Probably I was so tired that I even grumbled at having to eat supper alone; on these occasions, my sons were usually studying quietly.

"One night I overheard a Red Chinese program from the room of my second son, who had just entered senior high school. I turned off the radio and scolded him severely. When I found *Quotations from Mao Tse-tung* and *Instructions on Guerrilla Warfare* in his room, I again scolded him without concealing my feelings. My second son sharply opposed me. It was the first time he had disobeyed me, and I was shocked. Then my first son ran away from home, and I started to panic. My third son started to wear long hair. When I criticized him, he turned on me. Suddenly my obedient sons had changed. After all of them had run away from home, I read a book by a progressive university professor to try to understand my sons' ideology. The author irresponsibly connected revolution with violence. But why didn't I try to understand their thoughts earlier? . . . It was too late.

"I learned how to lead my life from my father. But now, after seeing Yoshitaka's body, I think I should have taught my sons how to lead their lives by themselves. We should cultivate children's ability to make the right decisions when they are small. We should raise our children to be open and unrestrained. In other words, I should have educated my sons to feel they could complain openly to their father. A generation gap? . . . Maybe so, but I don't know when it started. By the time I realized it, my sons were already far away from me.

"An officer of the Metropolitan Police Headquarters told me that my second and third sons grieved over the death of Bandō's father, thinking it was me. This made me feel a little better. . . . I was pleased to know they were still thinking of me. I will resign my position as a teacher, and when my sons come back some day I would like to get to know them again and be a true father."

Korean Residents
at Inoshino

In a society like Japan where lineage is very important, people of foreign ancestry often face social discrimination. One such group is the Korean community in Japan. Since the Japanese government follows the principle of lineage in determining citizenship, members of the Korean community, even those born in Japan, are aliens. A public school can reject Korean applicants because they are not Japanese. Honor students of a good university cannot get positions as public servants if they are not of Japanese lineage. Though marriages between Japanese and Koreans in Japan do occur, they are rare. The following excerpt is from an interview with a poet, Chong In, a man of Korean descent who makes a living in Japan as a writer. Chong was born and brought up in Inoshino in Osaka, the largest Korean community in Japan. He tells the interviewer what it is like to be a member of what he regards as an excluded group.

EARLY LIFE IN INOSHINO

Inuzuka: Could you begin by telling me why you moved from Korea to Japan?

Chong: It was not my decision to move to Japan from Korea. My father and mother came to Japan. . . . My father did various kinds of jobs. He was a laborer and a hatmaker. His life in Japan in those days was extremely unstable; he led a shiftless life and never stayed with one job very long. When he came to Japan, he found

From Jirō Iinuma, *Mienai hitobito: Zai nichi chōsenjin* (Tokyo: Kirisuto Kyōdan Shuppankyoku, 1975), pp. 167–185. Translated for this book by Yūji Yamamoto.

there was no room here for him to express his pride. Japanese society would not permit him to do so. He felt desperate and resented his situation in Japan, and he sometimes got into fights. In our family, it was not my father but my mother on whom we children depended emotionally. In our eyes, my father was a figure of contempt. He changed his residence more than twenty times before the war started. Until I entered high school, he moved at least once a year. Only later did I understand that his unsteadiness was a reflection of the instability of those days.

Inuzuka: When did you move to Osaka?

Chong: We lived there from the time we arrived from Korea. My father moved around because of his jobs, but our family always lived in Inoshino in Osaka. I was born there. . . . The environment of Inoshino had great impact on the second generation of Korean Japanese. I mean . . . that the second generation of Koreans who grew up outside of Inoshino, surrounded by Japanese society, had a strong tendency to be assimilated into Japanese society and give up their identity as Koreans. But those of us who grew up in Inoshino sensed we were different from the Japanese. Although we were too young to be fully conscious of the influence Inoshino had on us, still, because we were surrounded by Koreans, we naturally regarded certain things as being Korean, certain smells or customs. . . . It is because of Inoshino that I can identify myself as a Korean. Just after the end of the last war, I was a student in a Korean school for two years, and it was there that I learned the Korean language. I entered this Korean school in 1946. The school played a decisive role in the formation of my personality. I can no longer read or write Korean very well, but this short span in my life had great significance for me. It was as if it focused light on the unconscious world of my mind.

LIFE IN THE EVACUATION AREA

Inuzuka: To go back to an earlier part of your life, I understand that you moved from Inoshino as part of an evacuation during the last war. Would you tell me about that?

Chong: Japan was defeated in August 1945. My "period of

evacuation" lasted from June through August of that year. . . . In March 1945, Osaka was hit by heavy air raids. My family's house was destroyed, and I remember we walked around Mount Ikoma all day looking for a place to build a simple hut. It was all in vain. Finally, we were forced to depend on a relative of my mother who had borrowed a house in case of evacuation in Sakakibara, Mie prefecture. We knew all about the house because we had visited there the year before.

Several families were living there together, and since there were so many people in the house, we had to share a *futon** with several people. But there was no other place for us to go—Koreans do not hesitate to depend on even a distant relative. Some twenty children were living in the house; I was the eldest. There were relatives as well as nonrelatives. The best food we had was potatoes. I still have a habit of eating a meal very fast, a habit I developed in those days. At mealtimes all twenty children started eating at the same time. We had to eat as fast as we could to get enough food. . . . In front of the house was a school. I was treated very nicely by one of the teachers. This was the first time I was treated kindly by a Japanese woman.

Inuzuka: What do you remember about your awareness of being a Korean in those days?

Chong: Well, I was and was not aware of being Korean. In those days there was a general tendency among Korean children to avoid going out with their mothers because they were clearly Korean. (That is, the older generation of Korean Japanese had certain characteristics, such as their clothing and Korean accents, which identified them as Koreans.) But I did not hesitate to go out with my mother; I thought I should do so. However she might be spoken of by the world, she was my mother. In this sense I had a clear sense of identification as a Korean. But I doubt if it was a true awareness of my Korean ethnicity. It was very likely due as much to my affectionate attachment to my mother.

There was another thing about my Korean ethnic consciousness. I got into fights quite often—not only because I was Korean

---

*A Japanese bed spread out on the floor each night for sleeping.

but also because I was physically handicapped. All my fights were the result of these two problems. I never started the fights. Only when I was pushed again and again until I could not endure it any longer did I fight. Most of the time I was beaten. I did not cry at the time, but I started to cry as soon as I got home. I tried avoiding the situation by being absent from school. As a result of my resentment, I resolved to be a "better" Japanese than the Japanese. I would say to myself, "*You* are originally Japanese, and I can only imitate being Japanese—yet I'll do it so well that I'll be more capable than the genuine Japanese." I had a competitive urge. My school record was bad when I had a kind teacher and good when the teacher was nasty to me. This seems to have been a manifestation of my rebelliousness. There was a certain teacher I disliked. When he was put in charge of our class, however, my school record was very good. This was because I had the arrogance to feel I could make it whenever I wanted to. When a teacher liked me, I behaved very badly and didn't work hard. But this may well have been because of my personality rather than my Korean ethnic sentiment.

REACTION TO JAPAN'S DEFEAT IN THE WAR

Inuzuka: Were you still living in the evacuation area on the day Japan surrendered?

Chong: Yes. I can still remember that moment clearly. The housewife next door, Mrs. Hagino, was really a nice person, and very kind to me. She was typical of the good-natured middle-aged farm woman in the rural areas of Japan. She treated me fairly, or at least I believed so at the time. Because of this, I still vividly remember her words to me after she had listened to the emperor's radio message announcing Japan's surrender. She said, "My dear boy, you must be glad to hear it, mustn't you?" I can now understand the real meaning of her words, but at the time, they made no sense to me at all. I could not understand why the loss of the war should make me happy. I always had the feeling I was useless. Because of my physical handicap I would never be a fighter pilot or a soldier. I felt isolated, unable to become part of a group, and alone. In my elementary school days, whenever teachers asked my classmates what type of person they would like to be, they always said they wanted to become a fighter pilot or join the navy. I couldn't say that. Therefore, I deliberately held myself apart from my classmates and became an onlooker. Even today, I still have a psychological aversion to organizations and groups. I am afraid this comes from my childhood experiences. I avoid getting deeply involved in organizations. In other words, there is something in me which always reacts against groups.

Inuzuka: There seems to be something else besides your Korean ethnicity which is the cause of this aversion to organizations. . . .

Chong: Well . . . two problems seem to have interwoven themselves . . . my Korean ethnicity and my physical handicap. Both served to isolate me. In any collective activities during my elementary school days, such as school excursions or athletics, I had no choice but to be an observer. Especially in athletics, I was forced to be a spectator. In this respect, my mentality has remained unchanged since the old days. I fear groups and dislike them.

REFUSED ENTRANCE TO HIGH SCHOOL

Chong: While we were in the evacuation area, I did not really comprehend the fact that Japan had lost the war. After I came back to Osaka and began to go to the Korean school, I came to understand, little by little, the meaning of what the Japanese housewife had said to me.

I finished the sixth grade of elementary school in March 1945, and in August of the same year Japan was defeated. It was before the final defeat in August that I decided I wanted to enter Ikuno High School. Osaka Prefectural Ikuno High School was one of the most prestigious high schools in Japan. In those days there were no entrance examinations for any of the high schools. I wish there *had* been an entrance exam. I suppose, however, that few people studied properly in those days. Students were considered for high school on the basis of a recommendation from their elementary school which appeared on their school records. Of the students accepted at the school, a great many had worse records than mine. In my case, however, my school would not recommend me. My teachers refused to write the necessary report on my record. In addition, I was told I could not enter the high school because I could not get through a military training course—an obligatory course in the school. These were the two reasons why I was refused admission. . . . They never openly mentioned my Korean lineage. Instead, they found a compulsory course of military training as a justification for rejecting my application. Yet I was bright at my lessons and had the qualifications for high school.

I offered my advisor a bribe. I gave him sugar and dried cuttlefish, which were precious things in those days . . . and I don't remember how much I gave him in cash. My parents, despite their poverty, wanted me to have a high school education, regardless of the cost, to compensate for my physical handicap. They did not hesitate to offer a bribe. At last the advisor wrote a report on my school record for Jōhoku Technical High School. It was a very poor school. I was quite disappointed with it when I visited with my father. But they, too, refused to admit me as a student. We had been bled for nothing. Their reason was the same: I could not do military training. My father could not keep from crying on our way home from the school. I told myself that such a poor school did not deserve me as a student. I had my own pride. But my poor father seemed to think all was lost.

CLOSING OF THE KOREAN SCHOOLS

Chong: Immediately after the war, a Korean elementary school and high school were established. I was one of the first students in the high school. At the time I was quite cynical and thought I was too bright to attend such a small high school. A small kindergarten, called Rinpo Hall, had been remodeled to make our high school. There were five classrooms. The building was used not only for us but for various organizations as well. When my application to the Japanese high school was rejected, I had quit going to the Japanese elementary school and was not receiving any education at all. My mother was anxious, though, and kept telling me to go to the Korean school! At the beginning, I resisted her suggestion because I thought it was not good enough for me. Finally she took me to the school despite my reluctance. This was how I enrolled in the Korean high school; in the end, it proved to be an important part of my adolescence.

All the Korean schools were closed in October 1949, but by then I had already graduated from high school. Up to that time, the Korean schools had consistently improved, and enrollment had grown. Their closing had a great impact on the Korean residents. I took part in a sit-in demonstration during which a young Korean boy was shot to death. All this happened on the eve of the Korean War.

I CANNOT LIVE IN JAPAN UNDER MY REAL NAME

Chong: I run my business in Japan under my Japanese name, but I feel uncomfortable and resent having to do this. I want to use my real name, but something prevents me—logically speaking, I should do so in spite of the "something." The Chinese in Japan use their real names, but I think there's a vast difference between the Japanese view of the Chinese and their view of the Koreans. Though the Japanese have contempt for the Chinese and discriminate against them, they also feel something like awe of the Chinese as well as an awareness that China is a great country. There is no such awe of the Koreans. Instead, the Japanese feel only great contempt for us. In my case, my aesthetic sensibility and my sentiments are very close to those of the Japanese. This has caused me to develop an inferiority complex about Korean society. One part of me is proud of being Korean; another part feels inferior because I am Korean. Anyway, I can well understand the emotions of the Japanese. What I dislike about the Japanese is that they speak very softly. Perhaps this is due to their modesty. That's really a euphemism, though, since I really mean that there is some discrepancy between what they say and what they actually think or feel. I have been cheated by them quite often because of this. If I take what they say at face value, they suddenly ask me, "Why do you misunderstand me?" In other words, there is a difference between words and meaning.

Inuzuka: Do you mean they do not tell you an outright lie, but rather they manipulate the usage of conventional forms and meanings?

Chong: That's right.

Inuzuka: Are the Koreans direct and clear when they speak?

Chong: Yes. I am accustomed to Japanese ways of expression, but Koreans who were brought up in Korea and moved to Japan seem to have a hard time understanding the Japanese. Koreans are quite direct in expressing what they think and feel. In fact, we often start quarrels. In contrast, the Japanese are a very diplomatic people.

Maybe I'm being too severe with the Japanese, but it also seems to me that they have an intrinsic lack of affection. I'm saying they lack a sense of altruism. This is probably just my contentious view of the Japanese, but I feel this strongly. Certainly affection is expressed toward inferiors, but this is not the same as genuine love.

Inuzuka: In short, you're saying that the Japanese are egocentric and lacking in sensitivity toward others.

Chong: I believe that true affection is the understanding of others. I'm afraid that the Japanese are lacking in this ability to understand others. The Japanese think that others should be treated in terms of their relationships to themselves. It is not "Yesterday's enemy is today's friend" but "Yesterday's friend may be today's enemy."

UNDERSTANDING DIFFERENT ETHNIC PEOPLES

Chong: Mr. Inuzuka, you have tried to understand the Koreans through your conversation with me, but I am afraid it must be quite difficult for you to comprehend certain aspects of the Korean personality. It is probably impossible. But this is really not unusual—the point is, it's very hard to understand a different ethnic people. I have been deeply involved in Japanese society, but still I come across things I cannot understand about the Japanese. . . . I'm always impressed by my failure to understand why such-and-such a thing moves the Japanese, or why it makes them feel satisfied, or why it drives them mad. In other words, there must be a different flow of emotions in the Japanese than in Koreans. I can understand such emotional differences to a certain degree intellectually, but there are still differences that can't be breached by logic and knowledge. Therefore, social intercourse between different ethnic peoples must include mutual respect for other people's differences.

I hesitate to return to Korea . . . because I'm afraid I would feel like an outsider. I am an outsider not only in Japan but also in Korea. My personal aesthetics seem to be unusual in both countries. My daily impressions and my sense of beauty are not appreciated by either of the two peoples. If I were in my teens, I could accommodate myself to Japanese society. In this sense, I am very interested in how Japanese who have lived in foreign lands relate to Japanese society. I assume they confront the same feeling of alienation that I have. But I'm not sure.

Inuzuka: It may differ case by case, but I think it would be true to say that they reevaluate their country.

Chong: It is not exactly consciousness of being an outsider, but a sense of discord. . . . Osaka has always had a special significance for me. It was in Osaka that I fell in love, got drunk, got into fights, and wrote poetry. Because of these experiences, Osaka is an integral part of my life. Certainly there are memories of agony and resentment as well. But it is impossible for me to return to Korea and utterly discard my life in Osaka. It's part of me, and now I try to express my feelings through literature.

JAPANESE-LIKE KOREANS

Chong: When I talk with first-generation Koreans in Japan, I encounter a feeling of disharmony. At the same time, I have only respect for them. We (the second generation) clearly realize that we cannot live in Japan in the same way they did. They maintained a particular sense of their own identity. What can I call it? Genealogy, family, history . . . they give the impression that they are proud of their background. I have my own identity, but it's a very individual feeling. Theirs is somehow different from ours. The second generation of Koreans in Japan should no longer have a sense of being inferior to the first generation. Until now the second generation has always felt constrained by the first generation. I'm sure we feel inferior to the first generation because they were the ones who taught us about Korea. In my case, I feel an ambivalence in myself; for a long time I've suffered from a sense of shame, wishing I could be a true Korean but knowing I cannot. I feel that the younger Koreans should think about the problems of the second generation of Korean Japanese—that is, the problems of the Japanese-like Koreans—without feeling guilt toward the older Koreans. This may be difficult. But if we have no record of the Korean mentality in Japan it would certainly be a loss to us in the future. Surely it is necessary to record the voices of Koreans who tried to maintain their ethnic heritage but failed. We have no such record as yet, though studies have attempted to analyze Koreans in Japan. This work has its own significance.

Inuzuka: When economic or personal bankruptcy occurs, the Japanese are concerned only when it happens to Japanese. They do not care as long as it's the problem of the Korean residents.

Chong: The Japanese have a tendency to take it for granted that we have such problems.

Inuzuka: The attitude of taking things for granted can be found not only in the Japanese but in the Korean residents as well.

Chong: That's a very significant point. I hope I will be able to bring out that point very honestly in my writing. . . . We Korean writers in Japan have done some work on tracing the mentality of the Korean residents. But our writing has focused primarily on Korean intellectuals in Japan. . . .

Inuzuka: Recently a study examining the forced confinement of Korean residents during the war was published. But few works have examined the daily life of Koreans in the postwar Japan.

Chong: I'm afraid the intellectuals cannot write such works. Indeed there are many Koreans in Japan who lead a desperate sort of existence. They are concerned only with survival . . . and there is no room for literature. Yet we need to make a record of that kind of life.

Inuzuka: I agree. It would give us a vivid sense of the relationship between the Japanese and the Korean residents.

One Woman's Outcry

"One Woman's Outcry" is a letter to the editor of the *Asahi Shimbun* (Osaka) written in 1955 by a young woman from the group known as the *burakumin* or in the pejorative the *eta* (filthy people). Under law there is no discrimination against this group. In practice, however, there is considerable prejudice against them. They are often refused employment in any but menial jobs. Those who want to avoid discrimination sometimes try to hide their origin when seeking employment, marriage, or residence. The following selection illustrates the suffering of a woman whose husband discovered her identity after their marriage. She describes the breakup of her marriage and blames the Japanese government rather than the husband for the discrimination.

I heard someone say, "Akiko, what are you doing here!" I turned and saw that it was Kazuko, my old grade school classmate. "Don't you know? She's the wife of the factory manager," one of the workers told Kazuko. "What!" Kazuko exclaimed in amazement. "But she's an outcast. How can she be so high and mighty?" Kazuko's scornful words, spoken out of jealousy, spread quickly throughout the factory. It's true. I am an outcast. When I was in school and two of my classmates forgot their cups for lunch, the teacher lent them hers. When I forgot my cup the teacher said, "You are dirty. Go home and get your own cup." When I took an employment exam, I told the examiner the name of my village and

From Asahi Shimbun Osaka Honsha Shakaibu (ed.), *Buraku* (Kyoto: San'itsu Shobō, 1958), pp. 14–17. Translated for this book by Hiroko Kataoka.

my father's occupation. After that I received a failing grade. It was then that I learned to hide my birth.

Four years ago my husband begged me to marry him, and ever since then I had been very happy . . . but the day after Kazuko showed up my husband's attitude toward me suddenly changed completely. "You deceived me. You'll ruin my chances. I want a divorce." After burning me on my upper arm and left leg with red hot tongs, he left. He took everything but an old wicker trunk which he threw in the garden. In deep despair, I took sleeping pills and for seven days hovered between life and death. So many young lives have ended that way, marked only by a brief notice in the newspaper. A friend of mine fell deeply in love, but the man's father said, "You are just an outcast. If you love my son so much, I'll let you be his mistress." Trembling with rage, my friend killed herself that very night. People say there's no more discrimination. That is a lie.

We are no different from other people. People tell themselves it can't be helped—the birth and race of the outcasts are different from theirs. We are not a different race; we are not the descendants of captives. At the beginning of the Tokugawa period the government set up the distinction of outcast below the four feudal classes of warrior, farmer, artisan, and merchant. Since the middle ages there have been beggars, actors and actresses, and people in handicraft trades like leatherworking, gardening, dyeing, and blacksmithing. At the start of the Tokugawa era the government needed something to make the farmer feel superior to others so they would endure heavy taxation. Even though my ancestors had committed no crime they were rounded up by force and taken to the outskirts of town. Among them were warriors who had lost their masters and farmers who had absconded from their land because of illness or inability to pay taxes. I'm proud that I am an outcast. My ancestors never hurt anyone. They were good people. "Well, you might be right about the Tokugawa period," you say, "but isn't it your own fault that the outcast community continues to exist today? It was only in the hundred years between the Tempō era and the beginning of the Meiji (1868) that social divisions were so rigidly enforced. Certainly discrimination ended in 1873 with the order abolishing the old class system." It ended only on the surface—in our daily lives, discrimination is growing stronger. That is the problem.

Although all college graduates start at the same level, one will become a department head, many others will become clerks, and still others will be unemployed. That's the way our system works. While my ancestors were made to live in dried up riverbeds and beneath cliffs with no land to cultivate and no jobs, people were cheering, "Hurrah for the Meiji Restoration! Liberty! Equality!" What kind of liberty was there for us! We did not benefit from the land reforms even after the war. Most of us had less than an acre of land and were not recognized as farmers. What little land we had we salvaged from wasteland. We clung to our home industry, which was all we had, but we've lost even that. When capitalists saw that those industries were profitable, they took them over. We had no choice but to accept low wages from the capitalists for odd jobs. The capitalists said, "We're doing you outcasts a favor by hiring you at all."

Even at the highest levels of government discrimination exists. Do you believe phrases like "Let well enough alone" or "There's no discrimination any more"? A few years ago in Kyoto, where I live, there occurred something called the "*All Romance* incident." A city official wrote "The Special Village," a story that discriminated against outcasts, and published it in *All Romance* magazine. The story took place in one of the outcast communities in Kyoto. Everyone including the mayor called the story an outrage. But people from the Committee for Buraku Liberation would not let it go at that. They spread out a map of the city in front of the mayor and drew red circles around the areas of the city where housing was inferior and there was no running water or sewage system, areas that no fire truck could enter and where many people had trachoma and tuberculosis, areas where the incomes were low and unemployment high and many children did not go to school. In each case there was a circle on the map drawn around our outcast community. I felt as if my eyes had been opened for the first time—the official could write such a discriminatory story so easily because discrimination was practiced every day at every level of government.

Prejudice against the outcast community will not go away even if discriminatory words disappear along with the idea that outcasts are of a different race.

I remember vividly a time when I went with my husband to visit his home in Toyama prefecture. As we were going through a pass, my husband abused the people of an outcast community, calling them filthy pigs. His own family was incredibly poor. Unable to afford *tatami* mats they had only loosely woven straw. Only the feeling of superiority to the outcasts made life bearable for the miserable farmers. I no longer feel bitter toward my husband. Like everyone else he is the victim of a discriminatory government that acts as if prejudice were a matter of course. I am an outcast. I burn with anger when I think of all those who say with indifference, "Leave the outcast community as it is; there's no discrimination any more." Come and see the outcast community where I was born. See with your own eyes the very essence of discrimination.

Part 4

THE STATE

This part of the book shows, through fiction, interviews, and editorials, popular attitudes toward the state—which for purposes of this book means any authority above that of the family or community. The readings demonstrate not only Japanese views of the ideal state but also the way in which it is often believed to operate in practice.

In premodern Japan (Japan before 1868) the majority of the Japanese people had little contact with any authority above that of their family and community heads; the state was remote and only indirectly relevant to the daily concerns of the populace, most of whom lived in the countryside. The village headman acted as intermediary between the rural population and higher authority. As is evident in the story "Sōgo of Sakura," the headman was one of the villagers and hence shared their interests and grievances. He would side with the village against the government by underreporting tax yields or, if necessary, petitioning for the reduction of taxes.

In crisis situations, however, when famine, flood, drought, or crop failure caused hardship and suffering, the resentment of the common people was often directed against the state. In the Tokugawa period (1600–1868) there was a widespread belief, fostered by the government itself, that the people owed obedience to the state and in return the state owed them peace and a modicum of economic security. It therefore followed that when that security was severely threatened, the state was held responsible. When, as occasionally happened, unscrupulous individuals or rulers were widely held to be responsible for the suffering, then the people would feel themselves justified in rebelling openly against the state.

According to Confucian theory, introduced into Japan from China, the ideal government was a government that existed for the benefit of the people. Officials were to be virtuous themselves and were to govern by setting an example of ethical behavior. In their official capacity they were to be fair and incorruptible. They were to seek the underlying principle that governed all things and be guided by it. The Judge Ōoka tales illustrate this ideal, and their popularity among Japanese of all social levels indicates a wide acceptance of the ideal. Ōoka Echizen-no-kami (1677–1751) was in fact a magistrate of the Tokugawa government, but the stories about him are probably largely fictitious accounts written by unknown authors. In the tales the judge, because of his righteousness, can always distinguish between good and evil and the justice he dispenses is always equitable and based on the underlying principles he clearly and unfailingly perceives. His decisions are made on the merits of each case rather than according to precedent or statute.

In practice the state as represented by a government magistrate was the last place the ordinary Japanese would have turned to redress a grievance or settle a dispute in Judge Ōoka's day. It was the conscious policy of the government to discourage recourse to the courts and to encourage settlement of disagreements by conciliation and compromise. If parties could not settle their differences, they were often forced to do so by the magistrate, who could threaten them with imprisonment or torture if they did not agree on a solution. The lack of distinction between civil and criminal law in premodern Japan meant that the magistrate could treat a recalcitrant litigant as a criminal and the plaintiff might be no better off in the end for all his trouble than if he had settled his problems on his own. The association with criminal proceeding also meant that there was considerable stigma attached to involvement in litigation. A magistrate would refuse to hear complaints by inferiors against their superiors; in fact, one had to secure the permission of a superior before one could go before a magistrate in the first place. Hence "Ōoka justice" represented ideal justice to many people. In all likelihood, no one really expected such justice to be dispensed by an actual magistrate. Even today, under a modern legal system and an independent judiciary, most people in Japan prefer to settle disputes through conciliation and mediation rather than in court, and they are encouraged to do so by the government.

Few Japanese in the premodern period would have seen Judge Ōoka as the prototype of a real official. The attitude of many Japanese of that era and even in some areas today is expressed by the proverb "Officials are honored and the people are despised." It was commonly believed that officials above the village level were a privileged group concerned with the preservation of their own interests and those of the ruling elite, and not with the problems of the people as a whole. The story "Sōgo of Sakura" illustrates this view. When corrupt officials under an inept lord exact unreasonable taxes and labor from the farmers of the Sakura area, the headmen of all the villages in the region petition the officials to reduce the burden on the farmers, but to no avail. Finally the leader, Sōgo, waits for the palanquin of the *shōgun* and forces the farmers' petition on the *shōgun*'s guards. All efforts fail to bring relief for the farmers. Because the lord's family has loyally served the *shōgun*, the matter is kept secret and the lord is instructed to deal with the matter himself. Instead of punishing his officials or reducing taxes, however, he allows his advisors to persuade him to punish the petitioners and their families. The moral of the story is that even wise and honest officials would rather sacrifice the interests of the people than jeopardize the position of a member of the ruling elite.

If "Sōgo of Sakura" were a true story and the lord had continued to allow his officials to oppress the farmers, the situation would eventually have led to peasant rebellion and the central government would have been forced to intervene and punish the lord and his officials. The leaders of the rebellion would, like Sōgo, have been punished as well; but like Sōgo they would have been venerated as popular heroes. There is strong admiration in Japan for anyone willing to fight to the death for what he believes rather than submit to an authority he knows to be wrong.

"The Sinking Village," like "Sōgo of Sakura," is the story of a fight against the state by farmers who are destined to lose. The selection is taken from an autobiographical novel written by a man who was involved in a protest movement in the village of Yanaka near the Ashio copper mine between 1903 and 1908. The Yanaka protest was the last phase of the Ashio copper mine case, Japan's first great pollution incident. After the Meiji Restoration of 1868, national strength became a major goal of the state and industrialization was seen as essential. The rapid expansion and modernization of the copper mines at Ashio were part of the national drive for industrial growth. Waste from the mines was dumped into local rivers, and indiscriminate deforestation for the construction of mine shafts led to massive flooding of polluted river water that destroyed farmland and poisoned fish. Despite all efforts by the police to stop them, farmers from the Ashio area marched to Tokyo to protest the government's failure to close the mines and protect their livelihood. By 1900 their plight had aroused the sympathy of the public. The incident raised two questions: What sacrifices should the people be expected to make in the interests of national strength? And is it not the government's responsibility to protect the welfare of the people? Shōzō Tanaka, a leader of the protest movement against the government and the mine owners, charged in a speech in the Diet that the government had abandoned the people whose constitutional duty it was to protect. In "The Sinking Village" Tanaka is called the Honorable Noguchi and, as in historical fact, he is a spokesman for the farmers whose livelihood was destroyed by the pollution.

By the last phase of the protest, the Yanaka incident, the government was responding to the pressure of what had become a national movement by forcing the mine owners to take measures to prevent pollution. One such measure was to turn the area around Yanaka into a reservoir. Most of the villagers sold their land for the project because the prices offered were favorable, but a few, supported by Tanaka, held out even though they knew they would eventually be forced off their land. As in "Sōgo of Sakura" the farmers believed they were fighting for a just cause against an unsympathetic and powerful state. As one old man in "The Sinking Village" declares, "No matter what happens, we're in the right. Right will win in the end." Even if the police destroyed every house, he believed the village would live again. The excerpt ends with the government vacillating and the farmers waiting in frustration for the final confrontation with the police. Even after the village was, in fact, ultimately destroyed, some of the farmers went to live in the hills overlooking the flooded village as a final protest. Tanaka, too, lived there with them until he died.

Today, as at the time of the Yanaka protest, there is a widely held belief among many Japanese that the government is more responsive to the interests of business and industry than it is to the needs of the people for protection from the ecological dangers of unregulated economic growth. Yet, as in the Ashio pollution incident, the government has responded to demands for pollution control. Quality of life and social welfare are considered along with economic goals in political decision making.

To unify national power, a thorough centralization of government was carried out in the decades after the Meiji Restoration. In addition, the local autonomy of the premodern period was greatly reduced and the central government gained far more direct control over the lives of the Japanese people than ever before. With this increase in authority came a growing acceptance among government leaders that some political power should be shared with Japanese outside of government. The first national election in 1890 and the convention of the first Diet in the following year were followed by a gradual expansion of the electorate until in 1925 the passage of universal manhood suffrage allowed all adult males to participate in government through the election of representatives to the Diet. After World War II women, too, were given the vote.

The Japanese people consistently have a high voter turnout at elections. Yet studies by anthropologists indicate that few people believe that their representatives really represent their interests. Politicians are widely considered to act in their own interests or those of their political clique, and they are not held in high esteem. Certainly cynicism about their low moral caliber is evident in the editorials on the Lockheed scandal of 1976, in which eighteen men of influence in business and government (including former Prime Minister Tanaka) were indicted for accepting large bribes from the Lockheed Aircraft Corporation. The editorials also question the values of a society that would allow such men to become political leaders. Despite his indictment Tanaka was reelected to the Diet, but his Liberal Democratic Party has suffered serious defeats at the polls and the control it has held over national politics since the close of World War II has been greatly eroded.

While politicians come and go, the officials of the Japanese bureaucracy continue to carry on the business of government. Highly educated bureaucrats, especially those in the top echelons, regard themselves as an elite. They are recognized as competent by most people, but the attitudes expressed in "Sōgo of Sakura" still remain in the popular view of the bureaucratic official today. The phrase "Officials are honored and the people are despised" is today applied to bureaucratic arrogance and elitism. Complaints that the bureaucrat looks down on the ordinary citizen are not uncommon.

Throughout much of its premodern history Japan was ruled by military governments. In medieval times, farmers often took up arms to protect their fields and homes. Before 1600, some farmers fought for reward or social advancement. After 1600, with the freezing of social classes, the warriors became an elite, supported by a stipend and given privileges in dress, name, and status that set them off from the commoner classes. Directed to live in the castle towns of their lord or the *shōgun,* the warriors had no contact with people in the countryside, and they dealt with merchants and artisans in the towns from a position of legal and social superiority. In the 1870s the old class distinctions were abolished and the warriors lost both their stipends and their elite status. Conscription brought commoners into the military, and through their military training many Japanese were introduced to the national goal of a rich and powerful state. In the 1930s the military came increasingly (though never completely) to control that state. The Japanese people were asked to make considerable sacrifices to achieve the objectives of the military, and the military establishment was viewed with fear and awe. Today the people's estimation of the self-defense forces differs according to locality and social standing. In urban areas the military is generally disliked. In rural areas, however, where opportunity for employment is less than in the cities, young men still enter the military as they did before World War II and serving is considered an honor. Nevertheless, many Japanese hold the wartime military responsible for the years of deprivation and the national humiliation of defeat.

"A Protest Against My Charge" is a poignant statement of resentment against the military by a young soldier who is about to die for what he believes to be the cowardice of his superior officers. The soldier entered the army when entire classes of university students were mobilized during the war. His statement expresses in dramatic fashion the general feeling of betrayal and frustration many Japanese felt toward the military after World War II.

The Japanese people did not blame the emperor as they did the military leaders for war and defeat. Although nominally the head of state, throughout much of Japanese history the emperor did not exercise political power. He was primarily a religious figure who gave legitimacy to the political structure because of his claim of descent from the sun goddess, Amaterasu. With the Meiji Restoration the emperor was made the political head of the government, but, in practice, decisions were made and carried out by government leaders. The present emperor, Hirohito, asserted his political authority on only two occasions: once in 1936 when he insisted that the perpetrators of a military coup be punished, and again in 1945 when he broke a tie vote to decide that Japan should surrender to the allied forces. The Japanese people from 1868 on were consciously encouraged by government leaders to view the nation as analogous to a family and the emperor as head of that family. He was the symbol of Japanese culture and the focus of national loyalty. The interviews presented here demonstrate that because the emperor was removed from the actual decision making, it was not difficult for the people to separate him from responsibility for the war, and they continue to revere him as a focus for patriotic sentiment and loyalty.

For most people the important change in the emperor's postwar status was not his renunciation of divinity. As the interviews indicate, most people did not view him as a god. Instead, the significant change was the complete removal of the emperor from government power so that the imperial institution could no longer be used to give legitimacy to the government's actions. Before

World War II the emperor was remote from the people. He spoke a court Japanese which the average person could not understand. He seldom appeared in public, and when he did go out the people were required to bow so low that they could not see him. Today, in keeping with the more democratic institutions of the Japanese government, the emperor makes frequent appearances and personally addresses crowds in standard spoken Japanese. And, as these interviews demonstrate, he arouses considerable affection and loyalty.

In modern Japan, as in all modern societies, the state has come to touch people's lives to a far greater degree than ever before. Most people, even in remote villages, vote and are well informed about national events and problems. Many are increasingly politically involved as well. In the premodern and modern periods consensus had characterized popular attitudes toward the state for much of the time. Until the twentieth century there was little participation in government, but there was also little resentment. Yet today, as in the past, the state is the most visible and impersonal target for the expression of discontent and frustration, and those who write about the state often do so in order to attack the evils of their times as they perceive them.

The Judge Ōoka Tales

The following six tales have been selected from a contemporary version of popular stories known in Japan as the *Ōoka seidan* or Judge Ōoka Tales. Originally written sometime in the eighteenth century by unknown authors, the tales have aroused widespread admiration ever since. They are largely fictitious accounts of judicial decisions attributed to a Tokugawa official named Ōoka Echizen-no-kami who did, in fact, live between 1677 and 1751. Above all, they illustrate the principle of traditional Japanese law that reason should prevail over custom and precedent.

ONE PIECE FOR ALL THREE INVOLVED

There was a *tatami** maker named Saburobei at Reiganjima in Edo. Toward the end of one year, he borrowed three pieces of gold in order to prepare for the new year. On the way home from the moneylender, however, Saburobei lost the money.

In the meantime, a man named Chōjuro, a cabinetmaker, happened to walk in the bank of Yanagihara and find a purse containing three pieces of gold and a letter addressed to *tatami* maker Saburobei. From the letter Chōjuro had no way of knowing where Saburobei, *tatami* maker, lived. The New Year was the busiest time for everybody, but Chōjurō was determined to return the money to the owner. He put aside his own business and walked around the

---

From Tatsuya Tsuji, *Ōoka Echizen-no-kami* (Tokyo: Chūōkōronsha, 1964), pp. 3–5, 34–37, 46 51, 54–55. Translated for this book by Michiko Y. Aoki.
*Straw matting used as a floor covering in Japan.

town of Edo looking for the *tatami* makers in an attempt to find
Saburobei. Chōjurō spent four days searching: one day in the
Kanda district, another day in the Hongō area, and so forth.

Finally, Chōjurō found Saburobei, the owner of the purse, at
Reiganjima. Saburobei was stubborn, however. He declined to take
the money back, arguing that once he had lost it, the purse no
longer belonged to him. Chōjurō, on the other hand, had found it
while walking. "Why not take it as heaven's gift and keep the
money to yourself? It's yours."

Chōjurō was not to be persuaded. He had spent four busy
days looking for the owner of the purse with the intention of returning it. "I cannot take it. It's not mine." "Yes, it's yours." "No,
by god, no!" The argument grew into a violent fight. Saburobei's
landlord tried to intervene but to no avail. Neither party would listen to reason.

Unable to resolve the dispute, the two men went to the town
court, where Ōoka Echizen presided. Ōoka was impressed by the
honesty of the men. He therefore decreed that the three pieces of
gold in question would go into the government treasury. In return,
he arranged for the government to reward them by giving three
pieces of gold to the two men. They were happy to receive envelopes with the rewards.

When they opened the envelopes, Saburobei and Chōjurō
were puzzled. There were two pieces of gold in each envelope.
Didn't Ōoka Echizen say that the government was to give them
three gold pieces? We've got two pieces of gold apiece here. Altogether it adds up to four pieces. Where did the additional gold
come from? Who supplied it? Ōoka answered that the judge was
quite happy to see such honest people as Saburobei and Chōjurō,
and wanted to contribute one piece of gold himself. "It's a loss of
one piece of gold for me, of course," said Ōoka. "But Chōjurō has
found three pieces and is given two, so it's a loss of one gold piece
for Chōjurō," Ōoka continued. "Saburobei has lost three and is recovering two, so it's a one gold piece loss for Saburobei, too. The
case is settled by making all three, Saburobei, Chōjurō, and Ōoka,
lose one piece each.

Both parties, Saburobei and Chōjurō, were quite impressed and agreed to accept the money.

THE CASE OF THE CARPENTER

There was a carpenter named Hanshichi living on Owari-chō. Because of a long illness he could not pay rent for some time. When his debt had grown to something like three gold pieces, his landlord, Jirobei, demanded that Hanshichi leave the apartment and confiscated the carpenter's toolbox as security for the rent owed him.

Hanshichi moved to another apartment in Hatago-chō. His new landlord, a man named Jūbei, was a kind person. When he learned that Hanshichi could not work as a carpenter without tools, he lent him one piece of gold and told him to pay that much to Jirobei and negotiate the return of the toolbox. He added that Hanshichi could promise to pay Jirobei the remaining two when he earned it from his carpentry.

The carpenter went to his former landlord and did as Jūbei had suggested. But Jirobei would not listen. He insisted that he would not give up the tools unless he received the three gold pieces in full.

As a last resort Hanshichi appealed to Ōoka's court. Ōoka ordered Jūbei to lend another two pieces of gold to Hanshichi so that he could get his tools back. Jūbei obeyed. Then Ōoka asked Hanshichi how many days he had been unable to work because his tools had been confiscated. Hanshichi said, "Well, about a hundred days." "How much do you earn a day, Hanshichi?" asked Ōoka. Hanshichi's answer: "Well it depends, your honor. Somewhere between three and five ounces of silver, sir."

Thereupon Ōoka gave the verdict. "Jirobei, now that Hanshichi has paid up all his back rent, it is you who owe him the amount of money he would have earned over one hundred days. If he earned three ounces of silver every day, it would add up to 300 ounces altogether. That is five pieces of gold. You must pay that amount to Hanshichi."

Jirobei was not at all happy, yet he had no choice but to obey the order. He paid five pieces in gold to Hanshichi. Hanshichi paid three of them to Jūbei and the case was closed.

JIZŌ THE BOUND

A man named Yagorō was an employee of Echigoya dry goods store. One hot summer day he was assigned to carry a huge load of cotton cloth on his shoulder. By the time he came to some welcome shade under a tree at a place called Honjo, he was very tired and wanted to rest for a few minutes. Beneath the tree stood a stone statue of Jizō. Yagorō put his head on the pedestal, lay down, and inadvertently dozed off. He woke up toward evening and, alas, he found the huge package was gone! Yagorō was dumbfounded. He looked all around the neighborhood and made inquiries about the missing cotton cloth. No one could tell him anything about it.

Dispirited, Yagorō went back to Echigoya and explained what had happened. Nobody believed his story. "Yagorō, you filthy wretch, you must have sold the cotton and spent all the money gambling or going to a house of pleasure. You must pay for the lost merchandise."

Yagorō could not possibly pay such a large amount of money. Having no other alternative, he went to the town court for help.

At court Judge Ōoka ordered his men to go and arrest the statue of Jizō. The police surrounded the six-foot-tall stone statue. "Jizō, you are under arrest," they said, and tied the stone statue with rope. The spectacle drew quite a crowd of onlookers. The police with the help of the crowd loaded the statue on top of the cart and pulled it from Honjo to the courtroom at Sukiyabashi. The crowd followed the Jizō into court.

Thereupon Ōoka started questioning the Jizō. In the beginning he paid no attention to the crowd, but suddenly he turned to them and said, "It is most disrespectful of you people to come into court without permission. You deserve to be punished." The spectators were stunned. They tried to apologize for their behavior. But Ōoka would not let them go free. He had the court clerk record their names and addresses and released them on the condition that they stay home until further notice.

About two weeks later Ōoka summoned them and ordered that each of them pay a bundle of cotton cloth as fine. "After all the case started with cotton cloth, so you pay the fine in cotton cloth," said Ōoka. They all obeyed the order and paid the fine.

Then Ōoka had Yagorō inspect each bundle of cotton cloth carefully. Among the many bundles, Yagorō identified two as containing the same cloth that had been stolen. By finding the place where the cloth had been purchased, Ōoka then caught the real thief. From that time on, the Jizō came to be revered as "Wishing Jizō the Bound." And from this story came the belief that Jizō would fulfill the wish of anyone who tied him with a rope.

THE FISH VENDOR'S BILLS

At one time a fish vendor in Shitaya filed suit against eight Buddhist temples in his neighborhood. He charged that the priests of those temples had bought fish from him for a considerable length of time without ever paying. They owed him nearly one hundred pieces of gold in all. Ōoka ordered the court clerk to record the fish vendor's claim against each temple and dismissed the vendor.

Early the next morning Ōoka summoned all the priests and let them sit in the waiting room. There was no questioning whatsoever. As time passed the priests got restless. One after another, they started going to the restroom. In the restroom was a wall poster for them to read: a copy of the fish vendor's bills written in bold lettering! Priest So and So owes such and such amount of money for such and such purchase. . . . The priests, who were not supposed to eat any fish or flesh under the Tokugawa code, were in a panic, but they could do nothing. Toward the end of the day, Ōoka's deputy came to see them and apologized on Ōoka's behalf, saying that the judge was not feeling well and could not see them in person. "Please go home for today and await further instructions," said the deputy, and he released the priests. When they returned to their temples the priests in great haste paid their debts in full. All of them. Afterward Ōoka issued no summons.

THE TEN'ICHI AFFAIR

Long before he became the eighth *shōgun*, Tokugawa Yoshimune had a love affair with a girl named Sawanoi. At that time Yoshimune was living under the protection of Kanō Shōgen, an elder of the lord of Kii. Sawanoi, the girl he loved, was a chambermaid. When he realized that the girl was with child, Yoshimune gave her a dagger which had been handed down from Ieyasu, founder of the Tokugawa house, as a token of his love and proof of the forthcoming child's legitimacy. Yoshimune also scribbled a note and gave it to Sawanoi. The note said that if the child were a boy, Yoshimune would recognize him as his son and would arrange that mother and child could see him at an appropriate time. With these keepsakes the girl went back to her parents, who lived in the village of Hirasawa in the province of Kii.

In 1706 Sawanoi gave birth to a baby boy who soon died. When she learned of the premature death, Sawanoi became so disappointed that she succumbed also. Sawanoi was survived by her mother, Osan, who momentarily went insane and had to be entrusted to the village chief of Hirano.

Now a man named Harada Heisuke, a masterless *samurai* from Chōshū, had earlier drifted into the village of Hirano. He married a girl in the village who gave birth to a boy in 1705—that is, a year before Sawanoi's baby was born. Harada and his wife died young, and the orphan was raised by a temple priest in the village. The priest named the boy Hōtaku.

By the time he reached adulthood Hōtaku had learned from Osan, Sawanoi's mother, that she still kept Yoshimune's two mementos. Temptation was too great for Hōtaku to resist. Out of ambition he worked out a plan to kill Osan, get hold of the mementos, and then appear before Yoshimune claiming to be his child. Fearing discovery of his true identity, Hōtaku poisoned the priest after killing Osan and left the village on the pretext of going on a pilgrimage.

While on this feigned pilgrimage Hōtaku devised a plan to make it look as though he died while traveling. He concocted a story in which his boat was attacked by pirates, he was killed, and his corpse was thrown into the sea. With this scheme Hōtaku succeeded in convincing people that he was dead.

Then Hōtaku went to Kumamoto in Kyūshū, where he apprenticed himself to a rather wealthy merchant and gained the confidence of his master who then entrusted him with financial matters. Hōtaku stayed there for a few years. Then he stole a substantial amount of money from his master's treasury and fled eastward by boat.

En route the boat was shipwrecked but Hōtaku survived. He landed on the shore of Iyo province. In Iyo, Hōtaku met a man named Akagawa Taizen who felt resentment against the Tokugawa house because his father had been executed by Tokugawa Mitsukuni. This Akagawa had an uncle named Tenchū who was a member of a Buddhist order in Mino province. Akagawa talked to Tenchū and asked him to help in the conspiracy. Tenchū had a disciple named Ten'ichi, who happened to resemble Hōtaku. This was most convenient for the rogue. Tenchū killed this man and Hōtaku assumed the dead man's name, Ten'ichi.

Thereupon another villain joined the scheme. This was Yamanouchi Iganosuke, who had a talent for deceiving ignorant people. The swindlers made up a story that Hōtaku, now assuming the name Ten'ichi, was an illegitimate son of Yoshimune. By that time, Yoshimune was *shōgun*. The rogues then journeyed to Edo claiming that Ten'ichi was the son of Yoshimune and that he be made *daimyo* after seeing Yoshimune.

People on the roadside seemed to have believed those scoundrels' tales, partly because of the keepsakes and partly because of their own eagerness for reward. Ignorant villagers and townsmen donated money for Ten'ichi's cause hoping that he would reward them after becoming *daimyo*. Not only the ignorant commoners but the deputy officials in Osaka castle believed Ten'ichi's story. So did the deputy in Kyoto.

Finally, Ten'ichi and his retinue arrived in Edo. They presented the two pieces of evidence to the shogunate court and petitioned that Ten'ichi be granted an audience with Yoshimune. The council of elders at court carefully studied Ten'ichi's claim. The two mementos spoke for themselves. Yamanouchi presented Ten'ichi's case, and the council of elders concluded that Ten'ichi's claim was authentic.

There was one man, however, who did not believe the whole story. It was Ōoka Echizen. His intuition told him not to believe Ten'ichi's story. Ōoka's doubt was confirmed when he met Ten'ichi. He thought to himself, "This wretch cannot be Yoshimune's son." So Ōoka petitioned the council of elders to grant him the authority to reopen Ten'ichi's case. The council rejected Ōoka's appeal. For one thing, the elders were aware that Yoshimune himself wanted to see the man.

Ōoka tried to make a direct appeal to Yoshimune: perhaps he could be persuaded to wait until he could conduct a further investigation. Contrary to his expectation, however, Ōoka's appeal displeased Yoshimune. Instead of granting permission for further inquiry, Yoshimune ordered Ōoka to confine himself to his home.

Driven by the sense of crisis for the shogunate, Ōoka felt compelled to violate the shogunal order. He pretended to be a corpse and had his retainers carry him out of the house. He went to the mansion of the lord of Hitachi, Tokugawa Tsunaeda, to ask for help. Tsunaeda agreed that he would intercede with Yoshimune for Ōoka to persuade him to look into the case himself. Yoshimune listened to Tsunaeda's advice and the case was brought before Yoshimune himself. But alas Ōoka's justice was no match for the eloquence of Yamanouchi, who spoke on behalf of Ten'ichi! Yamanouchi won. Yoshimune was convinced that Yamanouchi was honest. Ōoka was utterly defeated.

Ōoka had lost the case and yet he still did not believe Ten'ichi. Excusing himself from the shogunal court under the pretense of illness, he hastily dispatched his retainers to Kii province for further information about Sawanoi and others.

While his men were still gathering information in Kii, Ōoka was put on the spot. He was forced either to resign from his office or to recommend Ten'ichi to Yoshimune as his real son. Ōoka could

do neither. He was sure that his emissaries would bring back the information he needed, and he had to buy time. Justice in Japan was
at stake! He would not even have minded committing suicide. If
he committed suicide as a gesture of admonishing the *shōgun*, the
case would have to be reopened by Ōoka's successor. If the case
were reopened, it would delay Yoshimune's formal recognition of
Ten'ichi's claim. Meanwhile Ōoka's emissaries would return with
the evidence against Ten'ichi. That was Ōoka's reasoning.

Just before Ōoka was to commit ritual suicide his retainers returned from Kii province with the evidence to prove that Ten'ichi
was a fraud. Ōoka had won. Ten'ichi was arrested. So were all his
accomplices except Yamanouchi. When he realized that he would
be arrested, Yamanouchi set fire to his dwelling and committed suicide.

THE HIKOBEI AFFAIR

At Dōjima in Osaka lived a man named Hikobei. Hikobei
had a store that specialized in women's furnishings and over the
years his business had slowed down. It was apparent that he needed to move to a new market. Mounting debts spurred Hikobei to
decide to try his luck in Edo. He left his family in Osaka and departed for Edo alone.

In Edo Hikobei did well and his business thrived. It was probably through his business that he came to be patronized by a
wealthy old woman called Yoneya no Inkyo who was the widow of a
successful innkeeper, Yoneya Ichirozaemon. The widow lived with
a maidservant in a separate house at the back of the inn, which was
located in Nihonbashi.

When Hikobei needed one hundred pieces of gold to finance
some business venture, he asked Yoneya no Inkyo to lend him the
money. The woman replied that she indeed had one hundred
pieces in gold but she meant to donate them to the temple. Instead of cash the woman gave Hikobei a suitcase full of valuables
and told him to take them to a pawnshop. Hikobei thanked her
and did as she suggested. The pawnbroker gave him fifty pieces of

gold. Hikobei managed to borrow the rest from various other acquaintances.

That evening the inn was very busy and needed extra help, so the old woman let her maidservant go to the inn to assist. The maid spent the night with other girls on duty. When the maid returned from the inn on the following morning she found her mistress dead. It was a case of murder and robbery. One hundred pieces of gold were missing.

The proprietor reported the deed to the police, who immediately suspected Hikobei and arrested him. Hikobei was brought to the court of Ōoka Echizen. To Hikobei's disadvantage it seemed that he was the only person who knew of the cash the slain woman had with her that night. The prosecution pressed him to confess. The inquisitors tortured him. After being subjected to repeated torture Hikobei finally broke down and confessed that he had killed the woman and taken her money. Hikobei was soon executed and his head was exhibited in public with the skin of the face stripped off.

It took some time for the news of Hikobei's crime and execution to reach his family in Osaka. When it finally reached them, his son Hikosaburō determined to go to Edo, collect his father's ashes, and perform the appropriate rites for the salvation of the dead soul.

On the night he arrived in Edo, Hikosaburō went to Suzugamori, where his father had been executed. Suzugamori was the famous execution ground located on the south of Shinagawa along the Tōkaidō route. Presently, Hikosaburō heard footsteps and hid behind a tree. Along came a pair of sedan chair carriers who wished to relieve themselves. When they approached the place where Hikosaburō was hiding, they started talking about the man who had been executed there. It was about his father!

"The poor fellow was innocent but he was executed here for someone else's crime. "Isn't that a shame?" said one. "You're damned right; Ōoka made a big mistake. I'm sure it was the work of Kantaro." Hikosaburō stealthily followed the two men to discover where they lived. On the following morning he visited both men, identified himself as the son of the executed man, and asked for their cooperation in discovering the real criminal.

The two fellows were Gonza and Sukejū who lived in Fukui-chō, Asakusa. They promised Hikosaburō whatever help they could give him. They knew the man Kantarō, who lived in their neighborhood, and recounted what happened on the night of the killing. They had come home late from work that night, and had seen a dark figure washing something in the roadside tub. They could not make out who the man was and went back to their apartments. While waiting for their landlord to open the front door for them, they saw a man pass by. It was Kantarō. Gonza and Sukejū went to look at the tub the next morning. They saw that the water had a faint trace of blood in it. Moreover, they detected a blood-stain on the outside of the tub! These two facts made them think that Kantarō was involved in some kind of crime in which his belongings had been stained with blood. Later that day the two men heard about the robbery and murder of Yoneya no Inkyo.

Gonza and Sukejū connected the crime with Kantarō and carefully watched his conduct. In the meantime, however, Hikobei confessed to the crime and was executed. The case was closed. Sure enough, afterward Kantarō's life-style became extravagant. Gonza and Sukejū were convinced that it was he who killed Yoneya's retired proprietress and took a hundred pieces of gold.

The two boys advised Hikosaburō to go to the landlord of the house where Hikobei had lived. When he heard the story, the landlord agreed to cooperate. He suggested that Hikosaburō go berserk in his house so that he could summon the police. "It's the easiest and quickest way to get Ooka's attention. Otherwise proceedings will take too long for you to wait," said the landlord. Hikosaburō heeded the man's advice and acted accordingly. He was taken to Ōoka's court and made a direct appeal to clear his father's name.

Kantarō was eventually arrested and his crime was revealed. But, alas, Hikobei would not return to this life! Hikosaburō brooded. Ōoka told Hikosaburō that he would give him a reward for his filial piety, and he ordered his subordinate to bring a certain man to court. The man was Hikobei! Alive! What kind of magic was this? Hikobei had been executed, his head displayed in public!

Ōoka explained to the court that he had not believed Hikobei's confession after all and therefore only pretended to execute him. Instead of killing the real Hikobei, Ōoka arranged for the corpse of a man who died in prison to be displayed as the body of Hikobei. The head displayed in public as Hikobei's also belonged to the dead prisoner.

Sōgo
of Sakura

Sōgo of Sakura, or Sakura Sōgo as he is known in Japan, is a folk hero whose selfless action has been told countless times since the eighteenth century. The story originated among the farmers who suffered from heavy taxation and injustice of local officials under a feudal lord, and it acquired widespread popularity among common folk. The characters as well as the incidents depicted in the story are largely fictitious although the personality of the obtuse and aloof feudal lord is attributed to a historical figure who actually ruled the territory. According to tradition, Sakura Sōgo, a village headman in the domain of Lord Hotta in Chiba, stood up against the corrupt officials for the cause of afflicted peasants and petitioned directly to the *shōgun*'s person, a crime that was punishable only by death. The following excerpts are taken from "Jizōdō Tsuya Monogatari," which was published in its earliest form sometime around 1700.

For many years the farmers in the territory governed by Sakura castle in eastern Japan had paid the same amount of rice in taxes on land and contributed the same amount of goods as annual tribute. Each year they worked the same number of days in service for the lord of Sakura. Everything remained unchanged even after 1626, when a new lord, Hotta Kaga-no-Kami, moved into the castle from Matsumoto. With the death of Kaga-no-Kami in 1651, however, the situation altered radically.

    Kaga-no-Kami's son, Kōzuke-no-Suke, succeeded his father

From Ken Shiratori (ed.), "Jizōdō tsuya monogatari" in *Gimin sōsho: Sakura Sōgo* (Tokyo: Nihon Shoin, 1931), pp. 2–37. Translated for this book by Takeo Hagihara.

as lord of the castle. He was immediately appointed to the *shō-gun*'s Council of Elders because of his father's great achievements. In Edo, where he served on the council, various *daimyō* as well as the *shōgun*'s vassals bribed his despicable subordinates, who became greedier as time passed. In their home province they imposed heavy taxes and labor on the farmers. As a result, whatever the size of their holdings, all the farmers sank into profound misery.

Some farmers could not pay the taxes on the date they were due. Hard pressed and in dire need, some sent their sons and daughters out to do service in other territories while requesting a postponement of payment. The officials refused to grant any postponement. Instead, they investigated the village headmen in charge of collecting the taxes and accused them of not performing their duties. Many farmers, after exhausting every means, sold houses that had belonged to their families for generations, turned over unproductive fields to their villages, and fled the territory.

On the seventh day of the tenth month in 1654, the village headmen in the territory of Sakura castle met in the village of Kōzu to discuss their plight. One headman proposed that they all assemble in front of the lord's mansion in Edo and appeal to the lord himself for the reduction of taxes and other duties. All agreed to this proposal except Sōgo, head of the village of Kōzu.

Sōgo advised the headmen to take the matter more seriously. He said, "We have had to meet in secrecy at various places concerning the reduction of tax levies and decided to give some money not only to low-ranking officials but also to high-ranking ones so that they would present our case to the lord. Despite all our efforts, our petition has never been presented. For that reason, I doubt that it will readily be accepted even if we go to Edo and make our plea for the reduction of taxes directly to the lord. We will just lose more money. If our petition is denied, we will be disgraced as well. Besides, the very act of going to Edo would immediately cause commotion. We must think about the situation more seriously and keep our plans secret. Secrets tend to get out no matter how hard one tries to keep them hidden. As the saying goes, 'Hedges have eyes and walls have ears.' Our arrival in Edo might be interpreted as a sign of a farmers' rebellion. Rumors that the farmers in our territory are banding together will spread and eventually get back here. You know what they say: 'Bad news travels fast.' People tend to exaggerate stories and make mountains out of molehills. It's clearly unwise for us to be open about this matter as if it were a mere quarrel or drunken brawl. We must realize that the main thing is to keep quiet about our plans." His words made sense to the others.

Sōgo suggested that they go to Edo in small groups and by different routes so they would not attract attention. Everyone agreed with him when he said that the proverb "Faith can move mountains" was wiser than the saying "You only die once." They also agreed to his proposal, and went on to discuss the trip to Edo. The matter was settled promptly; they decided to prepare a covenant which everyone would sign.

From early in the morning of the twenty-seventh day of the tenth month in 1654, more than three hundred village headmen gathered at the front door of the lord's mansion in Edo. They said to the doorkeeper, "We farmers are hard pressed by the heavy taxes and labor that have been increasing each year for the past several years. Now the situation is becoming unbearable. We have petitioned local officials in Sakura several times to excuse the new taxes and labor increases, but they have never even considered our petitions. Therefore, we have no other course than to appeal directly to the lord to have mercy on us."

An official in charge of finance appeared and told them to go to the back door where their petition would surely be examined. All the men were delighted and promptly moved to the back door. When they got there the same official demanded that they come inside while the petition was heard. No one went inside. The official and his men tried to force them in, but they did not dare to go because they were afraid of what the officials would do to them. After a while, the official came back and said the officials were too busy to take up the matter that day. He promised that they would examine the petition the next day at a detached house in Hyaku-nin-chō in Aoyama. He told them to return to their inns and report to the detached house the next day.

The next day, early in the morning, all the village headmen

gathered at the front door of the detached house in Aoyama. The same official appeared again and said, "Your petition really should be heard by the lord. We are not able to accept your petition here in Edo, however, because such matters have always been handled by the local officials in Sakura as they should be. That is what the local officials are there for. So return to Sakura immediately and ask the local officials once again to review your petition. As I have said, it is very difficult to deal with local matters from Edo. Go home to your village at once." With that the door was closed and the Edo officials never spoke to the farmers again.

On the next day the village headmen gathered for a conference. No one had offered any concrete suggestions for action. Their discussion went round in endless circles until someone suggested that they send for Sōgo. Messengers were hastily dispatched to seek Sōgo's advice.

Sōgo said to the messengers, "I was afraid that would happen. Our petition will not be considered if the officials in Edo are conspiring with those in Sakura. My fear seems to have been confirmed. Now we have no choice but to take this matter to a member of the *shōgun*'s council of elders. Even then, I doubt that our petition will be considered readily. At any rate, I must join the group. I will go to Edo with you." Sōgo and the messengers arrived in Edo on the same day the village headmen were still hotly debating the problem. Sōgo was asked to speak.

Sōgo said, "I first thought of submitting our petition to the *shōgun*'s council for solution. But on second thought I realized that it wouldn't be so easy, since our lord is also a member of the council. I therefore propose that we present our petition to Lord Kuze Yamato no Kami because he is widely known to be wise and influential. We can do that when he reports to the *shōgun*'s castle in the morning. That is a sure way." The village headmen agreed to Sōgo's proposal and decided to entrust the matter to Sōgo and five other village headmen.

On the following day Sōgo and the five headmen waited restlessly with the petitions in their pockets for Lord Kuze's palanquin to emerge from his mansion. They hid themselves in an alley next to the mansion. Before long the palanquin came out with many *samurai* in attendance. The six farmers rushed toward the palanquin and begged that their petitions be considered. The *samurai* pushed them aside. Frantically they tried to approach the palanquin again, and once more were pushed aside. Then Sōgo, in a thunderous voice, announced that all six of them would commit suicide right there unless they were allowed to give the petitions to Lord Kuze. Finally Lord Kuze responded by telling one of his attendants to take the petitions. Then his palanquin headed toward the *shōgun*'s castle.

On the second day of the eleventh month in 1654, a messenger from Lord Kuze came to the six village headmen to tell them to report to the Lord's mansion. The headmen were delighted.

As instructed, they went to the mansion early in the morning the next day. They were received by the secretary and superintendents of Lord Kuze, who told them that the petitions were perfectly absurd. The village headmen were astounded at their response. Lord Kuze's vassals continued, "Furthermore, it was wrong of you farmers to have stopped the lord's procession on the way to the *shōgun*'s castle. Nevertheless, because you farmers are ignorant about such etiquette, the lord has shown special mercy toward you and has decided to keep the matter quiet. He is therefore returning the petition."

Dispirited, the village headmen went back to the inn. For a while they could not even speak. It was Sōgo who broke the silence. "How can we return home without success?" he asked. "Although Lord Kuze did not take up our petitions, I am sure that what we have done has become known to the officials of our own lord. If we go home like this, we will surely be punished—all of us. We cannot let that happen, can we?" Sōgo looked determined. He continued, "Now look, gentlemen. I volunteer to take responsibility for the matter. You, gentlemen, please go home. If you are questioned by the officials at home, protect yourselves by saying that Sōgo alone led the petitioning. Then the officials cannot punish you."

The headmen listened to Sogo intently. They were quite

moved by his courageous statement. They said to themselves: "How can we let Sōgo alone take all the blame? No, that is not right."

One headman said, "No, you do not have to assume all the responsibility. Six of us were chosen by all the village headmen to represent them. It does not make sense that you alone should shoulder all the responsibility." Their statement encouraged Sōgo, and he began to believe that they might achieve their goal.

Sōgo and five other headmen determined to have a showdown with Lord Hotta Kōzuke no Suke. They resolved to sacrifice their lives for the cause of the suffering peasants at home. Thus they secretly worked over their plans and finally decided to present their grievances directly to the *shōgun*.

Meanwhile it was announced all over town that the *shōgun* would visit a certain temple on the twentieth day of the eleventh month. The six farmers discussed in detail the manner of presenting the petition to the *shōgun*. There was a technical problem in the plan's execution. "It will be very difficult for all of us to do it," Sōgo said thoughtfully, "because the route is carefully guarded on that day. Why don't I steal my way to the route alone and do it? I'm sure it would be better." The others consented to his proposal.

On the night before the scheduled visit of the *shōgun* to the specified temple, Sōgo hid himself under the bridge before the temple and waited for daylight. He tied the petition to the end of a long bamboo pole.

Day broke and finally the *shōgun*'s procession came to the bridge. When it reached the middle of the bridge, Sōgo emerged from beneath and ran up onto the bridge. "I beg your pardon, My Lord," shouted Sōgo. "I have a petition from all the farmers of Sakura." His mad dash at the procession caught all the retinue by surprise. A crowd of guards surrounded him and tried to drag him out of the way.

Sōgo, however, was so determined that they could not move him even an inch. A few officials finally gave in and ran to Sōgo to pick up the petition from him. Sōgo instinctively prostrated and the procession moved into the temple. The officials who were responsible for the security of the route were bewildered by what had happened. They considered it a very serious matter and were afraid of being blamed for it.

When the *shōgun* returned to the castle later on the same day, he gave the petition to one of the elders and ordered him to examine it. A conference was held in the castle and Lord Hotta was summoned the next day. Poor Lord Hotta knew nothing about what was happening. He hurried to the castle where his superiors were waiting for him with a stern letter of admonition. The letter read as follows:

> It is regrettable that disgraceful things have been said about you despite the fact that you are currently an honorable member of the *shōgun*'s council. In a case such as this, you would ordinarily face forfeiture of your castle and its territories. Since your late father, Hotta Kaga no Kami, had a distinguished record of service to the shogunate, however, the *shōgun* has decided to act with kindness and mercy this time and keep the matter quiet. He has ordered that the petition and those responsible for petitioning be referred to you. Be thankful for the *shōgun*'s leniency and examine the matter carefully by yourself.

Lord Hotta hurried home and immediately summoned his senior subordinates. He told them with indignation of his humiliation at the shogunal court. He ordered an investigation of the officials in Sakura.

At once the local officials were summoned from Sakura to Lord Hotta's mansion in Edo for questioning. The shameless officials all testified in unison that they had never inflicted harm upon the farmers. They went on to say that Sōgo was known to be a great scoundrel and recommended that he be punished severely. They proposed that Sōgo be crucified and decapitated, his head be displayed as a lesson to other peasants, and his property be confiscated.

Lord Hotta pondered the case for a while. Then he said, "I agree that Sōgo should be crucified. His crime of having presented such a petition is outrageous. There is no question about that." He then asked how the other five farmers should be treated. One county magistrate suggested that they should be banished from Sakura and their properties be confiscated. Lord Hotta agreed. He suggested that Sōgo's wife should receive the same punishment as the five men—banishment from the territory for life but not crucifixion—because she could not possibly have known the details of the crime.

The officials of Sakura disagreed with their master. They insisted that Sōgo's wife should be punished in the same way as her husband. Lord Hotta gave in. "But how about Sōgo's children?" said he. "They couldn't be responsible, could they? The death penalty is too severe for them. They probably don't know the meaning of 'direct appeal' or 'conspiracy.' If I lost face at the shogunal court, it was because you officials neglected your duty. We have to be lenient toward children. Perhaps a limited banishment is enough."

"No, My Lord," objected a county magistrate, "I respectfully disagree with your idea of mercy. To spare the lives of children whose father committed a grave crime against the *shōgun*'s person would be interpreted by the shogunate as an act of disrespect. That we must not do."

Lord Hotta Kōzuke no Suke was very indecisive. He generally used his father's records to handle domain matters and left everything to his subordinates. In this instance, too, he let his officials make the final judgment. He simply told his men to settle the matter "appropriately" and left the conference.

On the third day of the second month in 1655 the final verdict was handed down. It was decided that Sōgo was the principal leader and that he be crucified in Sakura. Lord Hotta's men made a makeshift cage for Sōgo and sent it from Edo to Sakura. Sōgo's wife was to be crucified, all his property confiscated, and his children decapitated. The other headmen were tied together with rope and sent to prison in Sakura. Six days later it was announced that the property of Sōgo and the other five men be appraised and surrendered to the lord. The five men were sent into exile.

As for all other peasants who had signed the covenant, they were presumed to have been misled by Sōgo. Hence, they were spared from severe punishment.

The Sinking Village

"The Sinking Village" is an excerpt from the novel *Rōdō* [Labor], published in 1909, by Naoe Kinoshita (1869–1937). First as a journalist and later as a freelance writer, the author was active in the protest against the Ashio copper mine pollution, a movement which reached nationwide proportions in the last decade of the nineteenth century and the early twentieth century. The excerpt presented here depicts the last phase of the protest. Residents were forced to sell their houses and evacuate their village. The man described as Noguchi in this story is said to be a faithful representation of Shōzō Tanaka, a politician who gave up his career as a Diet representative to devote himself to the cause of the farmers whose land was either destroyed by the pollution or taken away to be used as a waste dump for the mine.

When he heard that the remaining farmers were finally to be evicted from the village of Yanaka, Yōsaku Matsuyama decided to come out of his refuge immediately. However meek and docile a person may be, there comes a time when he cannot control his rage; his house, the very house that had been handed down to him from his forefathers, was now to be torn down. How could one be silent and meek? If the worst happens, there may be bloodshed, Matsuyama thought to himself. He could no longer sit still.

"I may be killed or, at the least, arrested. But I must go," Matsuyama told his wife, and he set out for the village.

The train reached Koga at high noon. It was hot. When he

From Naoe Kinoshita, "Rōdō," in *Kinoshita Naoe chosaku shū*, vol. 9 (Tokyo: Meiji Bunken, 1967), pp. 304–330, 333–342. Translated for this book by Michiko Y. Aoki and Hiroko Kataoka.

came out of the Koga station, Matsuyama went into a teahouse in front of the station. He wanted to find out the real situation. In the teahouse, Matsuyama found a familiar stout-looking man, the proprietor of the house. He was wearing a light cotton *kimono* and, sitting cross-legged, was cooling himself with a large fan.

"Well, welcome back, sir." A young girl emerged from within to greet Matsuyama. With a charming smile, she added, "Mr. Hasuike is in the back room."

"Oh, is he?"

Hasuike heard Matsuyama's voice.

"Here I am. I'm coming." No sooner had a booming voice reached Matsuyama's ear than a young man with a wide forehead appeared before him.

Matsuyama remembered that Hasuike was still a student at Waseda University when he came with some students to inspect the pollution caused by the copper mine waste. Since then Hasuike had become deeply involved in the protest and worked day and night for the cause of the victims. He would often be absent from school for long periods of time.

Hasuike was a great admirer of Nichiren, an ardent Japanese Buddhist leader of the thirteenth century. Like Nichiren, Hasuike was volatile. Fiery anger would suddenly give way to great bursts of laughter. Hasuike told Matsuyama that he had been working in Yanaka for some time and added that he had just come back from a short trip to Tokyo on Noguchi's behalf.

"I have just ordered my lunch," smiled Hasuike. His white vest stretched tightly across his chunky stomach.

"How are the villagers taking it?" asked Matsuyama.

"They are very determined," nodded Hasuike while wiping sweat from his forehead. "They've made up their minds, no doubt about that! After having suffered so much, they can take anything."

"But, Hasuike, don't you think some of them might be tempted to give in when the authorities use underhanded tactics?"

"Do you think so? Our worry at the moment is not that someone may give in. We are concerned instead about a riot. After all these years of suffering, they may fight back when cornered. That

is what the Honorable Noguchi is worried about. He insists that
not a single person in the village should be touched by the authorities. He will not even tolerate a broken finger. If such a thing happened, I am sure he would take his own life in protest. We can't let
that happen."

Hasuike's face burned with anger; his eyes shot sparks of fire.

"Look here, Mr. Matsuyama. When the debate on pollution
was going on in the Diet, quite a few dignitaries expressed their
sympathy with us. In the end, however, all of them withdrew their
support. Now, at the crucial stage when it is a matter of survival for
Yanaka village, no one comes to help us. What is going on? I just
can't take it."

He slashed the air with his fist, and tears flowed down his
cheeks. At that moment the girl, smiling, brought their lunch.
Hasuike's mood changed at once, and he smiled broadly. His face
was now bright as a rainbow after an evening shower.

The waitress told Hasuike and Matsuyama that the police
commissioner had come to the town of Fujioka to stand guard and
had summoned high-ranking officers from all over his area of juris-
diction.

"Still, they won't be able to destroy the village so soon," said
the girl cheerfully.

"Why not?" Hasuike asked with his mouth full of rice.

"Because they still don't have enough workers for that."

"They don't have enough workers? How do *you* know that?"

The girl blushed becomingly when Hasuike addressed her on
equal terms. But she calmly told them what she had heard: The
authorities of Tochigi prefecture had planned to recruit workers
from the vicinity of Koga to demolish the remaining houses in
Yanaka. Koga is not in Tochigi; it is in Ibaraki prefecture. The Tochigi government asked the Ibaraki authorities to have the Koga
police chief do the recruiting. The Koga police chief tried to recruit
workers, but the people of Koga did not respond. For Koga people
the Yanaka residents were long-time customers. They could never
destroy the houses of old friends no matter how wrong they might
be. In fact, the townsmen of Koga went so far as to decide to boy-
cott anyone who cooperated with the authorities. The Koga police

couldn't do anything about it. The authorities of Tochigi, therefore, had to seek help from afar.

"Hmm. . . ." Hasuike seemed quite impressed by the girl.
The girl concluded that the authorities would have to wait at least a
few more days. Matsuyama thought the girl's information depend-
able because he knew that her boss was quite knowledgeable about
such matters.

After lunch Matsuyama left the teahouse with Hasuike and
went as far as a pontoon bridge called Unahashi. There they saw a
man in a dark blue *kimono* watching passersby. The man was in a
traveler's attire with leggings and straw sandals, but it was obvious
that he was a plainclothesman. The two, Matsuyama and Hasuike,
hurried through the field under the scorching sun to reach an embankment near the Inari shrine called Tōkamori. There they found
a new vast stretch of water.

* * *

All the houses along the bank of the river had been torn down
with the exception of two that faced each other. In the courtyard
several farmers were hard at work threshing wheat. Among them
stood a slender, boyish figure in a black student uniform.

"Oh, that's Koshino," said Hasuike cheerfully. Koshino had
left school last spring to join the villagers' cause. As Matsuyama
and Hasuike approached, farmers stopped working and looked up.

It was painful for Matsuyama to face the villagers. As they recognized Matsuyama and Hasuike, the villagers took off their sun
hats and greeted them. Among them was a short man of about
fifty named Ichigorō.

"Tomorrow, sir. They are coming at last. Thank goodness,
they are going to demolish our houses!" Ichigorō broke into a loud
laughter. The wrinkles of his face sharpened.

"Hmm. . . ." Matsuyama muttered and lowered his eyes.
What else could he do? What could he say to this man? The
women standing behind Ichigorō wiped the sweat off themselves.
Their necks and foreheads were red from the sun. Leaving the men
talking to the visitors, the women soon went back to finish their
work.

"We have been ready for this for a long time," continued Ichigorō. "Waiting for something to happen has made us uneasy. If they don't come soon, we'll get angry. What has to be had better happen soon. Now that they seem to have decided on action, we're all delighted." Ichigorō was dressed only in his underclothes. He pulled out his tobacco pouch, put a pipe in his mouth, and then lit a match and began to smoke.

While Ichigorō was enjoying his tobacco and laughing uproariously, the young man, Koshino, quietly told the two men what had happened while Hasuike was away. Hasuike listened carefully.

An elderly man called Einojō came out of the house behind the building used for silkworms. Tall but feeble, he took faltering steps toward the visitors and invited them to his house.

Einojō insisted that even if the houses were demolished, the village would not die. He told the visitors about people who found it impossible to support themselves elsewhere after having sold their lands to the government. "They want to come back to their native village, of course!" said old Einojō.

According to Einojō, a man who had moved to Nasuno slipped back to Yanaka. "He said he had been deceived and regretted he had ever left the village. In tears this man said he would rather starve on his own land than try to live elsewhere."

"Those who have grown up on this fertile land can never survive anywhere else," said the old man as he bent over. "I always tell young people, 'So what if your houses are destroyed. My house was burned down three times and I didn't even have a pair of straw sandals left. Even if they demolish our houses, they can't take the soil away from us, can they? Then why should we be afraid of the government?

"This village is like a paradise. All we have to do is plant the seeds and we get a good harvest even without fertilizer. Those who left the village for a few hundred *yen* forgot the gift that heaven gave us here. They offended the gods. It is death for a farmer to leave his native village just as it is for a fish to leave water."

Einojō looked around at the faces of everyone there and continued. "Those who moved to the other side of the river now come back secretly to grow vegetables on their old land, to fish in the river, even to steal ducks from someone else. Those who stayed get mad at them. But I tell them not to condemn those who steal. After all, they're sorry they sold their land. We should be tolerant. If they want to come back, we should let them. It's their native village. As long as the natives live here, the village will recover. I have faith in that. I'm not worried."

Matsuyama listened with his head down.

"That's right! I agree with you," shouted Hasuike.

The old man cupped his ear with his hand and leaned forward to hear what Hasuike said. Koshino repeated Hasuike's words aloud in his ear. The old man mumbled something and nodded. "This village will live again, I'm sure. No matter what happens, we're in the right. Right will win in the end." The old man's feeble eyes gleamed.

"What do you think, Mr. Matsuyama?" Hasuike looked at Matsuyama proudly.

"I think you are right, Hasuike," nodded Matsuyama thoughtfully.

Ichigorō came to tell them the boat was ready. Matsuyama and Hasuike bid farewell to old Einojō and got in the boat to visit another farmhouse. Skillfully steering his own boat, Koshino followed them. On the water's edge, green rushes were thriving and white and yellow flowers were in bloom. Ducks were swimming around in the water and quacking. Beneath the water was once fertile soil. Here and there they could see gravestones and remnants of the past.

"We are sorry to trouble you when you are so busy, Mr. Ichigorō," said Matsuyama as the boat glided through the water.

"Oh, it's nothing," smiled Ichigorō lightly. "I was going to a meeting there tonight anyway."

"What meeting?"

"The people from the remaining houses are going to have a farewell party at the Miyatas' tonight. There'll be sixteen of us altogether. It's the last night we can sleep in our own homes."

"How can you be so meek that you let them destroy your houses?" Matsuyama asked.

"Well, sir, it wasn't easy," said Ichigorō. "We kept arguing until we finally decided on that course. To tell you the truth, some of us did want to fight to the end. There were those who even whet the edges of their tools. But Mr. Noguchi, Mr. Koshino, and Mr. Hasuike all persuaded the diehards not to resort to violence. They argued that we should value our lives. If we resisted the police and died, our deaths would be useless. In any case, the men who are coming to tear down our houses are just hirelings. There's no point in fighting with people like that and getting hurt. It's better to let them do their jobs. One hothead has already sharpened his chisel secretly for a fight, though," laughed Ichigorō.

The boats arrived at the Miyatas' where the farewell party was to be held that evening. It was a big house and served as a kind of headquarters for those who had remained in the village. The owner of the house, Kumezō Miyata, was intent on mending a fishnet in the shade of a tall tree.

"Where is Mr. Noguchi, sir?" asked Matsuyama.

"He has gone to Takasuna," replied Miyata. "Three families there fell into their hands, they say."

"Do you mean they gave in?" Ichigorō laughed out of disbelief.

"Then we had better go to Takasuna," said Matsuyama, who immediately returned to the boat. The others followed him. Ichigorō steered the boat again. So did Koshino. The ruined sites of the farmhouses looked desolate atop the hills. All the rest of the land was now under water. The boats crossed the vast stretch of water until they reached a small hill called Takasuna.

They moored the boats and waded through grass until they came to what had been the main road of the hamlet. There they saw policemen sitting under the trees. Some were in uniform and others in plainclothes. The four walked quickly up the slope which led to the door of a farmhouse. There, too, policemen were on guard. Matsuyama saw Noguchi standing sadly beside a well which was still bathed in sunlight. He was in formal Japanese dress. Matsuyama went up to embrace him.

"I heard that the families at Takasuna fell into their hands," said Hasuike bitterly.

"No, that's not true," Noguchi answered calmly. "It is only

the government's attempt at sabotage. The men in this hamlet were served notice from the town of Fujioka and had to report in haste. Nobody has returned from town yet. The authorities are already spreading rumors that those men fell into their hands. It's only a government trick to undermine our morale.

"Thank you for coming, my friend," said Noguchi to Matsuyama. "I, too, have to go to Fujioka now," he continued.

"What's going on there?"

"The governor's there," said Noguchi. "I've been told that he is anxious to see me. I must comply with his wish. I have nothing more to say to him, though."

"It's an insult to summon you like that!" shouted Hasuike. "He should come here himself if he wants to see you. There are all sorts of rumors going around. They must be scheming to arrest you; it's too dangerous for you to go there. You had better not go," said Hasuike.

Noguchi smiled faintly and said nothing.

"You never know what they might do," insisted Hasuike. "Why don't you tell him to come here if he has anything to say?"

"Well, Mr. Hasuike, don't worry," said Noguchi. "If they were to trick me like that, they would only defeat their own purpose. It would just prove their dishonesty, that's all." Noguchi unfolded an old-fashioned hat and put it on. "I understand there is going to be a village meeting tonight, but I may be late for it." Still arranging the chin strap of the hat, he hastened toward the shade under a tree. There a rickshaw was waiting. The vehicle had been sent to fetch him.

Soon Noguchi's broad shoulders stuck up above the rickshaw. The vehicle moved along the narrow road between the fields and disappeared behind an embankment. Anxiety showed in Hasuike's face.

*   *   *

The sunset reflected in the water as Miyata's two grown sons steered their boat home from a fishing trip. Another of Miyata's boys, much younger, was playing with Koshino in the courtyard. The boy did not seem to mind playing while surrounded by policemen. In the kitchen the women of the neighborhood were busy preparing for the party that night.

Miyata told Matsuyama how much the villagers had been harassed by the authorities during the past six years since the government had begun to buy them out. It was a story of such violence that, had it not come from the mouth of this honest farmer, Matsuyama would not have believed it.

Those who remained in the village had learned from long experience that they could trust neither the Diet nor the government. Not even the law. They fully realized that they could not rely on seemingly goodwilled people or on public opinion. They were no longer afraid of anything. Even small children had become tough. In the years of resistance, women found themselves more resilient than men.

"When I look back on what has happened," continued Miyata, "I cannot help wondering why those who were lucky enough to inherit large fortunes gave in first." Miyata had suffered a long illness a couple of years ago and was still not looking well.

"Those who inherited good land from their fathers sold it right away. They didn't even think of fighting back," said the ailing Miyata simply. "But those who started from scratch have held out this long. I wonder why."

Matsuyama could only mull over what Miyata had told him.

*   *   *

They heard a shrill voice echoing on the water.

"It's Matagorō, isn't it?" said one of the men who gathered at the Miyatas'.

"Yes, that's surely Matagorō," agreed another.

"And two other fellows from Takasuna. Well, they seem to have survived, then," said the third. They could all hear the boat as it reached the shore and then the sound of footsteps coming up to the earthen floor at the entrance to Miyata's house.

"Good evening!" Matagorō's voice reached the ears of people in the room. "Well, most of us are here now." He came up to the room and took a seat.

"I heard the Takasuna people finally gave in," one of the earlier arrivals said. "We thought we'd never see you again!" the man shouted in Matagorō's ear. Although Matagorō was in his early twenties, he had trouble hearing.

"What? Don't make me laugh," Matagorō shouted back hilariously, and he started telling them about the day's adventure at the government office in Fujioka.

"The officials said they would start tearing our houses down tomorrow," Matagorō reported. "They said we would be responsible for the cost of the demolition. They also said that if we give up, destroy our own houses voluntarily, accept the money from the government, and leave, we won't have to pay the expense. To hell with them!"

Matagorō told them about the government officials' scheme to get the Takasuna people to give in. According to Matagorō, the officials offered to pay the Takasuna people more if they would consent to sell the land and move out right away.

"Then my nephew asked the officials to write down the amount of additional payment so we would have written evidence. They agreed. Then they tried to persuade us to break away from the rest of the villagers.

"In time another nephew of mine arrived. He was away from home when the government summoned us, but he followed us as soon as he learned where we were headed. He arrived in Fujioka just in time. He saw us negotiating, and he questioned the officials carefully. You know, this boy is smart. He said 'This is a strange story. I hear the price of land was decided by the committee of land appropriations. How can you, mere officials, increase the amount as you like without instructions from the higher office?' The officials looked at each other. One of them groaned, 'Damn it! This brat knows a thing or two.' That was that, and the meeting ended."

"Even at this point they're still trying to deceive us," someone in the group said, gritting his teeth. The man who had sharpened his chisel for a fight shook his head violently. His lips were almost forming the words, "I told you."

"What did you do with the official document offering more money?" Koshino asked.

"I've brought it back here," Matagorō's nephew smiled tri-
umphantly.

Sake cups were passed around and before long the *sake* began
to take effect. One man started singing and others joined in.

"Hey, Fusakichi, what's the matter with you?" said one man
to a middle-aged man who was sitting quietly with arms folded in
the corner of the room. Fusakichi had a beautiful voice. He sang
"Matsumae" and the song filled everyone with delight. They all
clapped.

"Good, Fusakichi," said an old man. "It's been a long time
since I last heard you sing."

"I haven't sung for nearly twenty years," sighed Fusakichi.
"My voice is off now."

"Now it's Kin'ya's turn," someone shouted. The man named
Kin'ya was in his early forties. He was wearing a summer *kimono*
of faded blue and sat cross-legged with a faint smile on his stern-
looking face.

Yanaka used to be a rich village. Young men had had plenty
of free time and money for lessons. Some played the *samisen* and
sang ballads; some learned dancing and even appeared in village
theaters. In their slack season, they even went on tour with their
plays. Although they were amateurs, their costumes were as good
as those of professionals.

Kin'ya was a good dancer in his younger days. One day he fell
in love with a girl in the same village. Without knowing anything
about their daughter's love affair with Kin'ya, the girl's parents arranged a marriage for her with another man. The girl did not know
how to handle the situation, so she had no choice but to consent to
the marriage arranged by her parents.

The wedding night came. Having failed to break the marriage
arrangement, Kin'ya decided to take the girl away from her parents. By the roadside he lay in wait for the wedding procession,
waiting for a chance to snatch the girl away from the escorts and
elope with her.

The plan did not work; Kin'ya did not have the nerve to
snatch the girl. But he did not give up the idea. After the wedding
night, he attempted to take the girl away from her husband several

times. Although the family was always on guard against Kin'ya, he persisted until he finally succeeded in abducting the girl from her husband. The girl became his wife. A quiet and docile woman with a gentle face, she came to the Miyatas to help prepare the party.

Kin'ya seldom speaks. But when he does, his words affect people profoundly. When it came to the government's land purchasing plan, he simply said, "I will not move from my land. Even if I am the last person, I will not move." He would not listen to anyone even if they made a tempting offer.

Kin'ya did not sing. He just smiled.

"What happened to Mr. Noguchi? He's quite late, isn't he?" one villager said.

"I'll go and see," said Hasuike, standing up. No sooner had he stood than they heard a voice outside. When they opened the sliding door, they saw a boat with a lantern reflecting in the water. They could see Noguchi's white beard at a distance. Hasuike put on his sandals and ran out to welcome him.

"Hello, hello!" Noguchi's cheerful voice soothed everyone's ears. He was escorted by two plainclothesmen.

Noguchi was quite tired. They urged him to retire for the night. A man named Tsuruzō offered him a night's lodging. He lived close by the Miyatas. Matsuyama and Hasuike decided to go with them to Tsuruzō's.

Tsuruzō nimbly poled the boat. The boat glided on the calm water in the cool air. A breeze rustled the tall grass at the edge of the water. The stars were twinkling. They were now far enough from the policemen for Matsuyama to ask why the governor had wanted to see Noguchi.

"He doesn't have any business with me anymore," Noguchi said flatly, and as the boat reached Tsuruzō's place he told them about the meeting. Tsuruzō got out first and went home to make preparations for the guest. The other three remained in the boat.

"It is really restful on the water." Noguchi breathed deeply and looked up at the sky, his arms resting on the sides of the boat. The wind stirred his white beard. Noguchi sat there awhile, gazing intently at the sky.

"At the end I told the governor," Noguchi broke the silence, "you might know more about the law, but I know more about politics. You are a new governor and might not know very much about this issue involving the village. The central government has ordered the destruction of Yanaka. Your predecessor carried out the order this far and then was transferred. You came without knowing much about it." Noguchi took out his fan to drive away the mosquitoes.

"I told him that we even sympathize with him as governor for taking over such a contemptible task. But I told him that evil is evil, whatever the circumstances may require him to do. I said, 'You are a young man with a future. Don't stain your record by carrying out the order of an insensitive government by force. It will tarnish your reputation, your future. Why don't you change your mind, young man? Try to reverse the government's policy. Why don't you talk the politicians out of it? You may have to sacrifice your career in government, but if you are a man, summon your courage and do what you think is right. I'm telling you this for your own good, not necessarily for the sake of the villagers.'"

"What did the governor say?" asked Hasuike enthusiastically.

"Nothing. He just listened with his head bowed." Noguchi stretched himself in the boat. He closed his eyes and let the breeze blow over his stout body.

Having made preparations for Noguchi's lodging for the night, Tsuruzō came back to the boat to return to the Miyatas. When the boat passed the site of an old farmhouse, they saw many lanterns moving about in the Miyatas' courtyard. "Something must be going on there!" shouted Tsuruzō.

"Hurry!" said Matsuyama in agitation. Tsuruzō steered the boat with all his strength.

A crowd of policemen was standing guard. They were the escorts of the governor's official messenger. The messenger had been sent to deliver official notices to the villagers gathered there.

The messenger was sitting in the corridor outside the Miyatas' house filling out some forms. Inside sat Koshino and a friend writing the names and addresses of the villagers. All the villagers were to receive official letters of notice which they would acknowledge with their thumbprints as seals. As soon as he was assured that the villagers would receive the governor's letters of notice, the messenger hastily left the scene under police escort.

Each villager received two messages: one postponing the destruction of his house for five days and the other calling the villagers to the town office in Fujioka the following day. The governor had something to announce.

"They've postponed it again!" exclaimed one villager.

"Nothing will change our minds, even if they keep postponing it," said the other.

"I'd like to die soon if I have to. I don't want to wait for the crisis," said the third. The party broke up as each villager received his notices from the governor. They went home cursing the government all the way.

"Hey, are you going to Fujioka tomorrow?" one villager asked another.

"Like hell!" replied the other. "Why should I? We have nothing to do with them anymore."

"That's right. You're right."

A Protest Against My Charge

"A Protest Against My Charge" is an excerpt from a statement by Hisao Kimura (1918–1946). It was included in *Kike wadatsumi no koe* [Hear the voices of high seas]—a collection of writings by a number of students who were drafted during World War II and lost their lives in foreign lands. Kimura was sentenced to death by the Court Martial of the Allied Powers and was executed in Singapore in 1946. Kimura was not permitted to keep a notebook during and after the trial, so he wrote this statement on the margin of a philosophy book he was allowed to read before his execution. In this excerpt Kimura expresses his resentment toward his superior officers and his concern for his family and the future of Japan.

I have been sentenced to death. Who could have foreseen it? Not I. I could never have imagined I would have to leave this world at such an early age. I am not yet thirty and have not finished my studies. My life has been all ups and downs and now it will sink and disappear forever. I feel as if I am reading a novel about myself. When I realize that it is my fate to die, I suddenly see things as they really are. Whenever there is a great upheaval in history, there are many little-known sacrifices such as mine. When I think about my situation in light of history I realize that even my death, which otherwise seems so meaningless, has great historical significance.

From Nihon Sembotsu Gakusei Kinenkai (ed.), *Kike wadatsumi no koe: Nihon sembotsu gakusei no shuki* (Tokyo: Kōbunsha, 1959), pp. 200–204, 206–208, 211–215. Translated for this book by Takeo Hagihara.

I have done nothing to deserve death. It is others who have done wrong. In my case, however, that is no excuse. From the standpoint of the rest of the world I am no different from the others. At first glance it seems unfair that I should die for the wrongs of others, but when I stop to think that the Japanese have been far more unfair in one way or another toward the people of other countries, I cannot complain. I can only say that I was unfortunate enough to have attracted the attention of my superiors who gave me the assignment for which I was convicted. When I think that I am to die as a scapegoat for the Japanese military, I cannot accept my death. But when I think that I am going to pay for the crimes of the Japanese nation, I can take comfort.

I have done my best to prove my innocence both during and after the trial, but because I worked for the Japanese cause, I have to accept responsibility even though I myself have done nothing wrong. The soldiers who died during the attack on Pearl Harbor, once admired, have now become mere violators of international law. I am in the same position. When I discovered an American spy on Nicobar Island, everyone in the army thanked me; my superior officers praised my action; and it was even rumored that I was to be given a special letter of appreciation by the regional Japanese army. But Japan's surrender a month later changed all that. Under different circumstances what was once considered a great achievement is now the reason for my death.

I think that all Japanese are reconsidering what they have done. Their reflections will play a major role in a restored Japan. I am sorry that I must die before seeing it. But that is my fate. Japan failed to train its people in all the spheres—social, historical, political, intellectual, and humanistic. Blame will rest ultimately with the leaders who made us believe we were better than others in every way. But the Japanese people who supported those leaders are also responsible.

There will be a period of chaos in Japan. Japan will rebuild itself from all of this, and it will be good for the nation. It is a blessing for Japan that all the dogmas have been smashed. The day will come when profound theories such as Marxism and liberalism will be carefully examined and evaluated. With that, the true development of Japan will begin. I am sad that all this will begin after my death, but I trust that people with finer minds than mine will provide my country with leadership. To be sure, Japan must undergo a complete reorganization of its system. I pray for the dedicated participation of young students in Japan's reconstruction.

Please let my sister, Takako, marry soon. I hope my family will not be too despondent. My dear family, do not be brokenhearted because of my death. Live happily and in peace.

We war criminals are being guarded by Dutch soldiers who were once captives of the Japanese army. Because they were treated badly by Japanese soldiers, they take it out on us. Hitting and kicking are just the start of it. But we cannot complain because we Japanese have done much worse. Many of the high-ranking Japanese officers being held prisoner grumble about the guards. They forget what they themselves have done. They are simply paying for it now. It is unfair that a person like myself who has never dealt with prisoners of war or mistreated them should receive the same treatment as those who have. But in the eyes of the victors, I am no different from the rest. It is too much to ask the Dutch soldiers to distinguish me from other Japanese. Fortunately, I have never been hit or kicked. On the contrary the guards like me. We are normally given two meals a day—rice powder paste in the morning and rice porridge in the afternoon. We are hungry all day long and have only enough energy to walk about. I do not know whether it is because they like me or because they are just very kind, but soldiers on guard secretly give me bread, biscuits, cigarettes, and the like at night. Last night they brought me a bottle of soda pop. I was moved to tears—not because of the soda, but because of their kindness. One of the guards said that he might one day be stationed in Japan so I gave him a letter to take to my family. These soldiers know that I am the victim of a false charge and are sympathetic toward me. In general the Dutch soldiers are very anti-Japanese, but as individuals I find them to be very kind and humane.

One of the soldiers told me he was captured and imprisoned by the Japanese. The Japanese soldiers beat and kicked him and even burned his skin. He said he could not understand how they could do that sort of thing without remorse. He also said it was hard for him to understand why Japanese women are treated as so-cially inferior to men.

One by one my fellow prisoners are taken to the gallows. My turn will come soon. All my senses are sharpened by this realiza-tion. Even breathing and eating, which I have always taken for granted, have suddenly become meaningful to me. Soon—within the next few days—I will be called. Everything I have always taken for granted I now sense very keenly. One spoonful of rice in my mouth gives an indescribable sensation to my tongue; the rice melts and slides down my throat. When I close my eyes and savor this feeling, it is as if all the world's complexities were contained in this one sensation. Sometimes I want to cry, but I cannot allow my-self to indulge in even that luxury. Under the extreme pressure of death there is no anger, no pessimism, and no tears for me. I can only appreciate and accept what each moment brings. When I think of the moment of my death, however, I cannot help being terrified. So I have decided not to think about it until the time comes. When the moment arrives, I will die. Death is as simple as that. If I think of it in that way, I find comfort.

I have exhausted every way to prove my innocence. During the trial my superior officers ordered me not to tell the truth. I complied and as a result they received prison sentences while I was condemned to death. There is clearly no justification for this. It seems to me that my life is much more important to the future of Japan than theirs. Surely they are the ones who should be held re-sponsible for the charge against me, since it was they who gave me the orders. They realized this and so they ordered me not to tell the truth. After the verdict, though, I decided to appeal. I have a right to live and should be allowed to do so for the sake of my parents and the future of Japan. Therefore, I wrote a letter in English re-vealing the true facts of the incident, though I was not sure wheth-er my appeal would be heard since the trial was over and appeals are not allowed. I just wanted to make one last effort to save my life.

I perjured myself because of my sense of patriotism. Now I realize that I was wrong and my good intentions worked against me. That is why I changed my mind and decided to tell the truth.

If the appeal is granted, several colonels, lieutenant colonels, and subordinate officers may be sentenced to death. If that happens, it is only fitting. Besides, I firmly believe that if by their death my life is spared, it will be more beneficial to Japan than if I die and they live. I am disgusted by the fact that all their high-sounding words were nothing but a disguise for vanity and greed. I am convinced that they will be very little help to my country if they do not change. There may have been some great men in the Japanese military, but not many. Even among the generals it is hard to find anyone with a level of intelligence equivalent to that of a college professor. I have lived with former colonels and lieutenant colonels, and I know what kind of people they really are beneath their uniforms. I couldn't believe their vulgarity. No wonder we lost the war with officers like ours. Japan could never have won the war, even with sufficient technology and resources. Especially after the Manchurian incident and the occupation of South Asia, the Japanese army officers became greedier than profiteers. What became of their much touted loyalty and spirit of sacrifice then? Stripped of their uniforms they only revealed their true nature.

I just heard a piece of news. Our sentences may be reduced considerably since the laws that apply to war criminals have been nullified. Several days ago, I also heard from the guard that under a change of rules the soldiers who acted on orders would not be punished. When I think of that, a little hope wells up inside me. But in the end it will probably amount to nothing. I am writing all this down to show the inner turmoil that people feel when they are about to die. However prepared for death, a man cannot help clinging to life.

In the end, it is becoming apparent that my sentence will be carried out. How sad to have survived the war only to die here so soon. The course of world history has determined my death. I am dying for the good of my country. Please, mother and father, tell yourselves that I died nobly from an enemy bullet and take comfort in that. Ask Captain Eizo Fukunaka for the details of the incident that led to my death. I do not want to go into it here.

How are you, mother and father? How about you, Takako? You're almost twenty-two years old already, aren't you? I am sure you've become a beautiful woman. I am sorry I cannot have just a glimpse of you before I die. Takako, please marry soon and take my place in the family. After I die, you'll be the only one who can carry out our filial duty to our parents.

It is a very strange feeling to have lost all hope. There are no words to describe it in any language. I have already moved a step beyond this world. I have even lost all fear of death.

Japan must have changed a lot after the surrender. It will undergo many trials; ideas, political and economic institutions, all will change. I would like to see that. I am sad I cannot play a part in it, but the course of history has settled that. In the face of history I am insignificant, only one of the millions who gave their lives to the cause of history. There are many cases like mine—many brave soldiers died in the war and many people were killed by the atomic bombs. When viewed in those terms, my death takes on meaning, however trivial it may seem. When I think of the people who have died already, it seems ludicrous that I want to live. If I could go on living I might be able to make some small contribution to society, but I might end up doing nothing of importance. A life cut short, nipped in the bud, is a life nonetheless. But now there is nothing left but to die as the gods decree.

The thought of death no longer fills me with terror. I am not trying to show off my courage. A person who dies of a disease might feel the same way. Once in a while I cling to life, but only for a brief moment. Then the idea vanishes. In my present state of mind I can die a noble death. There is no trial in life equal to this.

I have no photograph of my mother, father, and sister, but every morning and every evening when I close my eyes, I recall their faces from memory. You too, my dear family, close your eyes and think of me.

My fellow soldiers are returning to Japan one by one and will tell you about me. If any of them write to you, please go and see them even if it means a long trip. It is the only way you can learn the truth of what happened. I will die with a clear conscience. I am sure I have done nothing shameful. Nevertheless, I have been branded a war criminal, and I am worried that it will hurt Takako's marriage prospects and my family's future. Anyone who was stationed at Nicobar until the end of the war can testify to my complete innocence. Believe what I say and take comfort in it.

If we really do live in the other world after death, I will be able to see my grandparents and the college friends who were killed in the war. I look forward to seeing them and talking about the past. From there I will watch over my parents, my sister, and her family to be. Perhaps to recall my unfortunate destiny will make you sad, but please think of me from time to time. Think of me in ways that will bring you happiness.

I am sentenced to die on 23 May 1946.

I have nothing more to write. I am ready to die. Goodbye everybody. Farewell.

Popular Views
of the Emperor

The imperial house in Japan has been a source of religious and political continuity throughout much of Japanese history. In the decades before World War II official doctrine emphasized the emperor's role as head of the Japanese state, father and protector of the Japanese people, and spiritual foundation of the Japanese nation. In the aftermath of war the reforms under the occupation divested the imperial family of its property and made the position of emperor subject to the "will of the people." The following interviews were conducted in 1950 by Takeyoshi Kawashima, a Tokyo University professor, in a small farming community near Tokyo. Professor Kawashima interviewed sixty-four men, women, and children of varying status in the community to discover their attitudes toward the imperial institution. This selection includes two complete interviews and a sampling of answers from a number of other villagers.

INTERVIEW WITH MRS. SHIMONI
Mrs. Shimoni, aged fifty, is a primary school graduate and the wife of a poor farmer.

Q: What do you think of the emperor?
A: He is the foundation of the state.
Q: Do you think the emperor began the last war?
A: I don't believe he started the war and now I feel he is working to rebuild our nation.

From Shunsuke Tsurumi, "Nihon no shisō no tokushoku to Tennō-sei," in *Tsurumi Shunsuke chosakushū,* vol. 3 (Tokyo: Chikuma Shobō, 1975), pp. 63–65, 67–68. Translated for this book by Keiko Sellner.

Q: Then you think we must have an emperor?
A: Yes, we need him.
Q: So you think the emperor is the foundation of the nation?
A: By foundation I mean . . . I imagine it is very difficult to be emperor and sometimes I think he must wish he did not occupy his position.

INTERVIEW WITH MR. KAZU KUMAGAI

Kazu Kumagai, a lawyer and landowner forty-two years of age, is a graduate of Meiji University School of Law.

Q: What do you think of the emperor?
A: It is sheer nonsense to think that people in modern times ever believed the emperor was really a god. I respect him and I support him absolutely as a human being.
Q: Why do you say that?
A: It's a feeling that's strong inside me.
Q: Do you think of the emperor as the symbol of the nation?
A: No, I do not think of the emperor as a symbol. I see him as the ruler of the nation. Personally, I think the word "symbol" is too vague a term to be understood by most people.
Q: Then you don't believe in him.
A: No, not in a religious sense.
Q: I don't understand what you are trying to say.
A: Basically, I feel toward the emperor much the same attachment that a child feels toward its mother and father.
Q: Do you think the retention of the emperor is contradictory to a democracy?
A: No, I don't think so.
Q: What do you mean? How can you have a president and an emperor?
A: The president is a servant of the people whereas the relationship of the emperor and the people is like that of parent and child. The emperor as head of our family is the major force uniting the nation.
Q: Are you talking about personal rule by the emperor—the kind we had in former times?

A: I'm talking about the present. Some people say the emperor's position has changed, but in fact we have not had a system of direct rule by an emperor since ancient times. In this respect the structure of the state has changed very little.

Q: Then can we say that the emperor watches over the growth of the people as a father watches over his children?

A: That's right.

Q: Well, what about the emperor's responsibility for the recent war?

A: I do not deny that the emperor shares some moral responsibility for the war, but so do all the Japanese people. Now that the war is over many people are discussing its rightness and wrongness. But we must not forget that it never entered their minds at the time to wonder whether the war was good or bad. People just thought that if war had to come, it would. I think our country was destined to follow its historical course and the last war was inevitable.

OTHER OPINIONS ON THE EMPEROR

The fifty-three-year-old wife of a poor farmer: "He is necessary to the rebuilding of the country."

A seventy-one-year-old landlord: "He's the mainstay of our people, their center and pillar."

A twelve-year-old high school girl: "Like a national flag, he is one aspect of the nation."

The fifty-three-year-old wife of a laborer: "When we look at a family, we see that it needs a father. When there's no father, the family cannot be happy."

The fifty-year-old wife of a poor farmer: "The emperor is like the father of a family. . . . We do not respect him anymore because we lost the war, but to me he is still a father."

A thirty-six-year-old landlord: "I think the emperor is the heart of the country because that's what I was taught in my boyhood."

A fifteen-year-old girl: "I think it is necessary to have an emperor because he provides stability for Japan."

A thirty-nine-year-old merchant: "We need him for the sake of our national consciousness."

A sixteen-year-old boy: "We need him as a symbol. He takes on the role of a symbol. We can see that when the emperor travels throughout the country, thousands of people go out to show their faith in him."

Another sixteen-year-old boy: "If he should cease to exist, our lives would lack direction."

A seventy-one-year-old landowner: "We've had an emperor since ancient times. . . ."

The twenty-five-year-old wife of a factory worker: "From school and newspapers I learned to respect the emperor as a great man."

The young wife of a poor farmer: "If there were no emperor, we would be plunged into confusion."

The wife of a Communist party member: "The emperor is necessary. If Chiang Kai-shek had possessed the power of the emperor he would never have lost continental China."

A ten-year-old boy: "Japan cannot be civilized without an emperor."

Another ten-year-old boy: "If we did not have the emperor, a foreign country might attack us because we did not have a superior person."

A forty-two-year-old landlord: "I think the emperor is descended from the gods."

The fifty-year-old wife of a poor farmer: "Even though people say the emperor is not a god, he is different from us and so I can't help but think of him as divine."

The Lockheed Scandal

The Japanese public seldom holds elected officials in high esteem. Rather, politics has been regarded as a necessary evil. When the United States Securities and Exchange Commission uncovered evidence of bribes paid by the Lockheed Aircraft Corporation to high-ranking Japanese government officials, the Japanese public was indignant. The ensuing scandal in Japan touched off a major political crisis and widespread public criticism of political leaders, particularly former Prime Minister Kakuei Tanaka, who was implicated in the Lockheed affair. The following selections are taken from the well-known column "Tensei-jingo" [Heaven's voice in human words] in *Asahi Shimbun* and other articles in Japanese newspapers in 1976 when the scandal was at its height.

"Tensei-jingo," *Asahi Shimbun* (Tokyo), 1 July 1976

One or two million *yen* is well beyond the reach of the typical Japanese employee. Who, then, would have imagined that a two-million-*yen* tax evasion would be possible? Bun'ichi Mizutani, one of Yoshio Kodama's henchmen, was arrested on just this charge. It is said that he had not declared any of his income for three years, holding secret property worth more than two million *yen*. The job of "intermediary" seems to be a very lucrative one.

In what is known as the Japan Line affair, Kodama maneuvered behind the scenes and bought up the stock of Sankō Kisen, the steamship company, to prevent their taking over Japan Line. At that time, Mizutani was Kodama's intermediary and made a large

---

Selections translated by Takeo Hagihara.

profit, taking advantage of the purchase and sale of the Sankō Ki-sen stocks. Although the National Tax Bureau had been investigating Kodama's tax evasion at about the same time, it failed to uncover his behind-the-scene activities. It is uncomfortable to think that Mizutani's tax evasion was not investigated at the same time.

What should not be overlooked is the fact that Kodama and Mizutani have worked together since the war. During the war when Japan was obtaining key raw materials from Asian countries in the Greater East Asian Co-Prosperity Sphere, many opportunists curried favor with the military authorities to obtain rights for procurement of materials and exploitation, and they took the lion's share. Kodama and Mizutani were among them.

Both Kodama and Mizutani had relations with the Nanking puppet government. Mizutani belonged to the Department of Materials Procurement in the navy and had a contact with Kodama's machine. Since then, the practice of seeking concessions and making big profits has gone on behind the scenes of the Japanese financial world. As a result of the Lockheed bribery scandal, such activities during and after the war have been disclosed one by one.

Kodama is also known to make his weight felt at general meetings of stockholders. At the time of the Japan Line affair, for example, he took an aggressive stance at a general meeting of Sankō Kisen stockholders to break up the gathering. At a general meeting of Marubeni's stockholders on 30 June 1976, some ten men held down and injured a man who shouted an objection to an item on the agenda. This incident reveals a profile of Kodama as a strong man at stockholders' general meetings.

The arrest of Mizutani led to three investigations: Marubeni, All Nippon Airlines, and Kodama. As the investigations develop, the taproot of corruption that produced the Lockheed bribery scandal is being uncovered little by little.

"Tensei-jingo," Asahi Shimbun (Tokyo), 17 July 1976

Corruption among officials is spreading throughout the nation. According to an investigation of the *Asahi Shimbun,* 189 people have been arrested since last April on the charge of corruption in local autonomous government. The police department also reported seventy-two bribery cases in the first half of this year, a number which more than surpasses that of last year. These figures indicate that one bribery case is disclosed almost every other day.

One local official accepted cash or tickets for merchandise in return for making allowances for an applicant taking an examination for a position in local government. The head of a town council was entertained at a resort spa regarding the sale of a town-owned forest. When we look at these "common" practices, it always seems as if briberies are isolated incidents done by special people. In fact, the blight which produces corruption is hiding deep inside all of us.

Paul Bone, a French businessman, wrote about his experience getting caught in a traffic violation. When driving his car to Haneda Airport to meet his friend, he was stopped by a policeman while going fifteen kilometers over the speed limit. He admitted it instantly, thinking there was no room for discussion. His Japanese secretary accompanying him did not agree, however.

Afterward the secretary told him he could have evaded the charge if he had just apologized and said, "It's because I haven't become accustomed to Japan yet." Hearing this, Bone realized that "disregard of the law" is hidden in the average Japanese. He wrote in his book, *Japan—A Mysterious Country:* "It is very strange from our point of view that both an apology and magnanimity are expected when a traffic violation is committed."

Bone's observations about Japan are very keen. He also wrote: "The Japanese regret that they have been unlucky when they are caught for traffic violations. They regret that they have failed to evade the law, not that they have violated it." The excuse that "everybody else is doing it" is heard in the case of bribery just as in a traffic violation. Probably both cases are the same in the sense of slighting the law.

Tanaka's bribery matter may have had an influence on the spread of corruption in local government. At that time, Tanaka, the former prime minister, repeatedly said, "I regret that I have given rise to sharp criticism." Nevertheless, he never mentioned a word about self-examination in his plutocratic government. Similarly, none of the suspects in the Lockheed bribery scandal have uttered a word of regret that they committed a crime.

"Tensei-jingo," *Asahi Shimbun* (Tokyo), 28 July 1976

It was a dramatic morning. Kakuei Tanaka, the former prime minister, suddenly found himself in jail. Although it was said that the investigation of the Lockheed bribery scandal would begin at the periphery, it went straight to the heart of the Liberal Democratic Party. Its impact on the political-financial world will be beyond measure.

What do you suppose the moment of his arrest was like? Undoubtedly no one said, in the style of novels and movies, "Your Excellency, I regret that I must arrest you." Tanaka's favorite phrase when he was premier was "I, who represent this country. . . ." What words are left to him now that he is in jail on the charge that he received a large sum of illegal money as a result of abuse of that very power?

Tanaka's arrest indicates that there is no capacity for self-cleansing in the present political world. The black cloud covering the bribery case that caused Tanaka to resign from his post as prime minister in the fall before last was, after all, never cleared away to reveal the truth. The Liberal Democratic Party was unable to rectify its plutocratic nature by itself and could do nothing but leave it in the hands of the court. How deplorable it is.

Company employees pored over the newspaper extras about the arrest while leaving aside their favorite horse-racing newspapers. Homemakers turned the TV channel to watch the news instead of soap operas or variety shows. All felt that the news had instantly taken a weight from their minds; they were irritated by "murky high officials" and had been eagerly awaiting a piece of news like that of Tanaka's arrest.

Still, in our hearts some bitterness remains. How on earth did we allow a person like Tanaka to hold a position that "represents our country"? Why did we naively believe his honeyed words and simply follow his dream of rapid national growth when nobody knew where it would lead? Aren't we the ones who mistook his gall

for vigor and his absence of convictions for practicality and only a while
ago applauded him?

"How can we revive clean politics in our country?" is a question we
sincerely ought to ask ourselves at this moment. The Lockheed bribery
scandal is an alarm bell warning both of the degenerate state of our democracy and of the "worship of money" that leads to the feeling that
anything can be done for a price. We must turn this alarm into the death
knell of the plutocracy and the government that ridiculed us, the ignorant people.

Asahi Shimbun (Tokyo Morning Edition), 2 August 1976

Reactions to Tanaka's Arrest:
A Flood of Letters to the Editor

It has been six days since Tanaka, the former prime minister,
was arrested. The investigation of the Lockheed bribery scandal has
come to a climax and soon will be settled. In response to this development, the Japanese are becoming more and more interested in
the scandal, as is evident from the drastic increase of letters to "The
Voice," a readers column in our newspaper, since Tanaka's arrest.

Reactions to Tanaka's arrest on 27 July began to appear in the
letters to "The Voice" two days after the arrest. Since the Lockheed
affair was made public at the beginning of last February, letters
have not stopped coming. They let up a little only after investigation began of those involved in bribery—Marubeni, All Nippon
Airlines, and Kodama. Suspicion concerning the involvement of
high government officials in the affair was rumored but had not yet
been substantiated. It was then that middle-aged or older people
who knew of past government scandals voiced their anxiety: "Will
the investigation go all the way to the top?" "How far can the Public Prosecutor's Office go?"

Because of our anxiety, Tanaka's arrest gave us a great feeling
of relief similar to that we enjoy after the rainy season is over.
Tanaka's disclosure of his finances did not restore confidence, and
there was a kind of deterioration in the nation's mental outlook. It
is not surprising that more than a hundred letters a day have been

pouring in to "The Voice" since 29 July. Eighty percent of them are letters expressing admiration: "Justice is still alive." "The Public Prosecutor's Office has done a good job." "I recognized that the executive, legislative, and judicial branches are clearly separated." The contributors came from all age groups: young teenagers, housewives, elderly people, and others. An eighty-four-year-old gentleman who is living in a nursing home praised the Public Prosecutor's Office highly: "It is now the country's moral support." Trust in the investigating staff seems to have been completely recovered.

On the other hand, we received several letters which suggested that we reexamine other areas of the political structure instead of simply giving cheers. Representative of these are opinions such as: "We must not forget that Tanaka's money has been used not only for the Liberal Democratic Party but also for the operation of the entire Diet." "The one-majority-party autocracy which has continued for more than thirty years has given rise to plutocratic government. Are the opposition parties doing anything to correct the situation? Nothing will be changed unless they actually do something and not just glory in the majority party's blunder."

Some letters call for self-examination: "Voters who have helped elect plutocrats must also reflect upon themselves." "Elections are not simply yearly events. I advocate a public movement which will purge politicians involved in the Lockheed scandal. We must make sure that we do not reelect untrustworthy politicians."

Some contributors have noticed in their daily lives the same elements as those found in the Lockheed scandal. A company employee deplores another kind of small-scale corruption: "I married a woman who is a teacher. In less than a year our house was flooded with gifts from students' parents. The number of gifts increases at the time of the entrance examination. Illicit money is spent here, too." A junior high school student wrote: "One evening my mother secretly went to see my teacher to ask for a favor. I wondered if it was not wrong."

Analysis of the Lockheed scandal seems to be interpreted as a matter of each individual's personal morality.

"A Politician's Lie," *Asahi Journal,* 3 September 1976

One of the alleged participants in the Lockheed bribery scandal, Carl Kotchian, former Lockheed president, has emphasized in his memoirs that he himself was victimized. He said that it was the Japanese people involved in the scandal who requested a bribe. What a shameful story!

Japanese ethics have been paralyzed. A policy of rapid economic growth has contributed to its demoralization. This demoralization started with the political leaders. The Lockheed incident was not the first political bribery scandal. In fact, long before the Lockheed scandal there were rumors of clandestine diplomatic relations both between Japan and Korea and between Japan and Taiwan. However, everyone questioned in connection with these rumors asserted his innocence saying, "I swear to heaven. . . ." It would seem from this that their ethical sense had not disappeared completely. At least, they seem to have known that they had done something wrong.

It is often the case, however, that the oaths made by most politicians turn out to be lies. Such was the case for all those accused of involvement in the Lockheed scandal. Many Japanese are not religious, and that probably gives rise to the belief that the ends justify the means.

To consider a lie as evil is supposedly the foundation of education both at home and at school. The Lockheed scandal is significant in the sense that it revealed that there were liars among the leaders in the political and economic world.

An oath taken at a hearing of the U.S. Congress is far more serious than one taken in Japan. A bill for preventing a repetition of the Watergate affair has been passed, and another bill intended to stop bribery of multinational enterprises is being considered. Americans hold the belief that high officials and politicians in general tend to do wrong by nature. Although it is questionable that this belief itself can eradicate corruption, we appreciate their strong and conscious efforts to do so.

There is no such movement in our Diet. It is now common knowledge that the Lockheed scandal resulted from the one-party control of the Liberal Democratic Party over the government as well as from its disposition. However, the party has been unsuccessful in its discussion of how to correct the situation.

Common expressions like "restoring popular trust" in the party are just another political lie. Actually, the party is just engaging in a political power struggle, a mixture of jealousy, private grudges, and obligations. Among the 277 members of the Diet who signed a petition to call a general meeting against Miki, for example, 88 of those who wanted revenge, in fact, belonged to Tanaka's faction. Unless all the powerful men in all the factions take responsibility and resign, we cannot call it "a true effort to restore trust in the party."

If we want to prevent a recurrence of the Lockheed scandal, we need to ban campaign contributions by large companies to members of the Diet. If the members of the Liberal Democratic Party hesitate to adopt this ban, voters can use this issue to refuse to vote for these candidates. We need a public movement to fight political evil.

🄷 *Production Notes*

This book was designed by Roger Eggers and typeset on the Unified Composing System by The University Press of Hawaii.

The text typeface is Garamond No. 49 and display typeface is Benguiat Book

Offset presswork and binding were done by Halliday Lithograph. Text paper is Glatfelter Offset, basis 55.